HOWARD KESTER AND THE STRUGGLE FOR SOCIAL JUSTICE IN THE SOUTH, 1904–77

Minds of the New South

A Series in Intellectual Biography

JOHN HERBERT ROPER
GENERAL EDITOR

■ HOWARD KESTER ■
AND THE STRUGGLE
FOR SOCIAL JUSTICE
IN THE SOUTH
1904–77

Robert F. Martin

University Press of Virginia
Charlottesville and London

THE UNIVERSITY PRESS OF VIRGINIA
Copyright © 1991 by the Rector and Visitors
of the University of Virginia

First published 1991

Library of Congress Cataloging-in-Publication Data

Martin, Robert Francis.
    Howard Kester and the struggle for social justice in the South,
1904–77 / Robert F. Martin.
        p.   cm.—(Minds of the new South)
    Includes bibliographical references and index.
    ISBN 0-8139-1294-6
    1. Kester, Howard, 1904–1977. 2. Social reformers—Southern
States—Biography. 3. Political activists—Southern States—
Biography. 4. Radicalists—Southern States—History. I. Title.
II. Series.
HN79.A13M28   1991
303.48′4′092—dc20   90-39702
                                                            CIP

Printed in the United States of America

FOR MY PARENTS
ROBERT CECIL AND
GEORGIA CULBRETH MARTIN

CONTENTS

ILLUSTRATIONS

FOREWORD

Robert F. Martin's biography of Howard Kester is the first in a series of studies of southern men and women who together form the minds of the New South. This series is not to be limited to any ideological perspectives, or by gender, or by race, though it is certainly the case that the thought and expressions of the modern South have been dominated by conservative white men associated with the New South elite. Plenty of such establishment figures will take their rightful place in our series, but so too will people such as Howard Kester.

Born in Martinsville, Virginia, Kester was a radical Christian who dedicated much of his life to the struggle for social justice in his native region. His fights were toughest, most dramatic, and most dangerous in Arkansas and Tennessee during the Great Depression, but for almost five decades, Howard Kester traveled on an intellectual and moral pilgrimage across the entire South. He did not publish much, and he is not a figure likely to be cited at a conference where scholars search for typical men or women who might be keys to the dominant southern identity. Yet there is no denying his southernness, for he spoke the speech, walked the walk, and otherwise exhibited the gestures and mannerisms associated with the people in that region of Appalachia which embraces the hills of Virginia, West Virginia, North Carolina, Tennessee, and Kentucky. Nor is there any denying his significance in his era, unless by significance one only means those who are clearly winners in their days. This was a man of radical temperament who kicked against the pricks and who made a difference just by protesting in such a way that he drew attention to serious social injustice and structural economic inequalities. Of course, Appalachia has been something of an embarrassment to some professional southerners; and this man, because of his probing questions and because of the unsettling answers he found to those questions, was particularly an embarrassment. After all, he insisted that not only southerners but also the whole world, including of course liberal Yankees, look at his people and take their problems seriously.

Possessing a good though somewhat brittle mind, Kester was conversant with the thought of modern theology and was friends with social theorists E. Franklin Frazier, Charles Spurgeon Johnson, and Reinhold Niebuhr as well as social activists Claude Williams, Norman

Thomas, and Walter Francis White. This was indeed a mind, energetic, dissident, dissonant, even prickly, but surely a mind; and one
which must be included in any series that intends, as this one does, to
capture the intriguing varieties of thought and expression in the twentieth-century South. In fighting as he fought and losing as many fights
as he lost, Kester demonstrated at once the reality of the existence of
radical protest and the extreme difficulties of waging such protest in
the 1930s and 1940s. As Martin aptly puts it, Kester understood well
the function of the Judaic prophet, that is, someone who reminds his
fellow believers of their fundamental obligation to social justice.

Such a role cannot be measured by contemporaneous political suc-
cesses or popularity in a community. As a matter of fact, much of what
Martin's biography does is to force us to rethink what we mean by the
terms *southern, Protestant, reformist, radical, conservative,* and perhaps
most important, *success* and *failure*. The biographer's meticulous research and his carefully spun story have here demonstrated that Kester
was at different times all of these things, was legitimately each of them
for at least some period of his life, though certainly not all at the same
time and not by comfortable or standard definitions of the terms.
Furthermore, Martin's work shows that Kester was influential, he did
make a difference, and, if eccentric in some ways, he was in no sense a
mere curiosity. Kester, while often lonely, was not at all alone, and his
efforts, while largely failing in his own career, did awaken other people
to the complex of societal problems of labor relations and race relations. Without at all denying the obvious importance of the reformist
Protestant clergy in the decades of the 1950s and 1960s, students of
southern culture must take account of this group which preceded the
more storied later generation. To the old saw that today we stand on
the shoulders of giants from the past must now be added the observation that the giants of the recent past themselves were hoisted up on
the shoulders of figures such as Howard Kester.

Martin gives us a sad but oddly moving story. In the final account-
ing, the radical theologian and activist is seen poised on a remarkable
irony, one which cuts in multiple directions. The man, with his friends
and coworkers so outnumbered in his South, finally met an obstacle to
reform which was much more of an immovable force than the legions
of his reactionary antagonists. This enemy was within, and it was Kester's own southernness, his oldest and most deeply held beliefs, which
kept him from becoming a thoroughgoing radical and which limited
and hedged the messages he preached. For all that, his mighty
struggles with his own conflicted soul and his struggles with the dif-

ferent local power elites of the South were not futile or without any effect. Prophets often lose the ear of the crowds and the king while gaining the much greater prize of the attention of younger prophets-to-come who will speak effectively in another day. Thus, a study of one mind in the New South: Howard Kester, prophet on a pilgrimage through a time of troubles in the South.

John Herbert Roper
General Series Editor

ACKNOWLEDGMENTS

Scholarship is a collaborative endeavor, and I have benefited much from the insights, knowledge, and generosity of others. I am especially indebted to the cordial, efficient, and knowledgeable staff members at the following libraries: the Southern Historical Collection and North Carolina Collection, Louis Round Wilson Library, the University of North Carolina at Chapel Hill; Manuscript Department, William R. Perkins Library, Duke University; Special Collections and University Archives, Heard Library, Vanderbilt University; Peace Collection, Friends Historical Library, Swarthmore College; Seeley G. Mudd Library, Princeton University; Speer Library, Princeton Theological Seminary; Disciples of Christ Historical Society; Manuscript Division, Library of Congress; Knight/Capron Library, Lynchburg College; Archives Division, the State Historical Society of Wisconsin; and the Donald O. Rod Library, University of Northern Iowa. The material from the American Civil Liberties Union Archives is published with the permission of Princeton University Libraries. Documents from the National Association for the Advancement of Colored People Records in the Manuscript Division of the Library of Congress are included with the permission of the association.

A number of friends and associates of Howard Kester corresponded or talked with me about his life and work. While I cannot mention all of them here, I do wish to acknowledge the assistance of a few individuals. The late Harry Leland Mitchell of the Southern Tenant Farmers Union and O. R. Post, a student and friend of Kester during his years at Montreat-Anderson College, not only shared with me their own insights but suggested other people with whom I might talk. Nelle Morton, Warren Ashby, and David Burgess of the Fellowship of Southern Churchmen provided information about the FSC for an earlier project that proved valuable in the preparation of this manuscript. Family members Nancy Kester Neale, Jane Kester, Maud Austine Paris, and Elizabeth Moore Kester facilitated my research by talking with me about the Kester and Harris families and making available papers and photographs in their possession.

Several friends and professional colleagues helped to make this a better book than it otherwise would have been. Professor Linda O.

McMurry of North Carolina State University shared some correspondence that she had with Kester as a part of her work on George Washington Carver and directed me to several Kester letters in the Carver Papers. Elizabeth Jacoway, who spent time with Kester during the 1970s as a part of her research on the Penn Normal Agricultural and Industrial School, provided valuable clues to his state of mind late in life. Professors Charles W. Eagles of the University of Mississippi and Gaines M. Foster of Louisiana State University not only discussed facets of this project with me on numerous occasions but also read a draft of the manuscript and raised thoughtful questions that helped me clarify certain issues and express my ideas more concisely. Professors Charles E. Quirk and David A. Walker of the University of Northern Iowa also read the manuscript carefully and called attention to a number of stylistic and substantive problems.

John H. Roper, editor of the series of which this book is a part, John McGuigan, Acquisitions Editor of the University Press of Virginia, and those who read the manuscript for the press suggested changes designed to add both breadth and depth to the study. Portions of two of my articles are reprinted here: "Critique of Southern Society and Vision of a New Order: The Fellowship of Southern Churchmen, 1934–1957," *Church History* 52 (1983): 66–80, with the permission of the American Society of Church History, and "A Prophet's Pilgrimage: The Religious Radicalism of Howard Anderson Kester, 1921–1941," *Journal of Southern History* 48 (Nov. 1982): 511–30, with the permission of the editor.

The University of Northern Iowa supported this endeavor by granting me a Summer Research Fellowship in 1982 and a Professional Development Leave in the fall of 1985. Over the past few years several students helped with the research for this project, most recently Michelle Wubben, Stephanie Steil, Jennifer Andregg, Gayle Lundgren, Kathleen Howell, and Jodie Stockberger. Judith M. Dohlman, secretary in the Department of History at the University of Northern Iowa, patiently, accurately, and without complaint typed several versions of the manuscript.

Katherine Finnegan Martin made sacrifices of time, energy, and money in order that this book might become a reality. She assisted in the research, offered constructive criticisms, and helped edit much of the manuscript, no small task given her husband's deficiencies as a typist and speller. All of this she did while pursuing her own career and serving as mother to Andrew, a toddler who will be very glad that his daddy's book is done. While it is hardly commensurate with the contributions that family, friends, and colleagues have made, I can do no more for the moment than to say simply, thank you.

INTRODUCTION

On Wednesday morning, 13 July 1977, residents of Asheville, North Carolina, who scanned the obituary column of their local newspaper noticed a brief item that read in part:

> Kester Dies; Former Dean of M-A College
>
> Howard A. Kester, 72, of High Top Colony, Black Mountain, died Tuesday in an Asheville hospital after a long illness.
>
> A native of Martinsville, Va., and a former resident of Beckley, W. Va., he moved to Black Mountain 30 years ago. Mr. Kester was a former director of Christmount Assembly and was former professor of Montreat-Anderson College, where he was Dean of Students.
>
> A retired minister of United Church of Christ, he was a former Sunday School teacher at Black Mountain First United Methodist Church. He was also a Mason.

With these terse lines the *Asheville Citizen* summarized what appeared to be a reasonably successful but rather conventional career. Although both the *Citizen* and the *Charlotte Observer* later carried brief articles highlighting some of the more dramatic facets of Kester's work, the tone and substance of the obituary suggest the extent to which this unusual man had been forgotten by the mid–1970s.

During the early 1920s Howard Kester embarked upon a quest for a life of Christian service which over the next forty years took him on a circuitous intellectual and emotional journey. This pilgrimage was marked not only by a number of jobs but also by a variety of theological and ideological phases that ranged from conservative Christian paternalism, to evangelical liberalism, to neoorthodox Christian socialism, and finally to an ill-defined religious liberalism tempered by neoorthodoxy and infused with some of the rural and small-town values of his youth. In the course of his journey Kester often found himself at odds with the secular and religious forces in his society while at the same time he was embroiled in an intensely personal struggle to transcend his own cultural limitations. He loved the South but hated much that was typically southern. He was profoundly religious but rejected much of the theology and practice of his region's brand of Protestantism.

Opponents viewed Kester as a fool or a fanatic. He considered himself a radical and a prophet. Certainly his vision of a South characterized by an equitable economic and social order was radical by the standards of his day. His radicalism was not essentially Marxian, although his reading of Marx and other theoreticians of the Left helped him formulate his ideas. There was more of Jesus and Jefferson than of Marx and Engels in his vision. Throughout most of his career, Kester was more a prophet than a revolutionary. His radicalism was generally one of ends rather than means. He measured society against what he believed to be a biblical ethic, and whenever it failed to measure up, he strove through word and deed to bring about change. During his most radical phase he accepted the possibility that violence might be a necessary weapon in the struggle for justice, condoning it in theory but usually warning against its use on practical and philosophical grounds. He accepted such forms of pressure as strikes, demonstrations, and legislation but never ceased to hope that men could be converted rather than coerced into righteousness. For much of his life this prophet, reformer, and teacher struggled to eliminate prejudice, curb the excesses of capitalism, revitalize rural culture, and awaken his region's religious establishment to a more sophisticated understanding of its social responsibility.

Kester's relative obscurity was due in part to the fact that he had gone about some of his tasks quietly, even covertly, in hopes of provoking as little opposition as possible. Another reason for his comparative anonymity was that his work, like that of other activists who labored in the South in the era before the civil rights movement, had been eclipsed by the dramatic events that unfolded in the region during the 1950s and 1960s. Only during the past two decades have authors such as Jacquelyn Hall, Morton Sosna, Frank Adams, Anthony Dunbar, John P. McDowell, and John M. Glen begun to give earlier generations of dissenters the attention their activities warrant, and only recently have they begun to recognize the degree to which religion motivated some of these advocates of change.[1]

Students of religion in the South such as Samuel S. Hill, John Lee Eighmy, Kenneth K. Bailey, and John Boles have generally regarded white southern Protestantism as individualistic, otherworldly, or complacent and consequently uninterested in or hostile to fundamental social change.[2] Most scholars would agree with Hill that Christians in the region sometimes engaged in religious benevolence but would also concur in his judgment that such good works warrant "no identification with the Social Gospel tradition."[3] While this interpretation is not inaccurate, it is somewhat misleading on two counts. It does not acknowledge the legitimacy of social action outside the context of the Social Gospel, and it does not do justice to the small but significant liberal and radical elements that emerged on the region's religious periphery between the world wars.

During the late nineteenth and early twentieth centuries, members of mainline churches in the South were not unconcerned with social issues but usually defined problems and formulated solutions to them in pietistic or paternalistic terms. They often viewed society as inimical to personal righteousness and sought to change it in ways conducive to the development of piety. The southern religious establishment's support of Sabbatarian, temperance, and other legislation governing private and public morality attests to its pietistic concerns. Many Christians in the region also felt it their duty to try to ameliorate the lot of the less fortunate within the framework of the existing socioeconomic order. The church's numerous charitable activities and the involvement of at least some clergy and laity in the crusades against such evils as convict leasing, child labor, and lynching provide considerable evidence of Christian paternalism among regional Protestants.

The prophetic conception of social responsibility judges society against what is believed to be a biblical standard of justice and, when necessary, strives for repentance and fundamental changes in the name of righteousness. It is true that this dimension of Christianity was almost nonexistent in the South. Undoubtedly, here and there a few people recognized their religion's implications for social as well as personal transformation. What was required if this realization was to become a significant force was the critical distance to enable individuals to grasp the contradictions between principle and practice in their region. This kind of objectivity was more likely to develop as industrialization and urbanization began to alter the traditional character of rural and small-town community life in parts of the South and as education and travel exposed at least some young southerners to new ideas and circumstances that gave them a better perspective on Dixie's problems.

By the 1920s and 1930s significant, though not ubiquitous, economic and social changes occurring in the region, and broadening educational horizons for at least some southerners, had begun to awaken a small number of young white men and women to the injustice and inhumanity in their society. During these years Lillian Smith began her work as writer and publisher. Myles Horton and Don West founded Highlander Folk School. James Dombrowski completed his analysis of Christian socialism in the United States and joined the Highlander staff. H. L. Mitchell and Clay East founded the Southern Tenant Farmers Union in Arkansas. Radical preachers Ward Rodgers and Claude Williams launched their labor and political work. Howard Kester began his service as secretary of the Fellowship of Reconciliation and later the Committee on Economic and Racial Justice, and hundreds of others joined or supported a variety of politically or socially active groups ranging from the Communist party to the Fellowship of Southern Churchmen. For some of these individuals, such as Mitchell and East, religion played little if any role in their work. For others, including Smith and Horton, Christian values were initially important in shaping their ethical convictions and sense of social responsibility, but as they matured they did not define either the problems they addressed or their own mission in religious terms. For still others, among them Kester and most of the people attracted to the Fellowship of Southern Churchmen, Protestant Christianity provided the primary impetus to, and major motif in, their activism. These men and women, some of whom like Kester chose to think of themselves as prophets, judged society against what they believed to be a divine standard; and whenever it fell short, they called the South's institutions and practices into question and dedicated themselves to a crusade for change in the interest of justice.

The story of Howard Kester's quest to find a meaningful way to serve both his region and his God is a complex, paradoxical, and absorbing tale. Beyond its intrinsic interest, however, it may also help to illuminate the struggles of the small but growing number of dissenters who appeared in the South during the 1920s and 1930s, especially those who emerged from the matrix of regional Protestantism. Kester's experiences elucidate the way in which social change, evolving cultural values, and training or work in other parts of the nation or abroad could produce unorthodox views. Yet his inability to define his own religious and social role satisfactorily also suggests the difficulty that activists born in the rural and small-town late Victorian South sometimes had in transcending their own cultural limitations as they confronted a wide range of economic and social problems.

CHAPTER 1

■ **"Train Up a Child** ■
in the Way He
Should Go"

oward Kester was born in Martinsville, Virginia, on 21 July
1904, the youngest of the three surviving children of William
Hamilton and Nannie Holt Kester.[1] Although William Kester
had spent most of his life there, he was not a native of the Old Domin-
ion. His father had been one of the numerous northern immigrants
who had come into the South in the aftermath of the Civil War. Howard's grandfather moved his family from Washingtonville in central
Pennsylvania to western Virginia sometime in the 1870s in search of a
healthier climate for his children. The émigrés moved first to Bristol
and then to the flourishing town of Roanoke in the mountains of that
state.[2]

The Kester ancestry is traceable to the early days of the colony of
Pennsylvania. The patriarch of the family, Paulus Kuster, with his wife
Gertrude and their three sons Arnold, Johanus, and Hermanus, im-
migrated to America around 1685 from Krefeld, located along the
lower river Rhine in the vicinity of Cologne. Fleeing Germany to escape religious persecution, they hoped to find in William Penn's wil-
derness refuge for dissenters the freedom of worship denied them in
their homeland. The Kusters were among the first settlers in the Ger-
mantown district of the colony and worshiped with Mennonite and
Quaker groups there.

The Kesters who settled in Virginia in the 1870s were descendants
of Johanus. A family tradition says that he was a surveyor who rendered
such valuable service to the colony that William Penn awarded him a
substantial grant of land near what is today Norristown. Johanus, out
of either apathy or ineptitude, lost the undeveloped grant to squatters
who settled upon, improved, and eventually gained title to the land.
His heirs were therefore yeomen, artisans, and craftsmen rather than
members of the Keystone State's landed elite.[3]

Nannie Holt Kester, Howard's mother, was the youngest of the twelve children of Elizabeth Brafford and Josiah W. Holt. Her family's English and Scotch-Irish roots were planted firmly in the soil of ante-bellum Virginia. Although not wealthy, Josiah, a farmer and carpenter, was prosperous enough in the prewar era to provide his wife and children with a measure of comfort and rural middle-class respectability. The extent to which the Civil War altered the family's economic and social condition is not entirely clear. Throughout her life Nannie re-counted stories she had heard as a child about the hardships of war, the scorched-earth policy of Union troops, and the way in which her family sank its silver and china in the river to avoid confiscation by Yankee forces. Yet while the war embittered the Holts, it apparently did not impoverish them. Although the census of 1870 described him as a landless agricultural worker, Josiah Holt was not simply a tenant or day laborer. He managed the John Daniels plantation in Amherst County near the present site of Sweet Briar College. This position, while hardly making them affluent, enabled the Holts to maintain themselves comfortably and to sustain their sense of pride and social status.

The death of Josiah Holt sometime during the late seventies or early eighties brought greater hardship than had the war. Several of his younger children were still either wholly or partially dependent upon their mother. Faced with the necessity of providing for her offspring, Elizabeth Holt moved to Roanoke where family connections and a booming local economy seemed to afford the greatest chance for secu-rity. There Nannie Holt met and, in September 1892, married Wil-liam Hamilton Kester.[4]

Shortly after their marriage the couple settled in Martinsville. At the time Kester was working as a traveling salesman for Bonsack Brothers, a Roanoke firm which manufactured and merchandised fab-ric. The job required that he be away much of the time. His absences became increasingly unsatisfactory as the family expanded with the birth of Jane Elizabeth in 1897 and the arrival of Holt in 1900.[5] Wil-liam came from a long line of merchant tailors but had never intended to follow in this family tradition. Now, however, the stability of a tailor's life-style and the opportunity to tap what appeared to be a lucrative market among the burgeoning business and professional classes of Martinsville made this occupation increasingly attractive. Consequently, in 1900 he attended a cutting school in New York City where he expanded upon and perfected the basic skills learned from his father. He then returned home and opened a shop in partnership with his brother.[6]

The prospects for such an enterprise seemed bright in the early years of the twentieth century. Martinsville was caught up in the enthusiasm for economic expansion that had been sweeping the South for more than two decades. Since the 1880s apostles of a "New South" had been preaching a gospel of economic diversification, industrialization, and intersectional reconciliation as a means of revitalizing the defeated and impoverished South. Advocates of regional redemption encouraged southerners to look to the future rather than the past and to take their economic destiny into their own hands. During the last decades of the nineteenth century, civic leaders and private entrepreneurs across the South began endeavoring to heed this advice. Motivated by dreams of community progress or personal profit, they began scrambling to mobilize human, economic, and natural resources in the name of local or regional advancement. By the turn of the century many southerners pointed with pride to what they regarded as the metamorphosis of their section. Confusing hope with reality, they sometimes refused to recognize the limited scope of their much-touted economic revolution and closed their minds to the fact that industrialization, when accompanied by episodes like the depression of the 1890s, was not an unmitigated blessing.

The *Henry County Bulletin*, the weekly newspaper serving Martinsville and the surrounding county during the early years of the century, provides evidence that the local citizenry was caught up in the fervor and boosterism characteristic of the New South and Progressive eras. The issue for 5 May 1910, devoted considerable space to an exposition of the community's assets and accomplishments. The editor boasted of its clean mountain air, pure water, and moderate climate, its modern hydroelectric and sanitation facilities, its proximity to other flourishing New South towns, and its excellent rail connections via the Southern and Norfolk and Western railroads. He pronounced its citizens public spirited, its labor force plentiful and intelligent, its religious life vigorous, and its schools excellent.

The *Bulletin* declared that Martinsville welcomed investors, settlers, and workers and was prepared to offer "special inducements to new industries." To demonstrate that the community's economic climate was as healthy as its physical and social environment, the paper reported that the area's industrial base already included companies manufacturing or processing textiles, overalls, furniture and other wood products, tobacco, and grain. The town of approximately four thousand also boasted two banks, two wholesale establishments, and forty retail stores.[7]

William Kester soon found himself a respected and successful member of the business community of which the *Bulletin* was so proud. For more than a decade the family tailor shop prospered as local residents availed themselves of the fine fabrics and quality craftsmanship that the Kester brothers offered. Not until the mid–1910s did problems develop that led to the demise of the enterprise.

Although they began their life together at the dawn of a new era in the history of the South and benefited from the economic changes occurring in the region, William and Nannie Kester were products of the nineteenth century. The values and attitudes permeating their household were in many ways typical of late Victorian America. Like most Victorians, they believed that the family was important both as a means of mutual economic and emotional support and as an instrument for inculcating moral and social values. This conviction had prompted William Kester to change his occupation from that of salesman to the more stable one of tailor, and it contributed to his decision to relocate his family on the outskirts of Martinsville, away from what he considered the disruptive influences of town. He was a craftsman and businessman, but he had a deep appreciation for the virtues of country life. In the early years of the century Martinsville, in spite of its industrial pretensions, was still hardly more than an overgrown country town nestled amid a patchwork of farms producing tobacco, corn, hay, and a variety of fruits and vegetables. Therefore, Kester had little difficulty finding the kind of semirural environment he wanted for his family. A year or two after Howard's birth, his father purchased a small tract of land about a mile outside of town and built a house there. Too small to constitute a farm, the property was large enough to allow the senior Kester to indulge his passion for keeping fine livestock, especially horses, and to provide his children with a wide range of what he regarded as character-building responsibilities.[8]

The world of Howard's childhood was, therefore, superficially little different from that of many other rural southern children of his generation. While he had closer ties to the nearby town than did most of his farm-boy contemporaries, he too had to attend to his daily round of rural chores, caring for the animals, working the garden, making repairs, and performing numerous other tasks around the homestead. In his spare time he roamed the surrounding fields and forests, becoming acquainted with the diversified agriculture of Henry County, getting to know the black and white farmers and tenants in his vicinity, and developing a familiarity with and lifelong appreciation for nature. Yet Kester's experience was fundamentally different from that of the majority of rural southern youth. His family never relied upon farming for survival. William exposed his children to what he believed to be the benefits of country life without forcing them to be dependent upon the vagaries of an agricultural economy. The relative security of this semi-agrarian environment fostered in Howard a somewhat romantic understanding of rural life in which he conceived of the farm primarily as a social rather than an economic unit.

The values that the Kesters sought to nurture in their family circle were characteristic of much of the white Protestant middle class in the Upper South during the late Victorian era. Believing in moral absolutes, personal and social progress, and the virtue of community cohesiveness, they tried to impress upon Howard and his siblings a sense of the importance of religious commitment, education, hard work, self-mastery, personal honor, and social responsibility.[9]

Religion was an important component of the South's cultural and social system, and the Protestant ethos permeated the Kester household. William's ancestry was Quaker, while Nannie had been reared in a devout and staunchly Presbyterian home. When the couple settled in Martinsville, they joined the local Presbyterian congregation and became active members. William Kester eventually served as an elder, and participation in the services and other activities of the church was an important part of the family's weekly routine.[10] The fact that at Howard's baptism, allegedly with water from the Jordan River, his parents dedicated their infant son to the ministry suggests the intensity of their religious commitment. The extent to which they thereafter actively sought to shape their youngest child's future is not clear, but they certainly encouraged every sign of interest in a ministerial career.

Nannie, a gentle but firm woman whose righteous indignation flared only in the face of insensitivity or cruelty, provided much of her children's direct religious and ethical instruction. By example and persuasion she labored to inculcate into them a strong sense of Christian morality and southern manners, as understood by middle-class rural and small-town Virginians. Her method of instruction, which included coercion only as a last resort, was calculated to build character, not merely to command obedience. In his seventies Howard remembered vividly his mother's approach to the nurture of her children's moral development:

> From the earliest days we were indoctrinated by what she conceived as the "marks of a christian man and woman"—and we were all surrounded by and immersed in a deep and profound love. When I failed, for example,

to be what she thought "a christian Gentleman and Virginian" should be—in terms of courtesy and good manners—the whip was not the corrective influence. Instead of the whip, she took me or all three of her children into the closet in her bedroom, closed the door and both loved us and prayed over us. She always explained *why* we had "misbehaved" and how important to man and God it was for us to be "gentle, gracious, and kind to all of God's creation"—to all living creatures. When the talk and the prayer was over we felt both cleansed, instructed and rededicated.[11]

Howard's general acceptance of his parents' religious values and hopes for his future attests to the effectiveness of his mother's methods. Although he flirted with the possibility of studying law or becoming a teacher, the idea of a life of Christian service captured his imagination. At an early age he began preparing himself for a religious vocation. He studied the Bible regularly and had read it through several times before graduating from high school. He also engaged in daily devotionals during which he recited the Twenty-third Psalm, the Lord's Prayer, Now I Lay Me Down to Sleep, and a personal appeal seeking forgiveness for his sins.[12]

The religious instruction, Bible study, and prayer that were such an integral part of Kester's childhood bred in him a profound but conventional sense of religiosity. He felt keenly the reality of God and perceived the deity as a loving father whose compassion for his creatures should be reflected in human relationships. His mind was filled with the rolling cadences of the admonitions of the prophets and the graphic simplicity of the ethical parables of Jesus; however, he did not yet grasp the social implications inherent in Christianity. As a child he lacked the detachment and powers of abstraction necessary to enable him to step back from the world of which he was a part and measure it against what he would later regard as the plumb line of divine justice. His youthful concern for the welfare of others was, therefore, largely a product of his parents' decency and the sense of mutual responsibility characteristic of the community in which he lived.

William and Nannie Kester considered intellectual growth almost as important as moral development. Both parents were literate and loved books. They tried to broaden their children's horizons and stimulate their intellectual curiosity by reading to them not only from collections of Bible stories but also from a wide range of other literature. Indeed, Howard believed that his first name came from a novel by Sir Walter Scott, whose works his mother loved, while his nickname "Buck" was derived from that of a Zane Gray hero. The Kesters encouraged their children to get as much formal education as possible and were able to avoid sacrificing their schooling to economic necessity.[13]

In the early years of the twentieth century, Martinsville had only begun to experience the erosive as well as the constructive effects of social and cultural changes upon community life. Racial prejudice was, of course, ubiquitous, and there were the first signs of industrial class consciousness, but the area retained many characteristics of an earlier, more organic society in which ties of kinship and friendship were important cohesive forces and economic and social relationships tended to be personal rather than bureaucratic and institutional.[14] The Kesters tried to equip their children with the integrity and sense of community responsibility necessary to function effectively in such a world.

In Martinsville a verbal commitment and a firm handshake still sealed many agreements, especially among the community's small businessmen. Therefore, personal success as well as the viability of this traditional way of doing business rested more on individual honesty and responsibility than on legal obligation. William Kester believed in and conveyed to his children the importance of being a person of honor whose word others could trust. He rarely signed a contract because he thought that a man's word was his bond and such formal legal arrangements were therefore unnecessary. Once parties to an agreement had pledged themselves, only mutual consent could justify breaking a commitment.

As far as the senior Kester was concerned, nothing, not even racial prejudice or peer pressure, took precedence over the principle of integrity. His convictions were occasionally tested, as, for example, when the only black doctor in Henry County needed a fast buggy horse in order to meet the needs of his patients. Aware that William Kester possessed a horse widely reputed to be one of the best in the county, he made the tailor an offer for it. Kester, recognizing the physician's need and judging the offer a fair one, sold the prized animal. Some members of the white community tried to persuade Kester to revoke the sale. However, he had given his word, and in spite of their entreaties, based on an appeal to racial solidarity, he refused to break the agreement.[15]

A deep sense of responsibility for the welfare of friends and neighbors was another characteristic of life in Henry County that the Kesters exemplified. Illness, death, or some other trouble in a neighbor's home would find Nannie there with food and an offer of assistance. During periods of community crisis, area residents could count on William to help those experiencing misfortune. When a scarlet fever epidemic swept Martinsville early in the century, the tailor worked days in his shop and ministered throughout the night to people suffering from the disease. [16]

The couple's largess was not restricted to members of their own race or class. Like most white southerners, they had daily contact with blacks and seem to have developed a deep, though paternalistic, affection for some of them, especially the several domestics and laborers whom they employed over the years. When their servants or hired hands required medical attention or faced other circumstances beyond their means, the Kesters provided for them. Black men who got into trouble with the law sometimes came to William for assistance, and he usually did whatever he could on their behalf. Furthermore, on several occasions the family assumed responsibility for the care of orphaned or deprived black children in the area. [17]

The Kesters' benevolence was extraordinary in degree but not in kind. The lengths to which they would go in extending a helping hand to people in need were unusual, but the fact that their charity was blind to racial or class distinctions was not. For them, as for many devout white southern Protestants of the era, Christian compassion for the less fortunate, not a spirit of egalitarianism, explains their generosity. Like their contemporaries, they took for granted the inferiority of blacks and suspected that the condition of most poor whites was a function of character rather than environment.

Yet in the Kester household, whenever considerations of race or class seemed to contravene fundamental principles of fairness and decency as the family understood them, principle usually triumphed over prejudice. One evening when Howard was nine or ten years old, he sat in his father's shop while William tended to his accounts. An intoxicated black employee staggered into the shop demanding immediate payment of his wages. When Kester's efforts to reason with the inebriated worker failed, he lost his temper, picked up a stick, and struck the profane intruder with such force that the blow sent him reeling through the front door into the street. As Kester's wrath subsided, he was overcome with remorse. The embarrassed tailor tried unsuccessfully to surrender to Martinsville's authorities, but community officials evidently regarded Kester's enraged assault on a black man as justifiable or at least acceptable. Nevertheless, his remorse and willingness to accept the consequences of his actions made it clear to his son that neither rage nor race justified irresponsible conduct. [18]

The religious and social values that the Kesters tried so diligently to cultivate generally were accepted by their children. Now and then inconsistencies between what he observed and what he was taught prompted Howard to raise questions about his region's mores. He wondered why the black boys with whom he played were considered inferior since he could discern no important differences between himself and them other than the color of their skin. In fact, in some respects, such as shooting marbles, they seemed clearly superior. Neither could he understand why many residents of Martinsville regarded local industrial laborers with such disdain. Several of his best friends came from the ranks of the mill operatives, and in so far as he could tell, they differed little, if at all, from anyone else. He was upset to discover that not even the Presbyterian church was free of this class consciousness. When a young boy, a cotton mill worker, tried to attend the Presbyterian Sunday school, its superintendent, who managed one of the local mills, ejected the poorly dressed child. At the urging of Kester and his classmates, a sympathetic teacher allowed the youth to continue attending the class.[19]

These occasional questions and protests arose out of a childish innocence and clarity of vision rather than from an essentially critical attitude toward the society of which he was a part. Kester's parents created for their children a secure environment exemplifying many of the best characteristics of their culture and sheltered them from much of the harsher reality of southern life. Only as Howard began emerging from this familial cocoon did he even begin to comprehend the fundamental problems of his region.

In the mid-teens competition from manufactured clothing and serious personal and business difficulties that developed between the Kester brothers led to the dissolution of their partnership. The experience was emotionally devastating for William and had financially catastrophic results for the family. They lost everything they owned in Martinsville except their home.

The collapse of the Martinsville enterprise shattered the relative security of the Kesters' world. For the first time, the children had to assume a significant part of the burden of providing the family's financial support. At the age of twelve Howard took his first job, that of water boy for a road construction crew working in the vicinity of Martinsville. In 1916 his father, in his middle forties and faced with the necessity of starting anew, went to the booming coal town of Beckley, West Virginia. Within a few months he had established a tailoring business, and the following year he moved his family there.[20]

As the train carrying the Kesters to West Virginia wound its way through the mountains of the state, passing through mining camp after mining camp, Howard witnessed poverty the likes of which he had not seen before. The mill workers of Martinsville were poor, but their condition seemed to the twelve-year-old boy infinitely superior to that of the people living in the shanty towns strewn along the valleys and up the hillsides near the mines. He thought the mountains beautiful, but the scars left upon that beauty by the mines and the squalor in which the miners lived appalled the apprehensive youth and convinced him that his family was moving into an area only "seven doors from hell."[21]

Conditions in Beckley were better than in the mining camps along the way, but they differed at least in degree from those Kester had known previously. He held a variety of part-time and summer jobs there: hauling cement, lumber, and bricks; laboring in a sawmill; serving as a baker's assistant; and working in a drugstore. These jobs in a new and different community enabled Howard to contribute to the shoring up of his family's sagging economic fortunes and at the same time gave him a new perspective on the world.[22]

Beckley was what Martinsville aspired to be but was not, an industrial center. The nation's manufacturing and transportation revolution and the outbreak of World War I had stimulated the demand for coal and hence economic growth in the area. The population of Raleigh County, in which Beckley was situated, had doubled between 1900 and 1910 and increased by approximately two-thirds during the next decade. In the mid-teens the city's newspapers carried numerous stories of record coal production, extensive road construction, new businesses, and expanding residential areas. This material progress was not, however, universal, nor was it free of the difficulties often associated with economic development.[23]

The growing affluence of Beckley's middle and upper classes contrasted sharply with the poverty of many of the miners and mountaineers who inhabited the coves and valleys of the surrounding Appalachians. The uneven distribution of wealth in the area produced considerable class consciousness and friction. The laborers of the region, believing themselves entitled to a larger share of the prosperity they helped to generate, were restless and determined to improve their condition. Their dissatisfaction and resentment erupted in 1919 in a major strike which resulted in the deployment of federal troops to guarantee the peace and the intervention of evangelist Billy Sunday to defuse the tension.[24]

Raleigh County's black population grew even more spectacularly than its white. In 1890 only seventy-nine blacks lived in the county.

Their number rose to 2,052 by 1910 and 6,393 by 1920. This dramatic increase contributed to considerable racial tension as well as class consciousness in the community. Beckley therefore afforded fertile soil in which the resurgent Ku Klux Klan (KKK) could take root. There, as elsewhere, the KKK thrived on white prejudice toward blacks and other minorities, wartime anxiety, and middle-class concern about alleged cultural decay. The Klan professed to be the guardian of Anglo-Saxon Protestant civilization and appealed to people seeking to integrate themselves into a tightly knit, culturally pure community.[25]

William Kester joined the organization shortly after arriving in Beckley. He shared its white, Protestant, middle-class bias and probably equated membership with good citizenship. He may also have found in it the camaraderie and sense of belonging that he needed in his new surroundings. Whatever his reasons for joining, Kester remained a member for a relatively short time. Never comfortable with the senseless violence that some of the rabid racists of the era perpetrated against blacks, he tolerated a limited amount of intimidation and coercion of blacks or lower-class whites if it seemed in the public interest. However, he objected to the increasing lawlessness and unrestrained violence of the Klan, especially when directed at middle- and upper-class citizens. A Klan attack on the son of a West Virginia judge who allegedly beat his wife precipitated Kester's withdrawal from the organization. He agreed that the young man's action was reprehensible but believed that there were alternatives to mob violence when dealing with personal problems among people of the victim's social station.[26]

In Beckley the Kester family could not shelter Howard, as it had in Martinsville, from the harshness of racism or class antagonism. Working at a variety of jobs exposed him to the problems, prejudices, and ideas of a wide range of people. Although he knew little of his father's Klan involvement, he understood well the principles upon which the organization rested and the kinds of activities in which it engaged. While he was never really a part of the industrial work force, he witnessed the poverty and felt the prejudice that were corollaries of the area's economic development. Slowly he began to comprehend the complexity of life and to raise questions about its inequity.

Out of his social, religious, and familial milieu Kester absorbed a complex and sometimes contradictory constellation of values and attitudes that would ultimately both stimulate and inhibit his future work. Predisposed by his childhood experiences to appreciate the virtues of rural life, he was also schooled to the benefits of the technological and industrial progress that threatened an agrarian life-style.

Reared in a culture in which religion served as an important cohesive force, he attended churches that talked of Christian brotherhood but condoned prejudice toward blacks and tolerated discrimination against the poor. Trained to exercise self-restraint and to respect law and order, he lived in one of the most personally and socially volatile and violent sections of the nation.

Yet Kester did not at first perceive the inconsistencies of his world. To be sure, he occasionally wondered about the presumed inferiority of his black playmates and about the de facto exclusion of factory workers from worship in his church, but his attitude was not essentially critical. The principles of kindness and courtesy preached and generally practiced by his parents, as well as the harmonious, protected childhood environment created by them in Martinsville, sheltered him from most of the harsher realities of society. Not until his family's financial crisis disrupted his secure world and exposed him to new circumstances in a different community, an experience that coincided with the questioning of values and mores that often accompanies adolescence, did he even begin to entertain doubts about his region's social and economic order. Only in his college years did these reservations begin to evolve into a thoroughgoing critique of, and challenge to, the deficiencies of southern life.

CHAPTER 2

The Evolution of a Liberal Christian Activist

When Buck Kester entered Lynchburg College in the fall of 1921, there was little about the energetic young West Virginian that hinted at social or religious heterodoxy. He was paternalistic in his racial views, conservative although not fundamentalist in religion, and unsophisticated in his economic and political thought. During the 1920s, however, a variety of educational and professional experiences began altering his perceptions of the church, the South, and the role he hoped to play in the future of both. By the end of the decade Kester, who believed himself to have been in 1921 "as green a freshman as ever bored a college president," had become a veteran activist whose theological, social, and political views were liberal by comparison with those of most contemporary southerners.[1]

Lynchburg College was scarcely two decades old when Kester enrolled.[2] This fledgling Disciples of Christ institution, nestled in the rolling foothills of the Blue Ridge Mountains of Virginia, seems an unlikely place for the evolution of a social activist to have begun. Southern Protestantism had rarely been a force for positive economic or social change in the region, and members of Disciples of Christ congregations were frequently among the South's most conservative Christians. While the intellectual and social atmosphere at Lynchburg was definitely Christian, the college community's understanding of the faith seems to have been somewhat less conservative than that of the Disciples as a whole. Indeed, in the mid-twenties one disgruntled Virginia churchman charged that the college was "a center of radical modern thought and teaching," that it "employed a rank modernist to teach in the field of religion," and that it "retained a professor who taught the theory of evolution." The faculty's response to these charges provides considerable insight into the educational milieu in which Kester found himself. The college issued a statement in which its teaching staff declared:

It is our earnest desire and purpose to present all subjects taught (whether Art, or Bible, or English or Education, or History, or Home Economics, or Language, or Mathematics, or Music, or Psychology, or Sociology, or Natural Science) in a constructive way that will be conducive to the building of Christian faith, Christian ideals and moral and religious character, and thus prepare the young people in our several classes to take their place in the world, in whatever profession or vocation, to live for Christ and His Church and to be actively engaged in the promotion of the Kingdom of God.[3]

While such an atmosphere might prove stifling to some students, for others with a religious orientation, such as Kester, it afforded considerable opportunity for growth. Although his college experiences were not entirely responsible for the changes in him, it was during his Lynchburg years that Kester began to recognize clearly the inequities inherent in southern social and economic relations and to grope for some means of making his Christian faith relevant to the resolution of the region's problems.

While his evolving understanding of social and economic issues and the actions to which this new insight gave rise occasionally alienated peers and faculty alike, Kester was anything but a pariah on the Lynchburg campus. The slender, athletic young West Virginian with dark wavy hair, remarkably blue eyes, and friendly demeanor soon won the affection and respect of many of his classmates. He held a number of student offices, including the presidencies of the sophomore class, Ministerial Association, and Young Men's Christian Association (YMCA); a seat on the Board of Athletic Control; an associate editorship of the yearbook; membership on the interracial committee and the Southern Regional Council of the YMCA; chairmanship of the Virginia Field Council of the YMCA; and a southern area directorship of the Student Friendship Fund. During the autumn of his senior year, the college newspaper, the *Critograph,* wrote of Kester, "There has probably never been a man numbered among the students of Lynchburg College who has entered into its life more fully, contributed more to its advancement or increased further its prestige while resident than Howard Kester."[4]

Kester might have added athletic prowess to his laurels had he chosen a football scholarship over a ministerial one, both of which the college offered him as a freshman. However, believing that his destiny lay with the church, he accepted the ministerial scholarship and began preparing himself for his intended career. He concentrated his studies in Greek, English, history, and Bible. In spite of his many extracurricular activities, Kester made better than average grades; and at least one of his professors, C. L. McPherson, remembered him many years later as "one of the most stimulating students" he ever had. McPherson helped Kester develop a prose style which, if occasionally florid, was also at times powerful. Virginia Harrison, a speech instructor, helped him develop his talent as a public speaker.[5] These writing and oratorical skills proved invaluable in future years when he labored as propagandist and teacher on behalf of a variety of causes.

The professor who had the most profound impact on Kester was Robert Kirshner, who taught him Bible during his first year at Lynchburg. Kirshner caused the young student to begin taking the New Testament more "earnestly and seriously," and he "electrified" him with the simple if ambiguous observation that to be a Christian is to "be a little Christ."[6] Kester's interpretation of this insight by no means led to his immediate transformation into a religious or social radical. His conception of the ministry and mission of Jesus during his Lynchburg years appears to have been relatively conventional, although he does seem to have begun placing a greater emphasis on its prophetic component than did many of his peers. Kirshner was probably responsible for his student's initial awakening to the social dimension of Christianity and for heightening his commitment to the religious life. However, it was an eventful student pastorate and his involvement with the collegiate work of the YMCA that gave meaning to Kester's classroom experiences.

Kester first served as a student pastor in the rural community of Grassy Meadows, West Virginia, in the summer of 1922. There is no evidence that either his experiences or the quality of his service were extraordinary. His second summer charge, at Thurmond in 1924, was, however, more eventful. Here he became directly acquainted with many of the problems inherent in capitalism and with southern Protestantism's apparent inability to cope with them. At first the aspiring minister did not want to go to this rough-and-tumble mining community a few miles from Beckley where there had never been either a Protestant or Catholic clergyman and where he could, according to all reports, expect to accomplish little. Indeed, he had been told that Thurmond, known locally as the "Monte Carlo of the East," was perhaps the roughest place in West Virginia, "a place where there was no church, no Sunday School, nothing but dance halls and gambling dens." However, Kester persuaded himself that it was God's will that he go and comforted himself with the thought that Jesus would be with him every hour. Within a short time after his arrival, Kester wrote to a friend: "I am so very happy in my work here. They told me that this was the very worst field in West Virginia but I thank God that he counted me worthy to send me here. I believe very confidently that God sent me down here to do a special work for Him and I am so very very happy that I am here."[7]

Not everyone agreed with Kester that his Thurmond ministry was divinely ordained. His difficulties stemmed not from the hostility of irreligious laborers but from the attitudes of conventional Christians. During his pastorate local miners went on strike. Kester considered their grievances just and believed management's treatment of its employees incompatible with the social teachings of Christ. Consequently, he sided with the strikers. Some of the members of the Beckley Presbyterian church that sponsored his work did not agree with the student minister's stance, and its pastor dispatched an elder to investigate rumors of the novice clergyman's unorthodox behavior. When the elder confirmed the reports, the presbytery queried Kester about his religious and social beliefs and subsequently reprimanded him.[8] Although neither he nor his adversaries knew it, the Thurmond pastorate was to be his last Presbyterian charge.

His work with the intercollegiate YMCA probably did more to broaden Kester's social horizons than did his experience at Thurmond. Important forces on southern campuses during the 1920s and 1930s, the Young Men's and Young Women's Christian Associations (YWCA) not only ministered to the religious needs of students but also helped to raise the social consciousness of many. They labored in a variety of ways to improve international relations and to promote social justice. In both areas, they, especially the YWCA, were often well in advance of the attitudes and mores of the day.

In the aftermath of World War I, young people in many parts of the world began working to prevent the recurrence of such a catastrophe. In the United States the intercollegiate YMCA played an active role in this effort. The organization published special texts for students seeking to familiarize themselves with international issues. In conjunction with other groups, the Y promoted contacts among students from different nations. The World Student Christian Federation, an international confederation of YMCA, YWCA, Student Volunteer, and similar student Christian groups, in 1920 began providing relief for destitute students in war-ravaged parts of Europe and the Middle East. Through the Student Friendship Fund the federation raised a substantial amount of money among American collegians. It also sponsored annual international student conferences in Europe at which delegates discussed a wide range of problems.[9]

In 1922 the YMCA began conducting a series of annual Pilgrimages of Friendship to Europe. Organizers of these trips intended that they acquaint American students with their peers in other countries and expose them to the social and economic devastation wrought by World War I. In 1923 Y officials invited Howard Kester to join fourteen other students on one such pilgrimage. For most of the month of August the group toured Britain, France, Switzerland, Austria, Hungary, Czechoslovakia, Poland, and Germany. In France the pilgrims visited the sites of some of the bloodiest fighting of the war, including Château-Thierry, the Meuse Valley, and the Argonne Forest. In eastern Europe they witnessed the poverty and dislocation to which the war had contributed. In Czechoslovakia their hosts invited Kester to preach. Although inexperienced, the youthful apostle appears to have risen to the occasion. One diarist among the American students observed, "No telling what I would give if I had the ability and the nerve to do what Buck is doing."[10]

While the opportunity to preach was for Kester undoubtedly one of the highlights of the European trip, he and others seem to have recalled most vividly their visit to the Jewish ghettos of Poland. They had first encountered such a bleak community in Krakow, but it was that of Warsaw which imprinted itself most deeply upon their imaginations. The students arrived in Warsaw on August 10 and rode through the ghetto late that afternoon. One of them, compiling a report on this trip years later, observed that in the students' diary accounts: "the description of filth, poverty and stench baffles description." For Kester the most disturbing sight was the chain that lay coiled at the entrance to the ghetto. Until thirty-five years earlier, it had been pulled across the street each evening at sundown to imprison the Polish Jews in their miserable quarter. Decades later, he recalled that seeing this chain caused him to begin drawing some troubling parallels between Polish treatment of Jews and white America's treatment of blacks.[11]

In Switzerland the students visited the headquarters of the League of Nations, the Red Cross, and the YMCA. The pilgrimage culminated with a visit to Germany where for several days they traveled about the country observing the social and political instability that plagued that vanquished nation.[12]

The next year, at the request of David Porter, international student secretary of the YMCA, Kester served as southern area director of the

Student Friendship Fund. The Lynchburg College administration authorized his absence from some classes, and the YMCA provided funds for secretarial assistance and travel. During the academic year of 1924–25, Kester toured many of the colleges and universities of the South on behalf of European student relief. Channing Tobias and William Craver, leaders in the "Negro" work of the Y, urged Kester to include black schools among those he visited. They warned him that his efforts on these campuses would yield only meager financial results but contended that black students must be informed about international conditions. Thus, during his senior year at Lynchburg, Kester traveled across the South describing economic and social conditions in Europe and, perhaps to his surprise, learning much about those in his native region.[13]

Kester's education began almost upon his own doorstep. One of the schools at which he spoke was Virginia Theological Seminary and College, a black Baptist institution in Lynchburg. In the course of enlightening his audience about conditions abroad, he acknowledged the inequity and inhumanity in American race relations but urged patience on the part of blacks striving to improve conditions. One of those sharing the platform with him was Channing Tobias, who proceeded to give him what Kester described years later as "the worst spiritual spanking one man could give another." When Kester had completed his remarks, Tobias rose and declared indignantly: "The young man speaks of patience. What does he think we have been practicing but patience for over 300 years."[14]

Tobias's "spiritual spanking" and other experiences at black institutions began awakening the fledgling liberal to his ignorance of the attitudes and aspirations of black southerners. Gradually he became convinced that interracial interaction and dialogue were the keys to the resolution of the South's racial problems. Other young southerners of both races were beginning to arrive at similar conclusions. Here and there throughout the South, small groups of college and university students were taking a look at their region's racial mores and were beginning to recognize the injustice and inhumanity inherent in them.

The intercollegiate YMCAs and YWCAs helped to nurture these stirrings of conscience on southern campuses. For some years a handful of Y leaders, most notably Willis D. Weatherford, had been in the vanguard of regional efforts to improve relations between blacks and whites. As early as 1912 Weatherford, then YMCA student secretary for the South, had told the inaugural conference of the Southern Sociological Congress:

A Congress like this has absolutely no meaning save in so far as we attach sacredness and value to personality. And when you say personality that means all personality; it means the bad as well as the good, it means the defective as well as the efficient, it means the unattractive as well as the attractive, it means the diseased as well as the physically sound—yes, more than all these, it means the black as well as the white. If it does not mean this, then this Congress is a mere mockery, and we, as delegates, are sham men and women trying to play at make-believe interest in humanity.[15]

Weatherford wrote books and articles on the subject of race and race relations and repeatedly told white southerners that their destiny was inextricably related to that of black southerners and that the races must stand or fall together.

The war and postwar years seemed to many to bode only ill for the future of race relations. The era was marked by the renaissance of the Ku Klux Klan and the eruption of violent race riots throughout the nation. Others of both races, although alarmed by these developments, believed there was reason for optimism. These individuals, many of whom had been associated with the war work of the YMCA and YWCA, were heartened by the unprecedented interracial interaction and cooperation they had witnessed during the conflict. In the 1920s these and other socially conscious southerners sought to tap what they perceived as a new mood of maturity and sensitivity among at least some of their region's young people.

There could hardly be a more inaccurate appellation than that of "lost generation" for many American collegians of the twenties. While far from ubiquitous, idealism and social activism were not so uncommon as has sometimes been assumed. Nowhere were these qualities more prevalent than among the members of the intercollegiate Ys and the closely allied Student Volunteer Movement. Many, though probably not a majority, of the young men and women who belonged to these organizations eagerly addressed the problems of their day and accepted responsibility for their resolution. Southern students were, on the whole, more cautious and less aggressive than their counterparts elsewhere, but in the South, too, small bands of energetic, committed youth labored to make Christian principles, as they understood them, relevant to their society.

Groups such as the YMCA and YWCA, and especially the Student Volunteer Movement, seem at first glance unlikely matrices for the nurture of social activism. While they played a much larger role on college campuses than religious groups usually play today, they had, at least until World War I, generally stressed piety, fellowship, service, or evangelism rather than the Social Gospel. During the 1910s and 1920s circumstances gradually began altering the character of these organizations.

Nowhere was this change more apparent than in the Student Volunteer Movement. It had originated in the late 1800s to promote foreign missions. Its founders, among them the revivalist Dwight L. Moody, dreamed of the "evangelization of the world in this generation." In 1891 the movement had begun quadrennial conferences to promote contacts between students and missionaries. The first postwar conference held in Des Moines, Iowa, in 1919 was, like its predecessors, intended to promote foreign missions. World War I had convinced some Christians that there was a greater need than ever before for evangelization. However, a growing number of students had become disenchanted with the traditional missionary emphasis of the movement. Their dissatisfaction stemmed in part from the fact that many of the delegates to the conference were chosen as much for their prominence on campus as for their religious zeal and in part because the postwar generation of students, not a few of whom were veterans, were more concerned with secular problems than with evangelism. Some of the disaffected conferees, believing themselves saddled with an antiquated and inflexible leadership, organized de facto discussion groups to consider national and international economic and social problems not addressed by the larger conference.[16]

The quadrennial meeting of 1923 was planned in conjunction with the intercollegiate YMCA and YWCA. It reflected, as that of 1919 had not, the changing attitudes and concerns of contemporary students. On December 28 approximately seven thousand black and white students from more than one thousand colleges and universities throughout North America and thirty foreign countries convened at Cadle Tabernacle in Indianapolis, Indiana. During the following three days, delegates relegated the issue of world evangelization to a position of secondary importance. Most of their deliberations revolved around the theme of the relevance of Christian principles to contemporary economic, social, and political problems. On the second day the conferees divided themselves into forty-nine discussion groups to consider the "concrete issues of the present-day World." The students, having more confidence in their own ability and intelligence than in those of the Conference leaders, barred them from participation in these sessions. Conferees in forty-four of the discussion groups selected race relations, especially those in the American South, as the primary topic of their deliberations. Delegates of both races generally agreed that "there was no such thing as racial superiority, that racial discrimination and prejudice were unchristian, and that the Negro should have equal opportunity for education, life, and justice." Students in a few of the groups declared themselves in favor of "absolute equality in all relationships." [17]

The biracial convention had considerable impact on southern students in a number of urban educational centers. It provided many of them with their first genuinely interracial contacts. This experience, so novel and for some, at least, so rewarding, precipitated a flurry of activity in such cities as Knoxville, Nashville, Atlanta, and Lynchburg. Students in these areas sought to promote the spirit of Indianapolis on the local level through the organization of biracial intercollegiate forums. [18]

Although a member of the Student Volunteer Movement, Kester does not appear to have attended the quadrennial meeting of 1923, but he certainly was aware of much that had transpired there. The enthusiasm for interracial student forums that emanated from Indianapolis probably inspired the founding of such a group in Lynchburg, for which he and a student at Virginia Theological Seminary and College were responsible. Small, composed mainly of middle-class students, and self-consciously cautious in its approach to race relations, the Lynchburg group nevertheless proved important because it gave participants of each race their first opportunity to meet on a basis which approximated equality. [19]

The growing enthusiasm for interracial interaction among a minority of white YMCA and YWCA students in the South soon posed problems for some Y leaders, especially those at the regional conference center at Blue Ridge near Asheville, North Carolina. For a number of years the YMCA and YWCA had held their summer conferences for white students at this site and those for black students at Kings Mountain, North Carolina, and Talladega, Alabama. These annual convocations served an important educational function in the lives of many southern students, exposing them to some of the outstanding leaders of their generation and giving them an opportunity to consider the important issues of the day in the light of the Christian faith. Among the issues which conferees addressed most frequently during the twenties was that of relations between the races in the South and nation.

W. D. Weatherford, director of Blue Ridge, was proud of the center's role in the promotion of better race relations. Officials there had cooperated with intercollegiate Y leaders in their efforts to bring educated, able black speakers before the conferees. They hoped that exposure to middle-class blacks, a novel experience for many white southern youth, would begin to break down stereotypes and to foster a thoughtful approach to racial issues. Weatherford believed Blue Ridge to be "the place that has done more for the colored people than any other single spot in America."[20] Some among the students and their leaders, however, did not share Weatherford's assessment. They recognized his and the center's past contributions but believed the time had come to go further. In the early and mid twenties, first liberal YWCA officials, then a minority of students and officers within the YMCA, began protesting the Blue Ridge policy of providing segregated accommodations for black speakers.

As early as 1922 and 1923 the southern leadership of the YWCA began requesting permission to entertain black guests at its conferences on an integrated basis. When Blue Ridge authorities denied its petitions, the YWCA considered moving its student conferences elsewhere but concluded that a majority of white southern college women would not support such a move. It therefore decided to invite black speakers for visits of no more than a few hours, thereby avoiding subjecting guests to the indignities of segregation.[21] Meanwhile, perhaps as early as 1923 and certainly by 1924, a radical minority within the regional intercollegiate YMCA began seeking ways in which to undermine the center's discriminatory policies. In the latter year Howard Kester offered to entertain George Washington Carver, a guest speaker at the summer conference for southern students, in the cottage of the Lynchburg College delegation. As a result, Carver slept among and dined with the Lynchburg men. This tactic enabled the Virginians to sidestep Blue Ridge regulations and strike a blow for the principle of equality and also led to a lasting friendship between the black scientist and Kester.[22]

While such actions prompted criticism from some conferees as well as center officials, they met with the approval of John W. Bergthold, YMCA student secretary for the Southern Division, who frequently and somewhat puckishly waged his own battles against regional prejudice. Bergthold incurred the wrath of students and leaders alike on several occasions. For example, in 1926 clergyman and educator Mordecai Johnson visited Blue Ridge as a guest lecturer. When Johnson, a black man with a very light complexion, arrived just in time for the evening meal, Bergthold rushed him into the main dining room, seated him among the conference leaders, and had him served. None of the black guest's companions realized that as they dined with this latecomer, they were breaking one of the South's oldest racial taboos. A few days later Bergthold struck again. Just as a photographer prepared to snap a group portrait of the student conferees, the secretary rushed up with three visiting black delegates and positioned them in front of the contingent from the University of South Carolina. The Carolinians were not amused. Neither were many of the other white collegians. As a result of protests from a number of Y secretaries, Blue Ridge authorities arranged for another photo session and demanded that Bergthold buy the original photographic plates and destroy them. [23]

Liberal students and their allies among the YMCA leadership in the South did not confine themselves to subversive activities. Sometime during the middle years of the decade, Kester, speaking for a radical minority, sought to address the question of segregation at Blue Ridge directly by proposing the integration of student conferences. W. D. Weatherford and other YMCA and Blue Ridge leaders believed that integration, whether token or total, was unwise given the social milieu of the South. Weatherford believed that Blue Ridge had a three-fold mission: promoting "the value of religion, the sacredness of personality, and the dignity and sacredness of work." To force integration not only would endanger this mission but also would constitute the kind of dogmatism he and his associates had traditionally opposed. He argued that the center should lead, not drive, the South toward constructive social change. To push the issue of integration would "be more unchristian than the attitude of doing less than we wish we could by our few colored guests." [24]

The Blue Ridge board of directors rejected Kester's proposal but did permit, beginning about 1926, the exchange of fraternal student delegates between Blue Ridge and Kings Mountain. However, they allowed no more than five black representatives to attend the white conference annually. Furthermore, although the Kings Mountain conference was completely integrated, that at Blue Ridge remained segregated. Kester was among the first white YMCA members to journey to Kings Mountain, attending the conference there in the summer of 1926. He also helped Benjamin Mays, secretary of the Black Student Division in the South, locate other white students willing to attend the black conferences. Both the YWCA and the YMCA experimented with this exchange program for a few years in the late twenties, but the inflexibility of Blue Ridge officials led to its termination by 1930. [25]

By the time Howard Kester had graduated from Lynchburg College in 1925, his ministerial and YMCA work had exposed the young southerner to circumstances and attitudes that left him uneasy about the relevance of the church as he knew it to the economic and social problems of his region. Yet since childhood he had felt keenly the conviction that his life was to be spent in Christian service. Despite his misgivings about the institutional church, he entered Princeton Theological Seminary in the fall of 1925. He had chosen Princeton because he believed it to be an outstanding institution which could equip him for the career he intended to pursue. To his chagrin, he found his year at the Presbyterian seminary quite disillusioning.

In the mid-twenties Princeton Theological Seminary was embroiled in a controversy among liberal evangelical, moderate, and conservative factions within the Presbyterian church. These groups disagreed over matters of theology and church polity. The liberals accepted certain aspects of the new biblical criticism. The moderates did not but were willing to tolerate theological differences within the denomination. The conservatives adhered tenaciously to what they regarded as orthodoxy and wished to exclude from the church those whose ideas they deemed heretical. When Kester began his studies at the school, several faculty members represented the church's moderate majority, but conservatives led by J. Gresham Machen dominated its intellectual and religious life.[26] Machen was a cultured, sophisticated, scholarly man who had little interest in the dispensationalist and premillenarian ideas that absorbed most of his fundamentalist contemporaries. He was, however, convinced that Christianity rested on unalterable historical facts that could not be interpreted away. He believed that the greatest threat to the faith lay not in atheism or agnosticism but in liberalism. Christianity, as Machen understood it, included belief in a transcendent God, a humanity corrupted by sinfulness, the infallibility of biblical authority, salvation by vicarious atonement to which man must respond in faith, the inherent imperfection of human institutions, and a church composed of the brotherhood of the redeemed awaiting the bodily return of Jesus. Liberalism, he believed, was characterized by a tendency to pantheize God, exaggerate human potential, locate religious authority in the experience of humanity, treat Jesus as example rather than savior, stress salvation through obedience to moral law, and preach the possibility of social improvement. The differences between Christianity and liberalism were therefore so profound that the two were irreconcilable. Machen thought that the church of his day emphasized the material at the expense of the spiritual dimension of Christianity.[27]

Buck Kester's Christianity was less doctrinally rigorous than that of most conservatives. Writing in the late thirties, he recalled that when he entered Princeton he was neither a modernist nor a conservative but merely "an ordinary American boy in search for something I knew I did not have but must have if my life was to be meaningful."[28] The one thing about which he was relatively certain was that the church, if it was to be true to the teachings of Jesus, had to minister to the physical as well as the spiritual needs of humanity.

Kester soon found himself at odds with many people in the seminary community over not only theological but also economic and social issues. Most conservatives had little patience with students who manifested his rather modest brand of skepticism. One professor dismissed him from his class when he refused to affirm his belief in everything in the Westminster Confession of Faith and the Bible. On another occasion Kester asked an instructor about the social significance of a certain passage in Galatians. The professor replied, "Young man, in this class we are not concerned with or interested in the social significance of the New Testament."[29]

Kester had difficulty with peers as well as professors. In 1925, after becoming disenchanted with what they regarded as the lack of orthodoxy of the interseminary conference sponsored by the Middle Atlantic Association of Theological Seminaries, students at Princeton had organized the League of Evangelical Students. Although seminary president J. R. Stevenson and a minority of faculty members opposed this new group, a majority of the conservative faculty and student body supported it. When Kester entered the school, he, like other incoming seminarians, was asked to join this organization. He and a few others declined, an action which immediately marked them for special attention. The Friars Club, the most conservative group on campus, invited Kester to join. He thought the invitation stemmed from the members' conviction that they alone could convince the sinner of the error of his ways. He recalled years later that each evening at mealtime most of the club's members engaged in prayer for the salvation of the heretic.

The fact that Kester did not share the theological and socioeconomic views of most of his peers, and his sense that faculty and students alike regarded him as something of an agnostic, caused him much anguish and loneliness. He gradually found solace and intellectual stimulation outside the seminary community. He sometimes worshiped in a nearby black church rather than in the seminary chapel. During the course of the year he made several trips to Yale Divinity School and Union Theological Seminary where he talked with faculty and students and acquired books not available to him at his own institution.[30]

By the spring of 1926 Kester had become thoroughly disillusioned with Princeton, and many among the members of the seminary community were not very impressed with him. President Stevenson, who was not among the conservative majority at the school, may have understood and sympathized with Kester's plight. Stevenson invited the troubled student to his home to talk over his problems. Although the seminary president was not a fundamentalist, neither was he as liberal as Kester appeared to be. During the course of the evening Stevenson gently reproached his student for having rejected eighteen centuries of Christian thought and practice. The charge troubled Kester, who believed himself to be attempting to recover the essence of Christianity. He returned to his room and after a restless night concluded that Princeton was not the place for him. He packed his bags and caught the train for West Virginia.[31]

On one of his visits to the Northeast, Kester had met William Simpson, a modern follower of Saint Francis. Simpson, a graduate of Union Theological Seminary, had chosen to become a barefooted, shabbily clad mendicant, working among the poor and espousing the virtues of a simple Christian life before groups of college and university students. He urged Kester to abandon his studies and become a disciple of Saint Francis, a suggestion that the youthful Presbyterian initially found appealing. His reading of works about Saint Francis caused Kester to become fascinated with this gentle Christian lover of nature and to adopt him as a kind of patron saint, but he ultimately rejected the idea of the simple celibate life of his idol. Steeped in traditional familial values and possessed of considerable physical as well as spiritual passion, he persuaded himself that "it was more natural and difficult for a man to marry and have a family with the home as the center of his life and still do what St. Francis demanded of his disciples than to remain single and do it." He concluded that "since the home has always been the center of life . . . it must of necessity be a fundamental part of any effort to live a full and complete life." Therefore, "what Christianity and modern civilization needed was an example, or at least the effort on the part of two people, or a family, to live the law of love in every relationship. . . . If a family could do this, other families could be induced to try it."[32]

Within a few months of his departure from Princeton Theological Seminary, Kester met the woman with whom he was to attempt to translate his ideas about the importance of a Christian home into reality. In the summer of 1926 he once again participated in intercollegiate Y activities at Blue Ridge. In order to take part in a preconference retreat, he and a number of other student leaders gathered there several days before the YMCA conference convened. When the men arrived, the annual summer gathering of YWCA students was in progress. Among the delegates to the women's conference was Alice Harris, an attractive young Georgian from Wesleyan College in Macon. She was one of the six children of Herman and Ruby Slappey Harris. Her devoutly Methodist parents were descended from two rather affluent and prominent families of Fort Valley, Georgia. Herman was a well-educated and innovative farm manager who experimented with the commercial production of a variety of crops. Ruby was a thoughtful and generous woman who took an interest in the problems of both black and white residents of her community. The Harrises, like the Kesters, appear to have endeavored to impress upon their children the importance of Christian faith and action as they understood them.[33]

Kester first met Alice on a Saturday afternoon in June at a meeting of YMCA and YWCA representatives on the lawn in front of Lee Hall on the Blue Ridge campus. The following morning, just before dawn, a number of students hiked to the summit of High Top, a mountain peak which was a favorite spot among Blue Ridge conferees. Alice had begun the hike with another man but ended it with Howard.[34]

The relationship begun that weekend blossomed quickly. Alice was a sensitive, compassionate young woman who had absorbed many of her parents' religious convictions and wanted very much to live a life consistent with the principles of Christianity. Yet she was plagued with uncertainty about precisely what constituted such a life. She seems to have found in Howard one whose idealism captured her imagination and whose intellect and experience might help her resolve her own uncertainties. Kester, on the other hand, believed he had found in Alice his "soul mate of God and Nature," one with whom he could share the frustrations of a Christian reformer in a misguided and callous world.[35] So rapidly did their relationship develop that in a few months the couple were engaged and within less than a year they married.

Although his initial exposure to seminary training had proved disappointing and did nothing to allay his doubts about the relevance of the church to the problems of the modern world, Kester still found it difficult to reject the idea that he must dedicate his life to the ministry. In the fall of 1926 he enrolled in the School of Religion at Vanderbilt

University where he hoped the intellectual and social atmosphere would be more congenial than that he had known at Princeton. His initial experience at Vanderbilt was less than satisfying, but he did find there an opportunity to engage in the kind of social activism about which he had become enthusiastic. When Kester entered Vanderbilt, he accepted a position as an associate secretary of the YMCA at the school. In this capacity he soon became involved in the interracial activities of the Student Forum in Nashville while continuing to participate in those of the regional YMCA and YWCA.

The Nashville forum with which Kester associated was one of the most vigorous of those organized in the aftermath of the Indianapolis Student Volunteer Convention. The young people who launched it aspired to "discover the mind of Christ as it affects human relationships, especially international, industrial and interracial relationships." They believed that if Jesus's teachings were translated into action, there would be "a new social order based on brotherhood and good will in which every single personality would have opportunity for fullest development." The Nashville students initially channeled most of their energy into an investigation of the condition of black residents of their city and an examination of the relationship between the two races there. During the academic year 1924–25 they broadened the scope of their activities to include discussions of social and economic conditions throughout the nation and abroad. Although the forum remained small and generated no dramatic economic or social changes in the Tennessee capital, throughout the mid and late twenties it helped to promote badly needed contacts across the color line and to broaden the horizons of students of both races.[36]

In October 1926, only a few weeks after he began graduate study in the School of Religion, Kester joined a small interracial group of students and leaders of the southern intercollegiate YMCA and YWCA in the inaugural meeting of a regional Interracial Committee. This body, which met at Fisk University in Nashville, planned a program to foster interracial cooperation and understanding among students from throughout the South. Members resolved to strengthen existing interracial forums and to promote others in urban educational centers, to encourage the exchange of speakers and artists among black and white institutions, and to establish a clipping service and circulating library to disseminate material about race and race relations throughout the South. Although the resolve of these students and leaders was great, their labors yielded meager fruits. Nevertheless, for socially minded individuals such as Kester the effort was perhaps as important as the results. Certainly an atmosphere in which this kind of endeavor could occur was much more refreshing than that which he had known at Princeton Theological Seminary.[37]

Given the social consciousness of at least some Nashville-area students and the precedent for interracial interaction among them, the events of Tuesday evening, 27 March 1927, should have surprised no one. Some internationally minded students were concerned about the recent intervention in China by several western nations, including the United States, to protect their interests against the rising tide of Chinese nationalism. The students believed this kind of military incursion to be immoral and hoped to find some means of stopping it. Having no direct access to the channels of power in the nation, they concluded that the only effective course of action lay in rallying public opinion against the policies of the government. Therefore, a small group of activists, including Kester, organized a protest meeting among college and university students in Nashville, hoping to ignite similar expressions of dissent throughout the nation and to force the Coolidge administration to modify its policy toward China.[38]

At Kester's invitation, the protesters gathered in Wesley Hall on the Vanderbilt campus. Approximately fifty black and one hundred white students assembled in the chapel on the appointed evening. They listened to addresses critical of their country's China policy by J. B. Matthews, a professor at Scarritt College; Malcolm Nurse, a native of Trinidad and student at Fisk University; and J. H. H. Berckman, a theology student at Vanderbilt who had worked for several years in Shanghai. Then, after a rather "spirited" discussion, the students adopted a series of resolutions. They opposed any militaristic or imperialistic policies of the United States, agreed to petition their government to remove its forces from China, and resolved to urge other students to study the China situation and make known their convictions. They sent a copy of these resolutions to Secretary of State Frank B. Kellogg and dispatched a telegram of support to student Christian associations in China.[39]

The gathering on the Vanderbilt University campus, described by Katharine Butler, a regional YWCA secretary, as "very sane and based on a high level of intelligence and Christian conviction," roused the ire of a number of Nashville-area citizens. According to Butler, "it was talked of by faculty and students, denounced from the pulpits and frowned upon by administrations." Vanderbilt authorities took a particularly dim view of the proceedings. It was the composition of the gathering rather than the students' criticisms of the country's China policy that troubled the school's administrators. Two days after the meeting, the conservative historian Walter L. Fleming, dean of arts and sciences, wrote to Chancellor James Kirkland expressing concern over the repercussions such interracial protest meetings might have for the school and arguing "that some step should be taken to secure responsible control of these bi-racial meetings." Fleming pointed out that this was the third time in recent months that an interracial gathering on the Vanderbilt campus had stirred controversy; the previous year a meeting of an interracial forum at the school had prompted criticism, and a biracial gathering of Tennessee Student Volunteers in January 1927 was said to have so angered some Vanderbilt undergraduates that they had threatened to break up the meeting forcibly, a development which he believed would have brought the university much undesirable publicity. Fleming noted that "there can be no objection to mature leaders of the races meeting for conferences looking toward cooperation, but I think that the public will rightly object to much display at so-called 'mass meetings' of students of both races who are probably not very competent to pass upon the questions which they select for discussion." [40]

Kirkland shared Fleming's concern for the school's reputation and moved swiftly to deal with those responsible for the latest potentially damaging incident. The chancellor suspected that the campus Y leadership was somehow involved. He already had the Vanderbilt YMCA and its secretary, William Jones, under close scrutiny, in part at least because of their role in promoting interracial contacts among students. In mid–1926 Dean O. E. Brown of the School of Religion, who was chairman of the board of directors of the YMCA, had promised Chancellor Kirkland to keep a watchful eye over the Y and to begin searching for new leadership if it showed no signs of making significant progress among Vanderbilt students. On 6 April 1927, the chancellor, believing that Jones had called the China meeting, informed Dean Brown that he could not recommend the secretary's reappointment. The following day, after Jones had denied responsibility for the gathering, Kirkland again wrote to Brown, requesting that he discover who was responsible. When Brown learned that Kester had called the meeting for the Wesley Hall chapel, he reprimanded the associate secretary for his role in the controversial affair. [41] Kester later claimed that he was then fired; if indeed he was dismissed from his Y position, his termination was little more than an embarrassment and an inconvenience since he had already decided to leave Vanderbilt to accept a position in New York City.

In 1925, while a student at Lynchburg, Kester had joined the
Fellowship of Reconciliation (FOR), an international pacifist organization which had originated in England during World War I. Kester
believed that he had found in the Fellowship, with its emphasis on
the unity of the human family, belief in the power of education, and
stress on the peaceful resolution of conflicts, an organization through
which he might give practical expression to his understanding of the
Gospel. He was therefore pleased when, in January 1927, the Fellowship asked him to become head of its Youth Section. The Youth Section had its genesis in the Fellowship of Youth for Peace (FYP). One
of the most absorbing issues at the Student Volunteer Conference in
1923–24 was peace in all its ramifications. Conferees in thirty-nine
of the forty-nine discussion groups addressed this issue. A majority
of the students, while refusing to declare themselves absolute pacifists, asserted their support for such agencies of international cooperation as the League of Nations, believing them to be the best means of
resolving international conflicts. However, from five to seven hundred
delegates took a more radical position, vowing that they would never
take part in war.[42] The pacifist students established a committee to
consider the creation of a permanent organization which would represent their point of view. This committee formed the Fellowship of
Youth for Peace.

The statement of principles of the FYP made clear the essentially
Christian character of the group's pacifism. It declared the Fellowship
to be an interracial, international body which recognized "the oneness
of the world-wide human family." It affirmed the membership's faith
that "the spirit of love disclosed in Jesus of Nazareth" was the "only
foundation for human society and the only power which can overcome
evil and call forth the undiscovered good in man." According to the
statement, the group was united in its determination to seek "such
changes in the spirit of men and the structure of society as shall make
possible the fullest expression of the spirit and principles of Jesus."
Change would not come through the use of force and violence but
through divine guidance and power, which members were confident
would be increasingly available as they sought to apply the law of love
in every relationship.[43]

The Fellowship of Youth for Peace affiliated briefly with the Fellowship of Reconciliation in early 1924. However, in an effort to
broaden its appeal, it soon chose to drop the commitment to absolute
Christian pacifism as a prerequisite for membership and to pursue an
independent course. For the next two years it had only modest success,

and in September 1926 it reaffirmed its previous position and merged with the FOR, becoming its Youth Section.[44]

Shortly after this merger, Paul Jones, secretary of the FOR, wrote to Kester at Vanderbilt asking whether he would be interested in directing the work of the Youth Section if the position of secretary was offered to him. Jones probably had learned of Kester's pacifist and interracial activities through reports from Y officials and George ("Shorty") Collins, field secretary of the FOR and the man responsible for Kester's enrollment in the pacifist organization in 1925. Familiar with Kester's enthusiasm and the breadth of his interests, Jones concluded that the southern seminarian would make a likely candidate for the job. He explained in his letter to Kester that the Youth Section needed "a person who will see the possibilities of such a youth group in the largest terms. It means on the one hand a person who feels not only the peace implications of those principles which Jesus taught us as they touch the questions of war and international relationships, but also is alive to their economic and industrial implications and where they touch the racial problems."[45]

Kester responded to Jones's inquiry in the affirmative although he had some reservations about his ability to do the job. In spite of his doubts he welcomed the opportunity because, as he wrote to Alice, "It is a challenge to you and to me to lay our lives down in real service." Furthermore, he believed it might "be the stepping stone to even larger service and even greater opportunities and responsibilities." In January 1927 Kester got a telegram from Don M. Chase of the Christian Youth Section Committee of the FOR indicating that he would soon receive a letter formally inviting him to become secretary of the Youth Section.[46] In February, four months earlier than originally intended, he and Alice were married and began making plans to move to New York City after the completion of his year's work at Vanderbilt.

Kester assumed his responsibilities with the FOR in New York in August 1927. During the next two years he traveled extensively throughout the East and South speaking before college and university audiences, participating in intercollegiate YMCA and YWCA conferences, and organizing or involving himself in the activities of special conventions dealing with international, industrial, or racial peace and justice.[47] As early as the mid-twenties, the Fellowship had begun seeking to promote interracial understanding and cooperation, especially among college and university students. As youth secretary Kester spent considerable time in the South championing this cause, and it was this facet of his responsibilities about which he was most enthusiastic. He coordinated the Fellowship's newly developed program of student conferences. These gatherings, usually held at black educational or community institutions, were characterized by the total integration of housing, dining, and conference facilities. Conferees discussed not only racial matters but a wide range of contemporary issues. By eliminating racial barriers and promoting thoughtful discussion of the problems of the day, the Fellowship hoped to awaken students of both races to their common humanity.

His thought and work during these years marked the zenith of Kester's liberalism. The Christian liberalism of the latter nineteenth and early twentieth centuries encompassed a rather wide range of views. Liberals were united in their optimism about human nature and society but differed on such other matters as their understanding of God, religion, the nature and function of the church, and biblical revelation. For example, the modernists within the liberal tradition were committed primarily to "the prevailing views of contemporary philosophy and the findings of science" and were Christian only in a "vague and sentimental way." Evangelical liberals, on the other hand, reinterpreted Christian theology only to the extent necessary for their faith to become a relevant vital force in the modern world. They were interested in recovering the theology and ethics of Jesus and generally understood the atonement in moral rather than substitutionary terms. They conceived of the church largely as a means of propagating a message of which ethics, Christian conscience, and the realization of the Kingdom of God on earth were central features.[48] It was this evangelical outlook to which Kester was committed, and his FOR work seemed to him an effective means of giving expression to it.

The members of the Fellowship of Reconciliation and its Youth Section were pacifists but not passive. Believing that "peace and positive good will" and not "force and evil" lay at the center of human nature, they wished to contribute to the creation of a world in which humanity could realize its full potential. Only by aspiring to follow the example of Jesus, who "was willing to lose his life rather than use any means other than love to combat evil," could they bring about the kind of revolutionary social change that the world so needed.[49] Commitment to a Christ-like way of life did not require Fellowship members to become dogmatic evangelists for their particular understanding of the Gospel. Rather, their lives would serve to inspire their contemporaries. Profound change, as they understood it, was the product not of force but of persuasion.

The Christian liberalism of the FOR represented precisely the kind of socially conscious expression of his faith for which Kester had been searching since his Lynchburg College days. His activities as youth secretary were often interesting, sometimes exciting, and occasionally gratifying, but for a variety of reasons he was not entirely happy with his position. A painful personal loss marred the Kesters' years in the Northeast. In August 1928 their first child, Howard Anderson, Jr., died at birth. While the void left by the infant's death was not the sole cause of Kester's discontent, the emotional strain it produced accentuated his sensitivity to several problems stemming from his work. One of these was the fact that the interracial dimension of his endeavors bred tension between him and both his own and Alice's families. William Kester viewed with alarm his son's growing concern about the character of race relations in the South and was upset by his fraternization with blacks on a basis of equality. A temporary but painful rift had occurred between the two when in the summer of 1926 Kester had decided to go to Tuskegee to spend some time with his friend George Washington Carver. Alice Harris's father, a man who was both socially and theologically very conservative, objected not only to Kester's unconventional racial views but also to his acceptance of such unorthodox ideas as the theory of evolution. He had been so violently opposed to his daughter's engagement to a man whom he considered a dangerous social and religious radical that he refused to attend their wedding.[50] While both Howard and Alice were convinced that their position with regard to the race question was correct, they were nevertheless troubled and hurt by their relatives' lack of understanding.

A second source of unhappiness lay in Kester's inability to get along with some of the personnel with whom he was associated in the FOR. The trouble stemmed from at least three factors: differences in style between Kester, a southerner, and his northeastern associates; dissatisfaction with his salary, which he regarded as meager when compared with that of other Fellowship officers; and Kester's independent nature. He resented what he considered interference with his work by some members of the Youth Section, and he rather quickly became "fed up with the many bosses he had" in New York.[51]

Perhaps the most important source of Kester's discontent was his strong identification with the South and its people. In the late thirties he wrote of his work in New York: "I never quite felt that I had any right to be in the east trying to do a job that many others could do better than I. I had a distinct feeling of being a sort of traitor to an earlier promise to myself to live and work in my native South." Less than a year after his move to New York, Kester began searching for some means by which he could devote most of his time to the South. At an FOR executive committee meeting in April 1928, he raised the issue of moving his work there. He suggested that either the head-quarters of the Youth Section be relocated or its work be divided, with its southern operations under his direction. The executive committee discussed the idea at length and finally referred the matter to a subcom-mittee for further consideration. The committee, composed of Kester, George Collins, and Paul Jones, was to investigate the need for a Fel-lowship secretary in the South and to consider ways in which such a position, if needed, might be funded.[52]

The committee's inquiries brought at least some favorable re-sponses. The reply of Wilson Newman, formerly one of the student activists at Vanderbilt and by the late twenties a teacher in Birming-ham, was typical. He wrote to Kester expressing his belief that there was indeed a great need for a Fellowship office in the South. Newman argued that an FOR secretary could help to nurture the glowing coals of racial liberalism in the region. Furthermore, a representative of the Fellowship might serve to minimize the causes of conflict between management and labor before these became chronic problems plaguing economic relations in the rapidly industrializing South. Although other groups were already addressing some of these issues, Newman believed that the region needed all the help it could get. A free-lance FOR secretary would have greater latitude of action than did such or-ganizations as the YMCA and YWCA and might also stimulate these and other groups to greater endeavors. Given the provincialism of the region, any secretary, to be effective, would have to come from the South. Although he did not say so directly, Newman clearly believed Kester would be just the man for the job.[53]

George Washington Carver too supported the idea of expanding the Fellowship's southern work. He wrote to Kester:

I have read with much interest and satisfaction your plea for an office in the South for the establishment of better race relations. It is a surprise to me that this has not been done before now. The beating on the tail of the snake may stop its progress a little but the more vital parts must be struck before his poisonous death-dealing venom will be wiped out. Just so with the poisonous venom of prejudice and race hatred. I believe that southern people will welcome such an office and many will lend their cooperative support.[54]

The Fellowship did not take any immediate action on Kester's proposal. However, in mid–1929, thanks to the generosity of Ethel Paine Moors of Boston, the FOR agreed to employ Kester as secretary for the South on a part-time basis while he resumed his seminary studies at Vanderbilt.[55]

Throughout the twenties Kester's educational experiences, service as a student pastor, and work with the intercollegiate YMCA and Fellowship of Reconciliation had nurtured within him a spirit of idealistic Christian liberalism. This sanguine outlook reached its zenith during the last years of the decade. In the early and mid thirties his liberalism would gradually give way to a somewhat less optimistic theological and philosophical position which transformed his conception of his religious and social mission.

CHAPTER 3

■ From Christian Liberal ■
to Prophetic Radical

W hen Howard Kester returned to the South in the late summer of 1929, he did so with feelings of both anticipation and foreboding. Dissatisfied with his work as youth secretary of the Fellowship of Reconciliation and somewhat uncomfortable with life in the urban Northeast, he welcomed the opportunity to return to his native region to complete his formal religious education and to serve the FOR in an area which he believed desperately needed its ministry. Yet his Fellowship work had begun to engender in him an understanding of the social, economic, and moral condition of the nation which caused him to be apprehensive about the prospects for liberal change in the near future.[1]

The onset of the depression within two months of Kester's arrival in Nashville seemed at first to justify his apprehension, but the ferment precipitated by the crisis ultimately provided greater latitude for the work of activists advocating economic and social reform than had the optimism and prosperity of the twenties. The early 1930s were important years for Kester's intellectual and professional development. His training at Vanderbilt and work as southern secretary of the Fellowship of Reconciliation, coming as they did at a critical juncture in the history of the South and nation, first tempered, then transformed his liberalism and cast his religious self-image in a new mold.

While at Vanderbilt Kester developed close ties with a number of socially conscious professors and students in the Nashville area. Among his friends and associates were E. Franklin Frazier, Charles S. Johnson, and Juliette Derricote of Fisk University, Albert E. Barnett of Scarritt College, and classmates Ward Rodgers, Don West, and Claude Williams of Vanderbilt. However, Alva Taylor, professor of social ethics at Vanderbilt, exercised a greater intellectual influence on Kester than anyone else in the academic community.

Taylor, an apostle of the Social Gospel, had joined the faculty of

Vanderbilt's expanding School of Religion in 1928. A native of Iowa, he had spent most of his life in the Midwest serving as minister, educator, and administrator with the Disciples of Christ. Although he was respected by his associates for his ability and dedication, Taylor's career was punctuated by controversy because he frequently took positions on economic and social issues well in advance of those of many of his fellow Christians. The new instructor soon found that Vanderbilt authorities, especially Chancellor Kirkland, had only slightly more sympathy for his liberal ideas than did most conservative churchmen among the Disciples. By the early 1930s his views had gotten him in trouble with the university's leadership, and in the middle of the decade the Kirkland administration used the financial stresses associated with the depression as an excuse to purge him from the Vanderbilt faculty.[2]

Taylor, under whom Kester wrote his bachelor of divinity thesis, impressed upon his students the inextricable relationship between the physical and spiritual dimensions of human experience. He taught that industrial capitalism was riddled with iniquity and inequity, that race relations in the South made a mockery of the principle of Christian fraternity, and that poor land produced poor people. Christians, he contended, had a responsibility to minister to every facet of life, and he encouraged his students to become involved in the liberal socioeconomic movements of the day.[3] Taylor's understanding of the relationship between the material and spiritual well-being of humanity was not new to Kester, yet the forcefulness with which the professor presented the message and his emphasis on the problems of labor and the rural poor helped to broaden the young activist's conception of his mission during the 1930s. So too did Kester's service as southern secretary of the Fellowship of Reconciliation.

While at Vanderbilt, Kester served the Fellowship only on a part-time basis. During these years his work differed little from that in which he had engaged as youth secretary. On weekends and during holidays he spoke on college and university campuses and at student retreats across the South. He continued to rely upon education as the most effective means of inducing constructive social change, and his primary objective remained the promotion of interracial justice and reconciliation. The only significant departure from his earlier endeavors was a shift in the emphasis of his message. He was now more inclined than in the past to analyze racial and other problems in an institutional as well as an ethical context and to argue that they could be resolved only through comprehensive economic and social reform.

Kester enjoyed his FOR work and hoped to devote himself exclusively to it after receiving his bachelor of divinity degree in the spring of 1931. Although he could see little evidence of an imminent transformation of the South's economic or social system, he thought that significant changes were under way in the region and that he, Alice, and the cadre of activists with whom they associated had an important role to play in them. Many FOR members apparently shared their agent's assessment of his efforts in Dixie. Fellowship leaders reported in May 1931 that they had received "numerous and urgent requests" to expand the work of the southern secretary. The widespread support for his endeavors, coupled with his dedication and experience, prompted the organization's executive committee to offer Kester a full-time appointment to begin on 1 July 1931.[4] His work during the next two-and-a-half years was both broader in scope and more radical in substance than that in which he had engaged previously and reflected the Fellowship's evolving interests.

During the latter 1920s, especially after absorbing the Fellowship for a Christian Social Order in 1928, the FOR retained its commitment to international peace but grew increasingly concerned with domestic social and economic issues.[5] The onset of the depression, and capitalism's apparent inability to cope with it, accelerated and intensified this reorientation. By the early thirties most Fellowship members had become deeply troubled by what they regarded as the economic, social, and political injustices in American life. As they grappled with the question of how they as responsible Christians might address these inequities realistically, many concluded that some type of socialism offered the best solution to the nation's problems and joined the Socialist party in hopes that it might become an effective agency for change.

Kester was among the Christian activists drawn to socialism during the early years of the depression. He read Marx, Engels, Lenin, and other theoreticians of the Left. These writers helped him begin "to understand the enormous implications of the economic factors in human relationships."[6] Yet it was not the persuasiveness of their arguments that prompted his ideological and political realignment. Rather, it was the tenor of the times and the influence of friends and associates such as Reinhold Niebuhr and Norman Thomas that affected the change.

Kester met Niebuhr while working with the Fellowship in New York, and the friendship that blossomed between the two men had a profound impact on the career of the young southerner. Although he was never really an ideologue, his training and experience during the twenties had propelled Kester toward a philosophical position which might be defined most accurately as Christian liberalism. Implicit in much of his work during these years were a faith in the rationality and potential for good inherent in humanity and a belief that moral suasion could be an effective instrument for social change. Niebuhr's evolving neoorthodoxy, with its emphasis on the reality of evil and skepticism about social perfection, challenged many of the FOR secretary's fundamental assumptions. The theologian's conviction that an approximation of justice, not the Kingdom of God, was the goal toward which activists should strive and his faith in the class struggle as the most realistic means to this end helped to transform Kester's liberalism into a kind of neoorthodox Christian radicalism. [7]

So too did his friendship with Norman Thomas, whom he also met while in New York. Kester felt a particular affinity for this gentle Socialist who had been nurtured in the church but had forsaken the parish ministry when it no longer seemed relevant to the problems of urban industrial America. Thomas's example may well have helped to confirm Kester in his rejection of a ministerial career in favor of other means of serving humanity. His nondoctrinaire, compassionate brand of radicalism most certainly encouraged the development of the southern secretary's nascent socialism. [8]

Although he had been gravitating toward the Left since the late twenties, Kester did not actually join the Socialist party until October 1931. Alice, who believed that socialism was "not merely a political theory" but "simply the religion of Jesus called by a new name," had already joined. Both Kesters feared that unless the impoverished and frustrated masses were presented with a realistic alternative, they might be drawn to communism or fascism. They felt that Christian socialism offered the most constructive alternative to a capitalistic system which had outlived its usefulness. [9]

Having joined the party, Kester with characteristic enthusiasm began working to establish the nucleus of a viable organization in Tennessee. He hoped to regenerate interest among former Socialists in the area and to recruit new converts from the pool of liberal southerners with whom he had become acquainted in the course of his FOR work. However, he soon recognized the enormity of his task.

Although there had been a significant grass-roots movement in the Southwest earlier in the century, socialism had never really been a vital political force in the South. The entry of the United States into World War I and the aura of prosperity in the postwar era had enervated the party even in those areas of Dixie where it had secured a foothold. In the late twenties Socialists launched a national membership and fund-raising campaign, but their leaders believed that work in the southern states would yield only modest results. Consequently, they offered little more than moral support and party literature to their comrades in the region. Inexperienced, inadequately funded, and laboring in an environment in which their cause was either an anathema or a mystery, these scattered Socialists had only their convictions and enthusiasm to sustain them.[10]

Kester's experiences seemed to vindicate the party's skepticism about work in the South. In spite of the economic deterioration and human degradation that the depression brought to the state, Tennesseans had little enthusiasm for socialism. In 1932 the Socialist party had only about thirty card-carrying members in the Volunteer State and no formal structure there. When, in February of that year, Kester brought in the noted New England Socialist Alfred Baker Lewis to speak at a meeting to launch a party local in Nashville, only twenty-five people turned out to hear him. Of these, only seven, including the Kesters, were sufficiently committed to socialism to petition for a local in the city.[11]

While disappointed by such an inauspicious beginning, Kester remained undaunted. He continued to devote a considerable portion of his time to Socialist activities. He wrote the party's constitution for Tennessee, acted as secretary of the Nashville local, served briefly as chairman of the state executive committee, and in the fall of 1932 ran for Congress on the Socialist ticket. His candidacy attracted only slightly more attention than had his organizing work. In what appears to have been the only local newspaper article devoted to his campaign, Kester told a reporter for the *Nashville Tennessean* that unemployment and war were inevitable under capitalism and asserted that the capitalistic system had failed modern man because it had produced the most gigantic war in human history and had filled the world with millions of unemployed men and women.[12]

The youthful congressional aspirant, who ran as a "wet" as well as a Socialist, knew that his election was unlikely but believed that his campaign and those of other Socialists in the state would generate votes for the presidential candidacy of Norman Thomas. Thomas did not do as well in Tennessee as his friend had hoped, but the returns confirmed Kester's doubts about the viability of his own bid for office. He polled only 677 votes, running behind both the Democratic and Republican congressional standard-bearers in Davidson County. Kester took his defeat in stride. As was often the case with Socialist office seekers, he rationalized his unsuccessful campaign as an educational exercise and a protest against the economic and social injustices perpetuated by capitalism. [13] Such efforts, though painful, were necessary steps in the process of raising the consciousness of the masses. Defeat, therefore, was not failure but a lamentably essential component of progress.

Officially, party activities consumed only a portion of Kester's time, but in fact socialism permeated every aspect of his Fellowship work. Throughout much of 1932–33 his efforts remained primarily educational but his message grew more radical. He spoke about the plight of the disadvantaged of both races before conferences of students, religious leaders, and social workers in the hope that a well-informed middle class might act more effectively to resolve the problems of the poor. Yet as he became convinced that significant social change rested not upon altruism but upon the development of countervailing power by the disinherited, he devoted a considerable part of his time to raising the class consciousness of workers. He conducted courses on economic and political issues for industrial wage earners in scattered localities across the South and participated in some of the educational projects of the Southern Summer School for Workers in western North Carolina and the Highlander Folk School near Monteagle, Tennessee. [14]

Although increasingly class-conscious and talking more and more of the struggle for economic and social justice, thus far Kester had had only limited exposure to the direct and sometimes brutal clash of interest group against interest group. However, in the depths of the depression he became involved in a prolonged, violent, and frustrating conflict between labor and management in the Tennessee coalfields. The experience affected him deeply and intensified his commitment to the radical causes he championed.

On 8 July 1932, miners in the communities of Wilder, Davidson, Twinton, and Crawford in Fentress County in eastern Tennessee went on strike after mine operators announced a 20 percent reduction in their already meager wages and refused to negotiate with the United Mine Workers local. In the fall the owners tried to reopen the mines with nonunion labor. Thereupon the hills came alive not only with the blazing colors of autumn but with the crackle of gunfire and the reverberations of dynamite as desperately poor men chose sides in what they perceived as a struggle for survival. Wilder, where the financially troubled Fentress Coal and Coke Company operated one of the largest mines in the county, became the focal point of the trouble. When violence erupted in October, Governor Henry H. Horton, acting primarily at the request of mining and railroad interests, sent Tennessee state militiamen to the vicinity.[15]

The unrest that prompted the governor to dispatch troops, the disorder that continued after their arrival, and the apparent destitution of the miners attracted the attention of a number of socially conscious liberals in Nashville. During the week of December 4 Howard and Alice Kester went to Wilder where they found an impoverished, demoralized labor force virtually reduced to peonage. Officials of the Fentress Coal and Coke Company indicated that the most a miner could make was roughly two dollars a day. The miners usually worked three days a week. This provided them with a monthly income of approximately twenty-five dollars, which under some circumstances might have been barely adequate; however, the conditions at Wilder were such that this amount was not a living wage. Various fees withheld from the miners' wages frequently amounted to more than half their earnings. Each month these charges included about five dollars for rent and approximately a dollar and a quarter for use of the bathhouse. The miners also had to purchase all their equipment and food from the company store where prices were often twice those they would have paid elsewhere. It was not unusual for miners to spend from fifteen to eighteen dollars for food and supplies each month. Records indicated that some employees had been in debt to the company for the previous four years.[16]

When the Kesters reported their findings to the liberal community in Nashville, a number of concerned citizens organized the Wilder Emergency Relief Committee. This group, along with several others, began gathering food, clothing, medical supplies, toys for the children, and money to assist the strikers. A few days before Christmas, the Kesters and two Scarritt College students went to Wilder to distribute a truckload of supplies. The Christmas expedition was only the first of many they would make into the Tennessee hills during the coming year. Howard served as the representative of the Fellowship of Reconciliation as well as the Wilder Emergency Relief Committee, the National Strikers Relief Committee, and the Church Emergency Relief Committee of the Federal Council of Churches. Alice acted as secretary of the Wilder Emergency Relief Committee in Nashville, coordinating the collection of donations of food, clothing, medicine, and money. The couple converted their dining room into a warehouse and soon had boxes of donated goods piled almost to the ceiling. By the spring of 1933 the Kesters had distributed three tons of beans, meal, sugar, coffee, meat, and other staples to more than three hundred families living in the vicinity of Wilder.[17]

As they worked in the Tennessee coalfields, the couple found poverty the likes of which they had never seen before. Howard reported, "On more than one occasion as my wife and I worked at the relief station we have seen four different women appear during the day in the same set of clothes, each one going home to take it off and lend them to the next neighbor who needed to come." Men's trousers were also at a premium, and the miners passed them around just as the women did their dresses. The poverty of the miners was compounded by the fact that the funds allocated for the support of the Fentress County workers by the United Mine Workers of America (UMWA) were soon depleted.[18]

The situation at Wilder, although deplorable for the miners, in a sense proved fortuitous for Kester. By 1932 the Fellowship of Reconciliation was feeling the impact of the depression. Declining revenues forced the organization to cut its budget, including the salary of the southern secretary, and the future of his work seemed in doubt. In November the executive committee voted to circulate a letter among the FOR's southern constituency in hopes of raising sufficient money to sustain its program in the region. However, in February 1933 FOR secretary John Nevin Sayre informed Kester that the future of the Fellowship's work in the South was uncertain and suggested that he consider the possibility of taking another part-time position while continuing to serve the FOR on a reduced basis.[19]

The scarcity of funds had already resulted in a curtailment of Fellowship activities in Dixie, and the diminished opportunities for service troubled the southern secretary. In late December 1932 Alva Taylor wrote to Sayre explaining the significance of the Wilder relief work and emphasizing Kester's importance to it. He indicated that Fentress County desperately needed both material assistance and a spirit of reconciliation and expressed the hope that the FOR would support its secretary's work there. He went on to explain confidentially that the limitations on Kester's activities were "beginning to depress him a lot" and suggested that his former student could "face the lack of funds for salary much more easily than lack of ability to keep on the road on behalf of the Fellowship." Taylor contended that the work at Wilder would not only sustain and hearten the suffering miners but also relieve Kester's depression.[20] The Fellowship somehow managed to find sufficient funds to retain the southern secretary on a full-time basis, and Wilder became the focal point of his activities.

As Taylor had expected, Kester's perception of the importance of his labors in the Tennessee coalfields had an exhilarating effect on the young activist, but the work in Wilder did far more than merely bolster his spirits. He discovered in Fentress County what he believed to be additional evidence of the decadence of modern capitalism. Coming as it did at a time when his economic, political, and religious views were in a state of flux, the Wilder crisis further radicalized the FOR secretary. Once he had believed largely in the power of education and moral suasion to bring about a better world, but by 1932–33 he had become convinced that the struggle of interest group against interest group and class against class was an essential component of constructive social change.

Kester may have allowed his growing commitment to radical socioeconomic and political change to affect his relief efforts. Alva Taylor, secretary of the Church Emergency Relief Committee, one of the groups providing assistance to the miners, complained to James Myers of the Federal Council of Churches and William B. Spofford of the Church League for Industrial Democracy that the FOR secretary wanted to distribute supplies only to the strikers rather than to all the unemployed miners and that he understood the relief work at Wilder as a Socialist rather than a social welfare endeavor. Taylor, who believed relief, not revolution, to be the objective in Fentress County, opposed using the committee's resources "to promote a socialist local or the Methodist church or the DAR or any other darned ulterior thing." While acknowledging that "Buck is the salt of the earth," he charged that "to him there is nothing worth doing unless it heads into socialism. He has turned his FOR work into socialist work and is, we fear, going to ruin it." [21]

Taylor understood and appreciated the commitment and compassion that motivated young zealots such as Kester as well as Myles Horton and Don West of Highlander Folk School, all of whom had become involved at Wilder, but he questioned the effectiveness of "these impassioned apostles of extremism." He thought that their political radicalism was interfering with their mission of ministering to the needs of the disinherited. It seemed to him that aid to desperate people in critical situations was becoming a means to an end rather than an end in itself. [22]

The degradation and bitterness they found in the Fentress County hills horrified the Kesters and many of the liberals and radicals with whom they worked. They were appalled by the poverty, angered by the injustice, and mystified by the inhumanity that they encountered there. Yet they were also impressed by the dignity, intelligence, and courage they sometimes found. No one impressed them more than the president of the miner's union, Byron F. ("Barney") Graham. Graham, a "slender sinewy man with stooped shoulders," had spent most of his life working in the mines. The laconic forty-year-old leader of the miners had little formal education but had read widely and possessed a native intelligence and common sense which served both him and the members of his union local well. Graham had counseled repeatedly against violence and was credited by Kester with having kept it to a minimum. The mining company, on the other hand, considered Graham the source of much of the labor unrest, and its private guards regarded him as a marked man. Some of the guards openly boasted that they had killed men and were in Wilder to get the union president. On Sunday evening, 30 April 1933, just after dark while most of the village was at home or at church, Graham was shot to death near the company store.[23]

The circumstances surrounding his death are not entirely clear, but the weight of the evidence points not toward self-defense, as company guards claimed, but toward cold-blooded murder. According to newspaper accounts, company physician Dr. C. A. Collins reported the day after Graham's death that he had examined the union leader's body and found ten bullet wounds, four of which were in Graham's back. "Two of the holes ranged downward as though Graham had been fired upon from above or while he was down on the ground. In addition to the gunshot wounds, the body showed that Graham had been struck heavily with some blunt instrument on the head, which left four gashes near the crown."[24]

The day after Graham's death, the Kesters went to Wilder to see how they might minister to the angry and grief-stricken miners. The condition of the Graham family posed the most immediate problem. Barney Graham's widow, who suffered from both epilepsy and pellagra, was unable to care for either herself or her children. Howard and Alice stayed with the family and experienced again the depths of poverty in which the miners lived. There was scarcely any food in the house, and the Grahams were so poor that there were no beds for the Kesters. The couple sat up all night before the union leader's funeral in straight chairs in a dilapidated shack with no light except that provided by a lamp made from a kerosene-filled Coca Cola bottle with a cotton string inserted in the mouth. The next day Howard delivered the eulogy of a man whom he professed to love "as a brother" and whom he described as "a symbol of unselfish devotion to the cause of working people."[25]

Authorities charged Jack ("Shorty") Green with Graham's death. Green reportedly had "an impressive reputation" among the miners for his quietness, coolness, and quick trigger finger. A native of Fentress County who had labored as a miner, he had in recent months worked as a mine guard in Illinois and Tennessee. After trouble developed at Wilder, the local sheriff employed him to conduct a one-man investigation of mine disorders in the area. The Fentress Coal and Coke Company subsequently hired him as a guard.[26]

Green claimed to have shot Graham in self-defense, but few of the Nashville liberals providing relief for the miners were convinced by his protestations of innocence. Yet they believed the significance of the case transcended the conviction of the union leader's alleged murderer. They thought the incident was another example of the use of force by those in power against the downtrodden and wanted to bring not only Green but the company itself before the bar of justice. Albert E. Barnett, a professor at Scarritt College and chair of the Wilder Emergency Relief Committee, wrote in an angry letter to Nashville papers: "Has it come to the pass that corporations can employ gunmen to shoot to death the leaders of those whose only proven offense is their effort to get a living wage for their honest labor? Let those who counsel non-violent methods for Labor look well into this killing of a splendid Tennessee leader of Labor by a 'private policeman.'" Barnett chastised the papers for the antilabor bias in their reporting and declared: "Who is responsible in the killing of Barney Graham? Will equally vigorous editorials be written calling for the fixing of responsibility? Is the man who fired the fatal shot into Barney Graham's body alone responsible, or do his employers share his responsibility? If the conditions were reversed, organized labor would surely be held to account! It is a poor rule that doesn't work both ways!"[27]

James Myers, the industrial secretary of the Federal Council of Churches who was in Tennessee at the time of Graham's death, wrote to Rodger Baldwin of the American Civil Liberties Union (ACLU): "It would appear to me that this case offers a very unusual opportunity to pin this crime where it belongs, on the higher-ups. . . . Might it not be possible to make the Company itself or its president criminally responsible for this deed?" Kester concurred, writing to Baldwin: "We have a great chance here to fix the responsibility on the Fentress Coal and Coke Company. . . . It would be a great victory for labor and civil liberties in general." Supporters of the miners petitioned the United Mine Workers of America for funds to hire a special prosecutor in the case. The UMWA had Earl A. Hauke, director of the union's legal department, personally investigate the question of Green's prosecution, and John L. Lewis assured Alva Taylor that the union was "anxious to assist in every way in the triumph of justice in this matter."[28]

Kester, who had been unimpressed by what he had seen of UMWA activities in Fentress County, doubted that the union would provide much assistance. Therefore, he also appealed to the American Civil Liberties Union for financial help, while making it clear that the organization should keep a low profile because of the provincialism of southerners. The ACLU agreed to accept the role of behind-the-scenes fund-raiser.[29]

The matter of funding the special prosecutor was, nevertheless, somewhat confused during the weeks following Graham's death. When the ACLU learned that the UMWA was willing to assume responsibility for the case, it believed its support unnecessary and withdrew its offer. Then in late July the United Mine Workers informed the American Civil Liberties Union that its funds for the Graham case had been depleted by the defense of several Wilder miners against a murder charge stemming from the ambush of two nonunion laborers. It would, therefore, be unable to honor its commitment to the prosecution of Green. This left the ACLU with the responsibility for providing as much assistance as it could. The situation became so complicated that the Kesters at one point tapped their own limited resources for use in the case.[30]

Ultimately, the Wilder experience proved disillusioning for the liberals and Socialists seeking justice for the miners in the vicinity. Green was tried but acquitted of murder. The company avoided having to accept any legal responsibility for Graham's death.[31] And the Socialists who wished to translate the tragedy of Wilder into a triumph for socialism failed.

A weak company in a sick industry, operating in one of the nation's most depressed areas, posed economic and social problems that were too great a challenge for liberals and Socialists alike. In late 1933 Alva Taylor wrote in despair: "The men and their families have starved, now the Co. has gone into bankruptcy—great pay for the battle. The Gov. told them both sides could be saved if they would arbitrate but the Co. refused. He then refused to send the guard. Three men have been killed including the union Pres. How beautifully a little Christianity would have worked."[32]

An infusion of Christianity, as this veteran proponent of the Social Gospel understood it, would have prevented the violence and bloodshed and might have ameliorated the human suffering. However, it probably would not have resolved the fundamental economic problems. To be sure, greed, insensitivity, and hatred were a part of the Wilder equation, but so too were depression, mechanization, and a declining demand for coal. By the early 1930s there were too many miners seeking a limited number of jobs. Such a situation tempted mine operators trying to protect themselves and their companies to take advantage of the workers.

Relocation, not religion or revolution, offered the simplest solution to Fentress County's labor problems, and it was this to which the miners' advocates ultimately resorted. Kester played a role in arranging the relocation. Among those present at one of his frequent public addresses concerning conditions in the South was an employee of the Tennessee Valley Authority (TVA) who arranged a meeting between Kester and Arthur Morgan, chairman of the TVA. Through the auspices of Morgan, a number of Wilder families eventually were resettled at the Cumberland Homestead near Crossville, Tennessee.[33]

The misery and degradation that Buck Kester witnessed at Wilder confirmed his growing conviction that "within the framework of capitalistic society any attempt to build a decent world is a dream and an illusion."[34] By 1933 such a pessimistic assessment of capitalism was prevalent among members of the Fellowship of Reconciliation. All but a small minority now accepted the organization's growing commitment to the struggle for economic and social justice. However, the practical implications of this commitment deeply divided the membership.

During the late twenties and early thirties, as they drifted to the Left, FOR members attempted to fuse the teachings of Marx with those of Jesus in their quest for a realistic approach to economic and social problems. As a result, they faced the challenge of reconciling social revolution and Christian pacifism. The majority of them appear to have resolved their dilemma by abandoning moral suasion for nonviolent coercion. They convinced themselves that class consciousness did not mean class hatred and that the class struggle did not require class warfare.[35] In the interest of justice, proponents of change could employ a variety of peaceful tactics such as strikes, boycotts, or demonstrations, while at the same time remaining true to the Christian law of love in every relationship. Such an aggressive pacifism seemed the only revolutionary strategy consistent with the teachings of Jesus.

A small but important minority within the Fellowship doubted the efficacy of this approach. While none of these individuals relished the use of force, they recognized it as a weapon ultimately at the disposal of both sides in the class struggle. It seemed to them unlikely

that those in positions of power would willingly surrender their advantage and equally improbable that the disinherited would acquiesce indefinitely in their lot. Therefore, the price of justice might well be
violence, and those unreservedly committed to an equitable social order
had to be willing to pay that price.

Throughout 1932 and 1933 tension mounted between the proponents of the two positions. Kester's activities among the miners of
eastern Tennessee catapulted him into the center of this philosophical
and tactical dispute. He summarized the Fentress County work in his
annual report to the Fellowship submitted in October 1933. He contended that his role in the strike, especially his efforts to hold Fentress
Coal and Coke officials responsible for the death of Barney Graham,
had made him "company enemy number one." As a result, the miners
took measures to assure his safety whenever he was in the vicinity. He
explained: "When going into the camp I was usually met by a group
of the strikers who accompanied me until I left. If our destination was
far from Wilder we went under cover of darkness. It was safer that way.
While I escaped all personal violence others were not so fortunate." [36]

Fellowship members recognized the danger in which Kester labored and appreciated his commitment and courage, but some of them
had reservations about his activities and the philosophy that underlay
them. FOR secretary Sayre pinpointed the problem when he wrote
Kester that

> although you do not say so, I presume that these strikers who guarded you
> had guns, (of course for self-defense). I must say that I consider it seriously
> wrong for a Fellowship secretary to have to depend on the "private gun-
> men" of his side to defend him. To admit the validity of such procedure
> would come pretty close to sanctioning armament for self-defense. It
> would not be what Jesus believed in when in the Garden of Gethsemane
> he commanded Peter to put up his sword. Therefore, I should feel that in
> the future no Fellowship secretary should go into situations of danger like
> those you describe *unless* he goes alone, unarmed, or with a group of friends
> who will also go unarmed and be prepared, like Gandhi's followers, to
> offer no violence themselves to opponents who may beat or shoot them
> down. [37]

Sayre's letter reflected the uneasiness of a majority of FOR members with what they perceived as the growing radicalism of the organization's left wing. The advocates of social change through peaceful
coercion were especially troubled by what appeared to be the militancy

of the other three FOR secretaries, Kester, J. B. Matthews, and Charles Webber. In his annual report for 1933 Kester wrote that "the task of the Fellowship is that of a revolutionary movement which must approach its work with the abandon, enthusiasm and realism of the revolutionary. . . . To attempt to emancipate the mass of white and Negro workers in the South, employed in mill, mine, farm and factory only through the methods of goodwill, moral suasion and education is to invite the continued exploitation, misery and suffering of generations yet unborn."[38] Precisely what the southern secretary meant by the "abandon, enthusiasm and realism of the revolutionary" was not entirely clear, but to many members his words suggested that there might come a time when the radicals would sacrifice the principle of pacifism on the altar of justice. In his work at Wilder Kester already seemed to many to be coming perilously close to abandoning nonviolence.

The southern secretary was both baffled and angered by what he considered the unwarranted criticism of his activities in Tennessee and elsewhere across the South. Nevertheless, he attempted to address the misgivings of the FOR moderates when he replied to Sayre's letter:

I have never entered Wilder or any other dangerous situation possessing arms or in any way relying upon the arms of associates or friends for protection. Everyone knows my position with reference to the use of violence in strikes. Non-violence is the only practical weapon for strikers to use. In my conversation with individuals and in talks before the unions I have repeatedly taken this position. . . .

. . . When men met me en route to Wilder they were at times armed I suppose. I don't remember ever seeing a gun on one of these trips though I have seen them at other times and have been in the homes of strikers possessing arms. . . .

. . . I have never asked to be defended and I accepted the risks involved. It would have been foolhardy for me, working as I was in and out of Wilder, and with a degree of status in society possessed by none of them to ask them to throw away their guns. Had I the time and had I been on the grounds all of the time the situation might be different. As it was I did as much with the situation as I possibly could.[39]

In spite of such affirmations of faith in the practical advantages of pacifism, the stance of Kester and other FOR militants continued to trouble the moderates. In late 1933, in an effort to clarify the Fellowship's position on the increasingly vexing question of the role of violence in the class struggle, the executive committee polled the FOR constituency. Approximately 80 percent of the respondents indicated that "the Fellowship should be primarily religious and emphasize the Christian approach," and roughly 90 percent believed that it should hold to nonviolence.[40] The results of the survey suggested that the vast majority of members believed that they should support labor in its legitimate struggle but should refrain from condoning violence under any circumstances.

Of the four Fellowship secretaries, only Kester and Matthews dissented. They took the position that if industrialists employed force against labor, similar tactics by the workers should be supported as long as these were necessary to achieve just ends. Since the majority of FOR members adopted a more passive stance than the secretaries, the executive committee dismissed Matthews in December 1933. At the time of the committee's action it had not yet received Kester's response to the survey. Therefore, the members, after considerable debate, voted to retain him but only on the condition that he accepted the majority position. When his reply arrived at Fellowship headquarters, it became clear that although he had never actually advocated or engaged in violence, he was philosophically more radical than most of his associates. Thus, his dismissal was automatic.[41]

Buck Kester believed that the Fellowship's uncompromising commitment to nonviolence and the dismissals that this position precipitated were "a horrible mistake" which would "have far-reaching consequences." The secretary resented what was, in his opinion, the intolerant abstract theorizing of middle-class pacifists in the Northeast who had little firsthand knowledge of the condition of the poor and oppressed in the South. He believed that his position on the question of the use of violence was not "born out of an emotional bias for the working class but was wrought from the furnace of southern life" and was the only one consistent with a realistic appraisal of the social and economic conditions in his region.[42]

Throughout the early thirties Kester had grown increasingly skeptical of the power of persuasion to bring about significant changes in society. By the middle of the decade he was convinced that reformers would be unable to "love people into the Kingdom" and had become scornful of those whom he described as "these cockeyed people who go about talking of love and good-will in the midst of all this oppression and hell." In March 1934 he wrote to George Washington Carver: "I am convinced that love, education, good will, moral suasion, et cetera et cetera are not enough. Something more rigorous and dynamic will be required to turn this hellish earth of ours into a fit habitation for man than these things. The force of circumstances have steadily driven me toward the left, politically and otherwise. The recent events in Germany and Austria, the break down of the NRA, the brutalities of white America, the stupidity of capitalistic America make of me a revolutionary socialist." [43]

But what did revolutionary socialism mean to this young southern idealist? Perhaps the question is best answered by determining Kester's place along the ideological spectrum of American socialism. During the first half of the 1930s the Socialist party in the United States was divided into three major factions. The most conservative element, the Old Guard, consisted largely of longtime party members who were Marxian in outlook but were committed to democracy as the vehicle for promoting gradual social change. The progressives, led by Norman Thomas, were generally more recent converts to the party. Their socialism was as much a function of compassion as of ideology. They hoped to build a political organization based on principles of economic and social justice which would represent the interests of the nation's laborers and farmers, and they were impatient with the gradualism of the Old Guard. The militants were a small but vocal minority comprised largely of young, middle-class, doctrinaire Marxist-Leninists who joined the party during the depression. These "romantic leftists" shared much with the Communists, including their suspicion of democracy, but were uncomfortable with the rigid discipline of the Third International and objected to Russia's denial of civil liberties. [44] Kester's socialism was essentially progressive in character, but for a time in the mid-thirties his perception of the deteriorating economic and political condition of the nation drove him further to the left.

When a small group of radical Socialists organized the Revolutionary Policy Committee (RPC) in March 1934, Kester took a keen interest in its activities. He was among the signers of the committee's "An Appeal to the Socialist Party," which reflected the sense of urgency characteristic of the party's left wing. Alarmed by ominous developments throughout the world, especially the rise of Hitler and the demise of socialism in Austria, the RPC called upon the party to become more aggressive in its efforts to secure political power because this was the only effective way to "transform capitalist society into Socialist society by means of the dictatorship of the proletariat." In doing so, it should make no "fetish of legality" and should be prepared for violence since its capitalist opponents would use force to prevent the establishment of a workers' republic.[45]

To Kester, each day seemed to bring the United States closer to "the dreaded Fascist dictatorship," and he was convinced that the South, with its "background of violence, deep-seated race prejudice and attendant evils," would probably experience its horrors first and most severely. The racist, anti-Communist hysteria that had begun sweeping Alabama and Georgia in conjunction with the Scottsboro and Angelo Herndon cases, along with what he interpreted as the beginning of a shift to the right by relatively liberal groups such as the FOR, National Association for the Advancement of Colored People (NAACP), Commission on Interracial Cooperation, and National Urban League, suggested to him that the tide of repression was already rolling in upon the forces of liberalism. If the South and nation were to survive and triumph over the "black terror of the reactionaries," collective action, not individual heroics, was essential.[46]

There appeared to Kester to be no social or political institutions in the South capable of effecting genuine change in the region. Southern Protestantism had the leadership, organizational structure, and popular support to address Dixie's problems but, thus far, lacked the critical perspective necessary to challenge the fundamental economic and social assumptions upon which southern civilization rested. The Communist party with which Kester sometimes cooperated and the Socialist party of which he was an active member sought to undermine a decadent capitalism and to challenge the conservative Democratic hegemony in the South, but neither seemed adequate for the task before them.

Kester thought the Communists' analysis of the deficiencies of the existing economic order sound and their stance on behalf of the disinherited correct, but the party's materialism, dogmatism, and ends-justifies-the-means philosophy troubled him. Socialism, as he understood it, was less doctrinaire and more practical, but by 1934 the party seemed to him so badly fragmented and its leadership so ineffectual that its creative potential was dissipated. Therefore, he doubted that it was capable of developing a significant constituency among the South's industrial and agricultural workers. He had hoped that the Fellowship of Reconciliation, with its fusion of religious and secular radicalism, might offer a constructive alternative to the shortcomings of existing social and political institutions. It seemed to him that as the Fellowship had grown more radical, it had begun to "make a really effective and most worthwhile contribution" in the South.[47] Consequently, the organization's apparent retreat from aggressive social action in late 1933 deeply troubled him.

Kester was not alone in his despair over the Fellowship's stance. The referendum on the use of violence in the class struggle and subsequent dismissal of the two secretaries prompted approximately sixty resignations as well as many expressions of disapproval from individuals who chose to remain within the Fellowship. Among the dissenters were some who believed commitment to absolute pacifism unrealistic in a world riddled with economic and social injustice and others, especially among the FOR's southern constituency, who considered most of the organization's leadership too far removed from the situation in the South to understand and direct the work there.[48]

In early 1934 a cadre of these dissidents who believed in Kester's philosophical and tactical approach to Dixie's problems established the Committee on Economic and Racial Justice (CERJ) and appointed him field secretary.[49] Reinhold Niebuhr served as chairman of the CERJ while Elisabeth Gilman, a prominent Maryland Socialist, acted as treasurer. Members of the new committee expected that their agent would continue the kind of free-lance activism in which he had engaged for the Fellowship and left to him the responsibility for developing his own agenda.

Kester appreciated the committee's vote of confidence and welcomed the opportunity to continue working in the South. He submitted to his new sponsors a plan of action which suggested that he intended to broaden the scope of his endeavors but would make few substantive changes in his work. He proposed to encourage interracial understanding among students, facilitate United Front activities, promote the Socialist party, develop educational programs for agricultural and industrial workers, investigate instances of racial and economic injustice, and generally champion the cause of the region's disinherited.[50] Committee members approved his program and immediately set about the difficult task of funding it.

The CERJ was to have only a limited impact upon the South, but its establishment was fortunate for Kester. The FOR secretaryship had been one of the few jobs in the region that offered even a modicum of the economic security and professional flexibility essential for the kind of activism to which he was committed. The loss of this position threatened not only to deny him the opportunity for continued service but also to deprive him of the means by which he had reconciled his religious and social aspirations. Thus, the establishment of the CERJ was both financially and psychologically important to him.

By 1934 Kester had arrived at a new understanding of the nature of the ills afflicting the South and of his role in the region's deliverance. Since 1929 his seminary training, experiences as southern secretary of the FOR, reading of a variety of social and economic theorists, and friendships with men such as Taylor, Thomas, and Niebuhr had enhanced his awareness of the importance of economic factors in human relationships and had engendered in him a new conception of the relevance of the prophetic and Gospel traditions. He was now convinced that not only had Old Testament prophets such as Amos railed against social injustice but Jesus himself had "definitely recognized the class struggle and set his face steadfastly against the oppressors of the poor, the weak and the disinherited."[51] His training and experience during these years had helped Kester to reconcile his sense of religious commitment with his social consciousness by enabling him to define his mission in life as that of prophetic radical rather than parish minister. Although this reconciliation was tenuous, it provided much of the ideological basis for what was to be the most dramatic and dangerous phase of his work on behalf of racial and economic justice during the mid and late thirties.

Howard Kester, secretary of the Committee on Economic and Racial Justice, mid-1930s (HAK Papers).

Fellowship of Reconciliation Interracial Student Conference, Le Moyne College, Memphis, 1932, organized by Kester, southern secretary of the FOR. *Front row (from left):* Howard Kester (*4th*), Claude Williams (*5th*); *middle row (from left):* William R. Amberson (*2d*), Alice H. Kester (*6th*) (HAK Papers).

Howard Kester with two unidentified men, Wilder, Tennessee, 1933 (HAK Papers).

Howard Kester watching clearing of land for Delta Cooperative Farm, Rochdale, Missis-
ppi, 1936 (HAK Papers).

Howard Kester (*5th from right*) and others constructing log house on Fellowship of
Southern Churchmen conference grounds, Buck Eye Cove, N.C., c.1956–57 (HAK Papers).

Sharecroppers protest march, Marked Tree, Arkansas, 1935. Kester organized and tographed this Southern Tenant Farmers Union demonstration (STFU Papers).

STFU leaders E. B. McKinney and H. L. Mitchell with Howard Kester, 1935 (ST Papers).

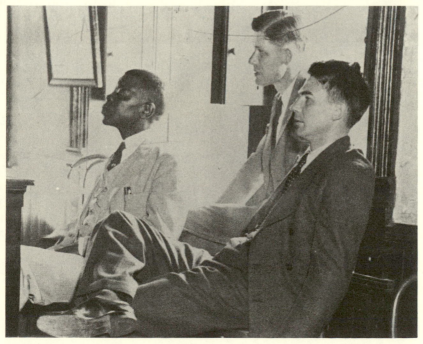

Alice and Howard Kester at Penn School, St. Helena Island, S.C., c. 1946 (HAK Papers).

Howard Kester, director, Displaced Persons Program, Congregational Christian Service Committee, New York, c. 1950 (HAK Papers).

Howard Kester at Piney Moors, the family home, High Top Colony, N.C., c. 1956 (HAK Papers).

Writer-activist John Beecher, former STFU secretary H. L. Mitchell, and Howard Kester (*at right*) promoting microfilm edition of the Southern Tenant Farmers Union Papers at the American Historical Association annual meeting, New Orleans, 1972 (STFU Papers).

CHAPTER 4

■ Race and Radicalism ■

An interest in the welfare of the black people of the South had inspired much of Buck Kester's passion for social change during the 1920s, and this concern continued to be an integral part of his activism throughout the following decade. Believing that Christians had an obligation to treat others with decency, respect, and fairness, he at first had understood the solution to his region's racial problems in terms of a personal ethical imperative. He had considered interracial justice and harmony possible if both black and white southerners became better acquainted with one another and practiced the golden rule of doing unto others as you would have them do unto you. During the early and middle 1930s, as the general tenor of his thought grew more radical, he began to place greater emphasis on the social and economic dimensions of racism. Before the decade was over, however, he had serious reservations about the adequacy of such a socioeconomic analysis.

As head of the Youth Section of the Fellowship of Reconciliation in the late 1920s, Kester had spent considerable time in the South promoting interracial contacts among students. A number of experiences during the course of this work made him more aware than ever before of the lack of understanding between the races and of the problems faced daily by black southerners. The way in which segregation prescribed roles for people of both races became very clear to him when at the depot in Old Fort, North Carolina, a group of blacks who noticed him in the Jim Crow car began crowding around the car to see what they assumed to be a white policeman escorting a black prisoner to jail. He frequently encountered prejudice on both sides of the color line. On one black college campus where the Fellowship ambassador was to deliver his message of reconciliation, several students were openly hostile and scornful of his efforts. Other circumstances were equally depressing. In Little Rock, Arkansas, a black YMCA official with whom he was traveling, Ned Pope, contracted food poisoning. There was no black doctor in the city whom Pope considered competent and no white one he thought likely to treat him. Kester, therefore, purchased medicine and ministered as best he could to the needs of his miserable companion until the crisis passed. Sometimes, however, the FOR secretary was heartened by the salutary effect of a simple act of kindness. Once when he and Pope were taking a train trip together, he chose to ride with his friend and coworker in the Jim Crow car. Such an action was both rare and risky. The black members of the train crew were so impressed by Kester's willingness to breach the color barrier that when the two young men, one of whom was unable to visit the segregated dining car, asked for something to eat, the porter brought what Kester remembered as one of the most sumptuous meals he ever had.[1]

Such episodes seemed to demonstrate both the necessity for and the potentially beneficial effects of the Fellowship's interracial endeavors in the South. It was this facet of his responsibilities about which Kester had been most enthusiastic, and his part-time work as southern secretary between 1929 and 1931 initially resembled, in intent, form, and substance, his earlier labors as head of the Youth Section.

His first major project as the FOR's southern secretary was a regional interracial retreat held during the Christmas holidays in 1929. On December 27 sixty-two persons, all but two of whom were from eight southern states or the District of Columbia, gathered at Le Moyne Junior College, a black school in Memphis, for a three-day conference. The participants, about half of whom were white, discussed a number of topics, including the varieties of racial attitudes found among Americans, the precarious position of blacks in an industrializing society riddled with prejudice, the development of effective techniques for undermining discrimination, and the question of interracial marriage.[2]

In this as in other such Fellowship conferences, Kester and most of the men and women with whom he worked believed the simple fact of bringing members of the two races into contact in an environment which minimized racial barriers and contributed to the erosion of the color line was as important as the intellectual content of their deliberations. Following the Le Moyne retreat, participants compiled a report which suggested that they believed the gathering had vindicated their faith in the beneficial effects of interracial interaction. They recounted with pride two incidents that they judged significant. In one, a black woman who had agreed to house some of the conferees had stipulated that she wanted no whites among her guests. Two young men, one of whom was white but who posed as black, stayed in her home. Before departing, the black youth informed their hostess that his companion was white. She was both surprised and pleased to find that a white person would stay in her home and treat her with respect and kindness. In another, a black Mississippi youth discovered among the conferees a young white woman from his state who invited him to sit down and talk with her. He was astonished by this simple act of decency because it was one of which he had believed white Mississippians incapable.[3] In retrospect such episodes seem to represent only modest gains, but the conferees, living as they did in a world almost devoid of genuine interracial interaction and communication, believed them illustrative of the potential for constructive change in the South.

Black activists appreciated the tentative efforts of moderate southerners, such as those in the Commission on Interracial Cooperation, to promote better race relations. They were, however, often critical of the caution of blacks and whites alike as they met somewhat self-consciously to extend a hand of friendship across the color line. Many Fellowship of Reconciliation members shared the conviction that such endeavors had often been "of the 'superficially good will type'" and strove to develop a more effective program.[4] Kester's carefully planned FOR conferences, with their young, educated, and committed conferees, generated a more favorable response among black participants and observers than did those of most other liberal groups.

In February 1931 the southern secretary sponsored a gathering in Birmingham, Alabama, similar to that which he had organized at Le Moyne. Fifty-three blacks and thirty-two whites from Alabama, Mississippi, Tennessee, Georgia, Illinois, and New York gathered in what was, by the standards of that southern industrial city, a most unconventional assemblage. There were conferees from eighteen schools and colleges as well as representatives from a number of social organizations interested in interracial activity. After the conference, Ira De Augustine Reid, director of the Department of Research and Investigation of the National Urban League and a member of the FOR, reported to the Fellowship:

I feel that we were quite successful in evading the shadow-boxing that is usually so typical of meetings of this sort. Both sides attempted to see their weaknesses and find a common ground and identity of interest whereupon they might meet.

Very frank talks with some adult members of other interracial movements have led me to conclude that we need not expect an elimination of this shadow-boxing on their part. Conservatism, in fact reactionism, in many instances, is the body and soul of their program. The Fellowship of Reconciliation appears to be in position to advance this program far better than anyone else, and I do not hesitate in commending Kester and those men and women in the South who have so valiantly fought for just such a meeting as occurred in Birmingham.[5]

Kester deeply appreciated such declarations of support for the Fellowship's interracial program. He was especially gratified by the affection and trust that many of his black associates seemed to have for him. Writing in the late thirties of the interracial dimension of his work, he recalled: "The problems of the Negro became my problems and I had a peculiar ability to make people understand what I was saying without always offending them. Negroes seem to trust me and to believe in me. This I coveted and appreciated and swore never to destroy." There were, of course, occasional difficulties with suspicious or prejudiced blacks as well as the prevalent hostility of southern whites, both of which retarded progress. Nevertheless, the secretary was convinced that "something of tremendous significance was happening in the South," and that he, Alice, and those with whom they worked were "having some small part in it."[6]

By 1931, when he became the Fellowship's southern secretary on a full-time basis, Kester's conception of the nature of the South's racism had begun to change. As a young Christian liberal during the twenties he had believed that it resulted from ignorance and insensitivity and could be eradicated or at least ameliorated through education and moral suasion. However, by the early thirties, the burgeoning Socialist Christian was becoming convinced that racism was part of a complex constellation of problems inherent in capitalism which could be resolved only through an extensive transformation of the social and economic order.

Kester's new understanding of the South's most persistent and vexing dilemma did not produce an immediate change in his tactics. For the moment, at least, he retained his faith in education as the most effective means of achieving social objectives. He continued to speak regularly before southern collegians and urban professionals and to organize periodic Fellowship conferences and retreats. However, the message he espoused as he traveled about the region began to change. Heretofore, although he had never excluded the subjects of peace or economic justice from the speeches he delivered or the discussions he coordinated, Kester had frequently made race relations the central theme of his gospel of reconciliation. Now he began to focus more on the injustices characteristic of the existing economic order and to interpret racism as merely one manifestation of this inequity.

His changing conception of society's ills was evident when the Fellowship secretary organized an interracial conference for the spring of 1931. The theme of the gathering that convened at Paine College in Augusta, Georgia, on May 1 was "A study of the assets and liabilities of capitalistic society and the technique for the realisation of the Kingdom of Right Relations." When in late March 1932 black and white men and women from several southern states gathered for a second FOR retreat at Le Moyne College, they discussed the international situation, especially the crisis in the Far East; the merits of capitalism, communism, and socialism; and the most effective means of resolving national and international problems. The causes and consequences of racism in Asia, South Africa, the Caribbean, and the United States were recurrent themes in the Le Moyne deliberations.[7]

While Kester believed that southern racism must be understood in the context of national and international social and economic conditions, he was equally certain that responsibility for the resolution of the problem lay with the people of the South. In the early thirties he was convinced that his region's traditional patterns of race relations were on the verge of disintegration. The means by which this transformation would occur and the consequences of the process were as yet uncertain, but he thought that if people of intelligence and goodwill did not act quickly, the South might soon be plunged into a violent racial crisis.[8]

Kester's perception of the critical nature of the southern situation sprang from several sources. One of these was his assessment of conditions in Alabama, which he visited in the summer of 1931 in the midst of the Scottsboro controversy. Another was the impression, shared with other activists in the region, that the depression was having a deleterious effect upon race relations. The third was his development of a kind of apocalyptic mentality typical of many young radicals of the era.

In late March 1931 local officials in northern Alabama took nine black youths from a Memphis-bound freight train and charged them with the rape of two young white women. Within less than two weeks a trial began in Scottsboro, county seat of Jackson County in which the arrests had occurred. In proceedings protected from mob violence by local police and a small contingent of Alabama National Guardsmen, an all-white jury, in less than four days, found eight of the nine defendants guilty and recommended the death penalty. The conviction of the "Scottsboro boys" was merely the first stage in a protracted and sometimes bitter legal, ideological, cultural, and racial conflict which lasted throughout much of the remainder of the decade.

In late July and early August 1931 Kester traveled across Alabama in sweltering heat, making plans for a fall Fellowship conference in Birmingham and attempting to determine what role the FOR might play in the Scottsboro affair. In the course of his work he talked with all sorts of people of both races, ranging from "university professors to bell boys and from plantation owners to maids," and developed a clear but troubling picture of the volatile situation there. In mid-August he wrote a general letter to Fellowship members sharing with them his rather gloomy appraisal of the turmoil in Alabama. He was certain of the innocence of the Scottsboro defendants but equally convinced that even if the Supreme Court overturned their recent conviction and granted a new trial, acquittal was out of the question. The closest approximation of justice that could be hoped for under the circumstances, according to Kester, was a ten- or fifteen-year sentence, and life imprisonment seemed a more likely verdict.[9]

There were, at the time, three principal groups active in the Scottsboro defense: the National Association for the Advancement of Colored People, the Commission on Interracial Cooperation, and the Communist party. Of these, Kester believed the peaceful, pragmatic, legalistic approach of the NAACP and Interracial Commission represented the only possible means of saving the lives of the eight black youths sentenced to death. He was extremely critical of the Communists' role in the case, charging that their International Labor Defense (ILD) was more interested in propaganda than justice. He believed that the ILD's activities were merely another facet of the Communist party's attempt to win black adherents. The Communists were, in his estimation, "trying to bulldoze the state and to turn the Negroes against everyone who is not lined up with them."[10]

The Communist party's tactics in Alabama struck Kester as those of "a crazy man," and for the moment at least, he doubted that its agents were winning many converts.[11] The greatest danger was that the party's activities in the state would further aggravate racial tensions already heightened by the depression. If this occurred, it would be difficult for the Fellowship of Reconciliation or any other group to work effectively there.

In the fall of 1931 the southern secretary painted a bleak picture of conditions not only in Alabama but throughout the South. In the Fellowship's annual report he declared that relations between blacks and whites were worse than at any time since Reconstruction and attributed much of the rising tide of tension in the region to deteriorating economic conditions. He contended that the depression had accelerated a process, under way for several decades, in which whites had gradually but systematically excluded blacks from occupations formerly open to them. Whites were now taking the most menial jobs once reserved for blacks, and as a result, the latter were becoming increasingly desperate. Kester warned Fellowship members that the conditions under which blacks lived in the South were so severe that it was questionable whether they would "continue to rely upon evolutionary methods in attempting to secure the rights and privileges guaranteed to them by the Constitution." [12]

Kester believed that the existing socioeconomic system must give way to a new order, but he thought that reliance by blacks upon revolutionary means, however desirable the ends, would result in "a colossal failure" and would be "suicidal." He reported that in the Deep South isolated outbursts of minority violence had already precipitated a wave of white repression which had led to the deaths of at least seventy-five blacks since the previous August. The region seemed to him much nearer an interracial civil war than most people realized. He feared that the disinherited and desperate black population of the South might resort to the kind of revolutionary violence advocated by the Communists unless they were presented with a constructive alternative. It was therefore "of paramount importance" that the Fellowship demonstrate "the effectiveness of aggressive pacifism for social and economic revolution." [13]

After formally joining the Socialist party in October 1931, Kester increasingly equated Fellowship work with Socialist activities. The party now seemed to him the most effective peaceful political means of bringing about the kind of fundamental economic and social change necessary if millions of impoverished Americans were to have a better life. However, he was convinced that it would succeed in Dixie only if it could triumph over the region's racial prejudice. Kester opposed the Jim Crowism advocated by some southern Socialists who argued they could never build an indigenous organization if they challenged the South's mores. He succeeded in getting party members in Tennessee to accept a clause in their state constitution condemning segregation or any other form of discrimination and giving the state executive committee authority to revoke the charters of locals that violated this provision. He believed that this constitutional affirmation of the principle of equality inspired party members in at least one other state to do likewise, and he claimed credit for having persuaded the national executive committee to deny a charter to one nascent state organization that refused to breach the color line.[14]

In early 1933 Kester wrote a letter to George F. Jackson, a Florida Socialist trying to build an interracial organization in that state, in which he explained his commitment to a thoroughly integrated party structure. In it he contended:

> To organise separate locals would be the most tragic blunder we could possibly commit. The consequences thereof would be far-reaching and would in the end contribute to the confusion, frustration and ultimate collapse of genuine socialism in America. By organising separate locals we not only forsake and compromise our fundamental aim of building a solid worker's party but we enhance the position of both capitalists and communists. Such a procedure would be immensely satisfactory and gratifying to communists as it would place them in the enviable position of offering the only political party where jim crowism is condemned. It would give them plenty of fuel for their fire. It is inevitable, furthermore, that sooner or later, the capitalists will seek to play the exploited, disfranchised, down trodden Negro over against his equally exploited white brother. By refusing to receive Negroes as genuine comrades within the locals we simply invite the capitalists to employ this ancient method of the ruling class and to their heart's content. Unless we socialists can achieve this principle of worker's solidarity and unity can it be said that we have greatly advanced upon the tactics or philosophy of capitalist society?

The desperate conditions in the South and his experiences during a decade of interracial work in the region persuaded Kester that there was at last a genuine opportunity for committed Socialists to transcend the barrier of racism and to build a united party in the South. He was convinced that "the walls of race prejudice which have held so long to keep the workers from being united are beginning to crumble" and that Socialists must capitalize on their opportunity before the status quo became "crystalized and frozen again."[15]

To hasten the collapse of these walls of prejudice, Kester not only worked directly through the Socialist party and Fellowship of Reconciliation but also continued his endeavors among black and white collegians in the region. On scores of campuses and at numerous state and regional student conferences, he stressed the pervasive effect of economic injustice on every phase of American life and encouraged his audiences to see racism as merely one manifestation of this fundamental problem.

As it had been for a decade, the Student Christian Movement continued to be the chief means by which he reached the colleges and universities of the South. The black YMCAs and YWCAs and the white YWCA were generally more receptive to Kester's message than was the white YMCA. In fact, he had become rather disaffected with the latter association. He had once believed it a potent force for change in the region, but after the departure of John Bergthold as southern secretary in the late twenties, he felt that student interracialism had been betrayed by "the reactionary leadership of the regime which followed." [16]

This perception, exaggerated but not entirely inaccurate, coupled with his opinion that much of the movement's leadership was thoroughly middle-class and inhospitable to genuine economic and social change, explains Kester's disenchantment. Yet he still had considerable faith that in the South's student population lay the best hope for the future. Therefore, whenever given the opportunity, he visited campuses and attended conferences in hopes of kindling interest in the kind of action he believed essential to the promotion of racial harmony.

The white intercollegiate YMCA was not the only group with which Kester became disillusioned as he grew more radical. Like many other young black and white social activists of the thirties, he became impatient with the philosophy and tactics of several organizations ostensibly committed in whole or in part to the cause of racial justice. Their dissatisfaction led a number of these radicals, including Kester, now secretary of the Committee on Economic and Racial Justice; George Streator, former managing editor of the NAACP *Crisis;* Julian Steel, a Boston social worker; Frank T. Wilson of the black YMCA; and Francis Henson of the International Student Service, to plan a conference to consider what constituted appropriate objectives in interracial work and to evaluate the activities of the various groups laboring in this field. The organizers envisioned the gathering as a United Front affair and invited a small cadre of liberals, Socialists, and Communists of both races to participate. [17]

The conferees gathered at Shaw University in Raleigh, North Carolina, on 30 November 1934. In the course of their discussions, they resolved that those working in the field of race relations should not be content with piecemeal gains but should strive for the complete economic, social, and political equality of the black. They charged that middle-class reformers had consistently neglected the disinherited of both races, and they admonished interracial workers to organize the masses in order to free impoverished blacks and whites alike from the bonds of prejudice and oppression.

The liberals and radicals who gathered in Raleigh judged organizations such as the NAACP, Commission on Interracial Cooperation, and National Urban League by these criteria and found them ideologically conservative and tactically timid. They argued that if these agencies wished to render effective service to black Americans, they must develop a more aggressive program and inclusive constituency. In hopes of stimulating such changes, the men and women assembled at Shaw decided to transform their gathering into a loose-knit association that they dubbed the Conference on the Social and Economic Aspects of the Race Problem. Through correspondence, publications, and meetings, Kester and the other members of the conference planned to keep one another abreast of developments in their respective localities. They also expressed their intention to further the cause of social and economic justice by participating in such activities as interracial worker education projects, unionization drives among black and white agricultural and industrial workers, and efforts to promote greater economic and social sophistication among the students of the South.[18]

The Raleigh meeting was significant because it provided the dedicated idealists who attended a forum in which they could express their dissatisfaction with the limited scope of current interracial work and afforded them an opportunity to reaffirm their commitment to a more comprehensive program of action. However, beyond this immediate psychological impact it was of little importance. The Conference on the Social and Economic Aspects of the Race Problem survived for only a short time and never became the radical alternative to existing reform groups that its organizers had envisioned.

One of the established organizations of which the Raleigh conferees were highly critical was the National Association for the Advancement of Colored People. Kester shared his peers' frustration with what they regarded as the conservatism and cautious pragmatism of the NAACP but was somewhat more tolerant of its shortcomings than were many of his colleagues. Over the years he had worked with Walter White, secretary of the association, on several occasions and had developed a cordial relationship with him. In spite of the fact that by the midthirties his economic and political views generally were to the left of those of White and most other members, Kester believed that the NAACP had made and continued to make an important if limited contribution to Afro-American life through its campaign against racial violence.

It was the association's perennial crusade against lynchings and other atrocities that had first prompted White to call upon Kester for help in the summer of 1931. In early August he arranged for the FOR's southern secretary to investigate a lynching which had occurred the previous April at Union City, Tennessee. A few days after completing his inquiry into the racial tensions surrounding the Scottsboro affair, Kester began an probe into the violence in the Volunteer State. Meanwhile, White read the young southerner's report on conditions in Alabama and immediately wrote to him again asking permission to use portions of it in the NAACP's propaganda battle with the Communists and other critics of its role in the Scottsboro case. He explained: "Your report comes like a breath of cool clean air, and coming as it does from an impartial and reliable source, it will do an immense amount of good in helping colored people to think straight and not to be mislead. Our story is to go only to the colored press and I hope you will give your consent." The FOR secretary enthusiastically complied with White's request, writing in early September "you are welcome to use anything I write any time." [19]

Kester's account of the lynching in Union City was neither as sophisticated nor as useful to the NAACP as his analysis of the situation in Alabama. [20] Nevertheless, Walter White was impressed with the novice investigator's work. He believed that he could count this zealous young champion of social justice among the small band of able white southerners to whom the NAACP could turn for assistance in its struggle against lynching. Therefore, on several occasions during the next few years, White sought Kester's help in the association's efforts to bring lynchers to justice and to secure passage of federal antilynching legislation. Among the investigations that Kester undertook for the NAACP and other organizations were probes into some of the most notorious incidents in the region. None was more indicative of White's confidence in him or more crucial to the NAACP's antilynching campaign than his inquiry into the death of Claude Neal in late 1934.

On the afternoon of October 18, petite, attractive Lola Cannidy set aside the family ironing and stepped out of her parents' farmhouse near Greenwood, Florida. The nineteen-year-old girl walked across a field toward a pump and watering trough and was never seen alive again. About 6:30 the following morning searchers found her strangled, bludgeoned body hidden beneath a pile of brush and logs in a wooded area not far from the Cannidy home. Jackson County author-

ities quickly pieced together considerable circumstantial evidence link-
ing a twenty-three-year-old black neighbor, Claude Neal, to the
murder. Within a few hours they had arrested the young black man for
the crime. Then followed a complex, protracted, and ultimately violent series of events as vigilante and institutional power struggled for
the right to administer conflicting versions of justice.[21]

Rumors of the death of a Caucasian girl at the hands of a black
man spread quickly over northwest Florida. The story roused the white
South's traditional fear of the violation of white womanhood by black
men and kindled in some Floridians a lust for blood in reprisal for such
an outrage. Aware of the potentially volatile nature of the situation,
the sheriff lodged Neal only briefly in the jail at Marianna, county seat
of Jackson County, before transferring him to Chipley, about twenty
miles away. After a mob tried to remove the prisoner from the jail there
on October 21, officials removed him first to Panama City, then to
Pensacola, and finally to Brewton, Alabama, approximately 210 miles
from Marianna.

In the early hours of the following Friday morning, a small band
of vigilantes crossed into Alabama, seized Neal, and returned with him
to a lonely wooded area of Jackson County where they intended to hold
him until arrangements for his execution were completed. They
planned to turn him over to the Cannidy family for retribution, but,
as was the custom, the punishment was to be a public affair. With the
help of the media, word of Neal's seizure spread quickly across north
Florida and nearby areas of adjacent states. Headlines in the Friday
afternoon edition of the Dothan, Alabama, *Eagle* declared "Florida to
Burn Negro at Stake: Sex Criminal Seized from Brewton Jail, Will be
Mutilated, Set Afire in Extra-Legal Vengeance for Deed."[22] Dothan's
radio station repeatedly announced the impending event.

On Friday night a crowd later estimated at from several hundred
to several thousand assembled on the Cannidy farm. Bonfires flared to
dispel the encroaching darkness as the swelling and increasingly fren-
zied throng milled about waiting for its victim. The men who had
seized Neal now became reluctant to surrender him to the Cannidys.
Their hesitation probably stemmed either from the fear that they
might incriminate themselves by publicly delivering Neal to the mob
or from the fact that they had begun to succumb to their own sadism.
In any case, they assumed the right to torture and murder Neal.

This change of venue denied the executioners assembled at the
Cannidy farm their opportunity for retribution. When the lynchers
delivered Neal's body to them shortly after one o'clock on Saturday

morning, they savagely vented their anger and frustration on the corpse. Men, women, and children, some of them hardly more than toddlers, repeatedly shot, stabbed, and slashed his remains into a repulsive mass of flesh. They then turned their unslaked thirst for vengeance against the living. Fanning out from the Cannidy farm, they burned the shacks of several black families in the vicinity. Finally, in the wee hours of the morning some of the lynchers took the mutilated body of Neal into Marianna and hung it from the limb of a tree on the courthouse lawn as a grotesque announcement to whites and warning to blacks that justice had been and would continue to be served in Jackson County.

The lynching of Neal did not immediately restore order to the area. On Saturday the streets of Marianna filled with people, many of whom were not local residents but outsiders who had come to participate in the lynching bee. Disappointed that they had missed the preceding night's festivities, most were now in an ugly mood. Tensions ran high and soon erupted into violence. Angry crowds of whites first attacked blacks they found on the streets and then began searching for them in stores and private residences. Quickly losing control of the situation, local police requested the assistance of the Florida National Guard. Guardsmen arrived in late afternoon and gradually restored order, but not before some two hundred blacks were injured and hundreds more forced to flee their homes.[23]

The violence in northern Florida came at a time when the number of such incidents across the South, after declining during the twenties, had begun to increase. As the depression deepened, many black activists and white liberals believed the passage of federal antilynching legislation was essential to stem the rising tide of lawlessness. Consequently, in early 1934 the Costigan-Wagner bill was introduced in Congress. Designed to intimidate mobs and to encourage state and local authorities to prosecute lynchers, it defined a mob very broadly as "three or more persons, lacking a legal basis, who set about to harm another or deprive him of life." The bill called for the imposition of a $10,000 fine on counties in which lynchings occurred. State or local officials who failed to arrest or prosecute lynchers were subject to a fine of up to five thousand dollars and a prison term of up to five years. Federal district courts were to assume jurisdiction in suspected lynching cases if county or state courts failed to initiate action within thirty days.[24]

As it had in the past, the NAACP assumed an important role in the effort to generate support for federal antilynching legislation. Association officers wished to prevent leadership in the crusade for such legislation from passing to more radical groups and believed that with Franklin Roosevelt as president chances for securing passage of an antilynching bill were better than at any time in recent years.

Walter White was disappointed but undaunted when the Costigan-Wagner bill failed to come before Congress for a vote in 1934. As he prepared to resume the struggle in the next legislative session, the NAACP secretary decided to try to translate the tragedy in north Florida into a triumph for black America. To do so, the association would have to launch a massive propaganda campaign to publicize the incident. The effort necessitated gathering as much information as possible about the circumstances of Neal's death and the violence that followed it.

Walter White knew Buck Kester to be an experienced and reliable investigator of interracial trouble in the South. Although he had reservations about some of Kester's economic and political views, he regarded him as "a first-rate young white man, who is absolutely right on the race question." Therefore, a few days after Neal's death, White wired Kester asking him to look into the Marianna violence. When he agreed, the NAACP secretary wrote to him, explaining: "We would like to get all the gruesome details possible together with any photographs of the body, crowd, etc., and as much evidence as is possible as to the identity of leaders and movers of the mob. As the capacity of the American people for indignation is great but short lived, get the facts to us as soon as you can, won't you. If you have a camera, send us some views of the town. Also find out if you can whether there is any evidence that Neal actually did or did not rape and murder Lola Cannidy."[25]

Recognizing that immediate action was indeed imperative, Kester wasted no time in launching his investigation. Within a few days, he had arrived in northern Florida and was traveling about Marianna and Jackson County searching for pertinent information. He talked informally with all sorts of people of both races, casually introducing the subject of Neal at opportune times but divulging to only a handful of sympathetic and trusted informants the real reason for his presence in Marianna. Kester occasionally had to muster tremendous reserves of strength to maintain his composure as he listened to local residents recount the sordid details of the lynching. On November 7 he wired White: "Last night I talked for one hour and forty minutes with a member of the mob which lynched Claude Neal. He described the scene in all of its horror down to the minutest detail. I was quite nauseated by the things which apparently gave this man the greatest delight to relate." [26]

Gathering the details of a recent lynching from the citizenry of the community in which it occurred was not only distasteful but also difficult and dangerous. In late 1933 Kester, part of a group investigating a lynching in Alabama, wrote of the problems and perils of the job:

The strain has been terrific on all of us, being watched and spied upon at every turn has caused us to be quite jerky.

We have gotten some 'hot stuff.' . . . Much of our work has been on the surface but a lot has been underground and secret. We've had to be as careful as could be everywhere. Today I got in a jam and in the twinkling of an eye became a book salesman from the Methodist Pub. House. We've got our 'dope' from headquarters as well as from underground.

Since I have had such a pronounced Southern accent I've had to be the spokesman. I started with the Governor, Attorney General, Sheriff and others. Last night was my first night of sleep. We have to see most of our people around mid night in various places. Life is hell, hell, hell! We are afraid there will be an epidemic of deaths among our informants after we get away.

The investigator could never be absolutely confident of the reliability of his sources, nor could he, if working undercover, be entirely certain that the cause of justice would not fall victim to the malice or fear of someone to whom he had entrusted the secret of his mission. So great were the dangers that George Washington Carver allegedly taught Kester to prepare a poison to be taken if he someday faced an agonizing death at the hands of a vindictive mob. [27]

The hazardous nature of the job became very clear to Buck Kester in Marianna. He had hoped to begin his assignment by gathering as much information as possible from the faculty and staff of Florida A & M College. However, when he arrived at the campus, he learned that the school's president feared that cooperation in an NAACP investigation might endanger the institution's state funding and that he had instructed college personnel to have nothing to do with the inquiry. Kester did manage, through the auspices of a faculty member with whom he was acquainted, to arrange a meeting with a student at the school who pastored a black congregation in Marianna. The young man, obviously reluctant to become involved, finally agreed to talk with him a few days later at his church.

On the appointed evening an apprehensive Kester decided to walk rather than drive to the designated rendezvous site. As dusk faded into darkness his uneasiness grew, and he slipped into the shadows on the north side of the church to await the arrival of his contact. Hardly had he moved when a caravan of a dozen or so cars with lights burning brightly turned into the churchyard. He could tell by their voices and the boldness of their approach that the occupants of the automobiles were neither worshipers nor informants, and he knew he was in trouble.

As a substantial party of whites emerged from the cars and began searching the church and its grounds, Kester quickly retreated into the nearby woods looking for some means of escape. His only option was to drop into a ravine filled with brush and briars and to move cautiously through the darkness and tangled undergrowth toward the lights of Marianna. Scratched, bruised, and frightened, he made his way through side streets and alleys back to his hotel where he slipped unobserved through a side door and up to his room. With the help of a black porter who knew his mission, he bathed and dressed. Then he attempted to establish an alibi for himself by going down to the hotel lobby, talking with the desk clerk, and walking conspicuously onto the front porch where he could be seen.

Frightened by his narrow escape and troubled by the appalling story his investigation had uncovered, Kester slept little that night. Early the next morning he left town, stopping only long enough to buy gas at the service station where he had previously purchased a picture of Neal's mutilated body hanging from a tree on the courthouse lawn. The attendant, unaware that his customer was preparing to beat a hasty retreat toward the Alabama line, warned him that he had better get out of town since a number of people had begun to suspect that he was in Marianna to investigate the lynching.[28]

Kester's departure was somewhat precipitous, but he did not leave before gleaning sufficient information to compile a horrifying report describing in graphic detail humanity's capacity for brutality. As he portrayed the incident, death had not come easily to Neal. His captors held the alleged murderer for ten to twelve hours and during a good part of that time subjected him to hideous tortures including emasculation, amputation of fingers and toes, slashing with knives, burning with hot irons, and periodic quasi hangings in which the victim was hoisted up over a limb until almost dead and then released and revived to undergo further torture. Finally, the lynchers, their sadism satiated, murdered Neal. They then tied his body behind a car and dragged it to the Cannidy home.[29]

Although conceding that the evidence was inconclusive, Kester believed that Neal was probably guilty of Lola Cannidy's murder. He gave considerable credence to rumors that Neal and Cannidy had been having an affair and that the young white woman's decision to terminate the relationship had provoked her lover to murder.[30] On the other hand, he was certain that the lynching and subsequent rioting were not merely crimes of passion, the results of indignation and outrage run amuck. Rather, they were the violent manifestations of complex economic pressures that had developed in Jackson County during the depression. Shortly after returning from Florida, Kester wrote to the Bergtholds that of all the lynchings he had investigated in recent years the Neal case had "the most complete economic basis." He reported to White:

> The basic factor in this whole beastly affair is economic. Jackson County's population is about fifty percent Negro. In Marianna it ranges from forty-five to fifty percent. There has been constant agitation on the part of a disinherited white element for the jobs of Negroes. Employers who give work to Negroes when white men could do the work are boycotted and threatened. A sustained effort has been made to get all Negroes off the relief roles and turn the relief entirely to the whites. A semi-fascist organization called the "Purification League" . . . has been doing most of the agitation. One man remarked "There ain't enough jobs to go round and niggers ain't got no right to have a job when white people are out of work." Another man said "This lynching was used to scare the Negroes away from the jobs and to make the white men give their jobs to white men out of work."[31]

In his official report Kester contended that "while the feeling against Claude Neal was certainly very great because of the crime which he was alleged to have committed, the lynching was to a large extent a surface eruption. Beneath this volcanic eruption lay the pressing problem of jobs and bread and economic security. A very competent observer said to me: 'The lynching had two objects, first, to intimidate and threaten the white employers of Negro labor and secondly to scare and terrorize the Negroes so that they would leave the county and their jobs could be taken over by white men.'"[32]

The NAACP's determination to make the case a weapon in the struggle for federal antilynching legislation and Kester's skill in gathering and conveying the facts combined to make the lynching of Claude Neal the most publicized episode in the long history of violence against blacks in America. The grizzly story provided precisely the kind of material that association leaders believed they could use to rouse the indignation of the American public against lynchers and in support of the Costigan-Wagner bill. As soon as their investigator was safely out of Marianna, they began releasing to the press his preliminary account of the circumstances surrounding Neal's death. When the final horrifyingly graphic report arrived at NAACP headquarters in New York, Walter White, although sickened by its portrayal of human degradation, recognized its usefulness. He immediately began distributing mimeographed copies to members of the Roosevelt administration, congressional leaders, American and foreign journalists, and other influential persons. Meanwhile, he initiated preparations for the printing and mass circulation of the report in pamphlet form. Ultimately, he hoped to produce a hundred thousand copies to be distributed throughout the nation to ministers, priests, rabbis, and other molders of public opinion.[33]

The publicity that the NAACP gave the Marianna affair provoked swift responses from many quarters. Not all the reaction was favorable. White sent a copy of the report to Governor David Scholtz of Florida who passed it on to John H. Carter, state's attorney in Jackson County. The attorney wrote the governor, "From what information I have been able to gather concerning the lynching of Claud Neal, I find this report to be grossly inaccurate, extremely exaggerated and founded mainly on false rumors floating about the country." Carter was particularly upset by Kester's suggestion of sexual intimacy between Cannidy and Neal, an idea that he branded "a lie of the whole cloth." Much of the reaction, however, reflected the indignation for which the association had hoped. Dr. A. A. Brill, a New York psychiatrist, declared: "After reading the report of the Florida lynching, it occurred to me that de Sade in all his glory could not have invented a more diabolical situation than was actually enacted in this southern Christian community in the United States of America. . . . One is forced to conclude that a large section of our southern whites are nothing but primitive sadists forever looking for new victims."[34] A businessman wrote to White, "The report on the Neal lynching you sent me almost made me ill, and the unavoidable contemplation of it has tormented me ever since." H. L. Mencken, after thanking the NAACP secretary for the report of the "Marianna Fiesta," observed: "It seems to me the brethren are showing a steady advancement in technique. Certainly no other recent lynching in the Bible Belt has been carried out with so much professional zeal and ingenuity. Needless to say, I'll be glad to have as many copies of the printed report as you can spare. It will be a pleasure to circulate them in Christian circles."[35]

The thousands of copies of Kester's report distributed by the NAACP in late 1934 and 1935 probably had a greater impact on white opinion than any other exposé in the organization's campaign to end lynching. After the publication of the pamphlet, a number of southern newspapers abandoned their traditional opposition to federal anti-lynching legislation, and the Commission on Interracial Cooperation for the first time endorsed federal action. In the late thirties a Gallup poll found that even among southerners a majority of people favored a national antilynching statute.[36]

Of course, the story that Kester helped to popularize in *The Lynching of Claude Neal* did not bring an end to extralegal violence against blacks. It did, however, serve as a catalyst, accelerating a trend toward public revulsion against such crimes which had begun earlier in the century. As the South became less isolated and more desirous of integration into the national economic and social mainstream, it grew somewhat more receptive to values and attitudes emanating from outside the region. Deprived of public sanction, even in many parts of Dixie, the number of lynchings each year declined after the mid-thirties.[37]

Although shifting popular sentiment gradually undermined the practice, the NAACP failed in its bid to eradicate lynching by means of a federal statute. It simultaneously lobbied Congress and wooed President Roosevelt in an effort to secure passage of the Costigan-Wagner bill. Walter White, who suspected that some of the president's staff members were unsympathetic to the measure, sent a copy of Kester's report directly to Eleanor Roosevelt, hoping that she would show it to her husband and intercede on the bill's behalf.[38]

The association, like the Commission on Interracial Cooperation, Association of Southern Women for the Prevention of Lynching, American Civil Liberties Union, and Writer's League against Lynching, also tried to persuade Attorney General Homer Cummings to prosecute Neal's lynchers under a federal law prohibiting kidnapping across state lines. Cummings refused to invoke the so-called Lindberg Act of 1932 on the grounds that it applied only to cases of abduction for ransom or reward. Action by the Justice Department in this instance would have required a broad interpretation of the kidnapping statute, but Cummings's reluctance to move against Neal's lynchers was probably more a product of political than legal considerations. He wanted to push a comprehensive federal law enforcement program through Congress and did not wish to alienate powerful southern legislators by intervening in the case.[39]

The Costigan-Wagner bill also ran afoul of the political realities of the mid-1930s. Franklin Roosevelt packed his legislative agenda for 1935 with the economic and social reform measures later dubbed the Second New Deal. The president abhorred lynching and sympathized with the NAACP's efforts to eliminate it, but he was unwilling to risk destroying his precarious coalition of congressional support for the sake of a single, rather specific issue.

The antilynching bill came before the Senate for debate in the spring of 1935. Thanks in part to the reaction generated by the Neal case, the NAACP had rallied a substantial number of senators and congressmen to the cause. By April 43 senators and 123 congressmen had gone on record in support of the measure. White believed that if the bill was brought to a vote, it would pass; and he was confident that Roosevelt would sign it. Unfortunately for its supporters, southern senatorial opponents staged a filibuster which prevented a vote, thus killing the measure. Although the bill was reintroduced in subsequent sessions of Congress, with its failure in 1935 the momentum had passed, and the legislation languished and ultimately died.[40]

Kester played a pivotal role in the NAACP's legislative campaign against lynching in 1934 and 1935. He not only investigated and helped to publicize the Neal case, but during the previous February he had been among a group of knowledgeable southerners whom the association had marshaled to testify before congressional hearings on the need for federal antilynching legislation. Kester told members of a Senate judiciary subcommittee that lynching created "fear, mistrust, and suspicion"; made for "bitterness and contempt"; and created "social forces upon which no government can stand." He argued that a federal law was desirable because it would act as a deterrent to mob violence, thus offering protection to "the most exploited and oppressed, the least privileged and protected body of our citizenry." It would also help to end the brutalizing effects of lynching not only upon those who participated in the crime but also upon the entire white population of the South.[41] Yet, in spite of his contributions to the cause, the CERJ secretary had misgivings about what he regarded as the essentially palliative nature of such measures as the Costigan-Wagner bill. Now at the zenith of his radicalism, he viewed racism and the violence it produced as manifestations of profound economic and social disorders. Laws that addressed crimes against blacks while ignoring the matrix from which they emerged might be of value in bringing criminals to justice, but they did nothing to eliminate the underlying conditions of unrest.

In late November 1934, shortly after returning from Marianna, an exhausted and despondent Kester wrote to an associate in Pittsburgh explaining his position:

> My personal feeling is that we are at the beginning of a long and terrible interracial conflict which will gradually grow in severity and intensity until a very definite crisis has been reached. A federal law will be helpful but it will not touch the basic factors which are creative of the sort of thing which occurred in Marianna, Tuscaloosa and elsewhere. I rather feel that our tactics of working from the top is misplaced emphasis and that increasingly we shall have to direct our attention and efforts to the exploited and disinherited whites and Negroes among whom the conflict now rages, which is due, to a large extent, to a total misunderstanding of the economic, social and political forces at work among them. We must not forsake the upper and middle classes in either group but we must develop among them a larger intelligence, imagination and social conscience than we have succeeded in doing thus far.[42]

Given his conviction that in the education and mobilization of the masses lay the key to the eradication of racial violence and scores of other social evils, it would not have been surprising had Kester simply dismissed the antilynching crusade of the rather conservative middle-class NAACP as inconsequential. Yet, he was rarely so doctrinaire that he sacrificed limited practical objectives to ideological purity. Furthermore, by mid-1935 he believed that his philosophical differences with the leaders of the NAACP were growing less pronounced. He thought the organization showed definite signs of becoming, if not radical, at least more liberal. In July he wrote to Francis Henson, mastermind of the conference at Shaw University the previous November, that

> in my opinion the NAACP did move to the left, that it has attempted to do so continuously, and that it is increasingly becoming the sort of organization we might wish it to become. I think I am in a little better position to understand the situation than I was a year ago and I am considerably more hopeful than I was then. I think Walter White is less inclined to follow the bourgeois group he seemed to follow so closely some time ago. He seems to be genuinely concerned for the NAACP to identify itself with the working class and its organization.[43]

The reasons for Kester's reassessment were twofold. His work on the Neal case strengthened his ties to the association and its leadership. In this instance, familiarity bred not contempt but mutual understanding and respect. He was also heartened by the fact that the activities of the Southern Tenant Farmers Union (STFU), to which he was now deeply committed, had captured the imagination of many NAACP members. In late June 1935 he spoke before the association's annual convention in St. Louis on "The Struggle against Farm Peonage." He stressed the interracial character of the STFU, declaring that for the first time in the history of the South black and white workers had come to the conclusion that "color made no difference." They recognized that they had common problems and goals and that "together they must be saved or together they must be lost." He challenged the delegates to make the struggle of the landless farmer their struggle and to so identify with the oppressed that "when the voice of the sharecropper is raised in distress, it immediately and forthrightly becomes the voice of every Negro in America."[44] The enthusiastic response of his audience strengthened the speaker's conviction that the NAACP was beginning to adopt a more realistic approach to the nation's racial problems than it had in the past.

During the following fall and winter Walter White raised the funds necessary to subsidize the publication of Kester's *Revolt among the Sharecroppers,* a lengthy pamphlet describing the plight of the disinherited black and white farmers of the Arkansas delta. The NAACP secretary's contribution to the production of this slender volume may well have reflected something of the shift to the left that Kester thought he perceived. Yet, there was more to White's support than mere enthusiasm for the Socialist-oriented STFU. Frances Williams, secretary of the labor division of the YWCA, illuminated his motives when she wrote to Alice Kester: "I cannot tell you with what joy and enthusiasm Walter has worked on this project. It was a tangible way for him to express his appreciation of Buck's and your very significant contribution to the race situation in this country."[45]

The work of which White, Williams, and many other blacks were so appreciative continued to be an integral part of Kester's activities during the latter half of the thirties. As his address in St. Louis suggested, no aspect of the Southern Tenant Farmers Union was more important to him than its interracial character. He believed that only through unity could the disinherited effectively challenge the present possessors of the earth. He thought that groups such as the STFU were a step in the direction of a society which was not only classless but also casteless. Therefore, he devoted much of his time to the union.

Meanwhile, he continued to serve as an investigator of interracial disturbances for several organizations, including the NAACP, American Civil Liberties Union, and Workers Defense League (WDL). During the last half of the decade Kester gathered information about lynchings, riots, alleged peonage, and the resurgent Ku Klux Klan in widely scattered sections of the South from the Carolinas to Louisiana.

Although the NAACP, ACLU, and WDL used much of the material he gleaned in congressional testimony and exposés of injustice in Dixie, Kester began to have doubts about the efficacy of much of his investigatory work. These misgivings stemmed from frustration, frail health, and questions about the nature of the violence he studied. He suspected that his efforts to undermine lynching had done little more than help to drive the practice underground. In 1939, after his investigation of the murder of a black man near Canton, Mississippi, he wrote to Walter White: "I have a strong opinion that lynching is entering a new phase and one much more difficult to deal with than the open mob. I was told that after the exposure of the double lynchings at Duck Hill that word was passed that all fu[r]ther trouble would be handled by a 'small number of men' designated by the mob to do the job for them. It is my judgment that Negroes are being disposed of in this manner." Kester expressed his willingness to do what he could to ascertain the extent of this new manifestation of racial violence, but he warned White that he would soon have to give up such detective work because the emotional strain involved seemed to induce severe attacks of asthma.[46]

The psychological tension of which he wrote was in part a result of the danger that was almost always a corollary of serious investigations of lynchings. But in Kester's case it was also related to growing questions about the source and meaning of the violence into which he delved. These questions began to plague him as early as the spring of 1937. In April he made an inquiry into a double lynching near Duck Hill, Mississippi. Next to the Neal episode, this blowtorch murder of two black men, Roosevelt Townes and "Boot Jack" McDaniels, was probably the most horrifying such incident of the decade. Authorities in Montgomery County, Mississippi, arrested Townes and McDaniels for the murder of a rural storekeeper near Duck Hill. After the prisoners' arraignment in Winona, county seat of Montgomery County, a small band of conspirators seized the two men from the sheriff and took them back to the vicinity of their alleged crime. There, a vengeful mob consisting largely of friends and relatives of the dead storekeeper watched with satisfaction as their leaders repeatedly applied the white-hot flame of a blowtorch to the flesh of their living victims, searing gaping holes in the bodies of the screaming, writhing men. The lynchers terminated this fiery ordeal with a volley of shots into the body of one man and the immolation of the other.[47]

The report of this incident that Kester submitted to the NAACP differed significantly from that which he filed after his examination of the Marianna murder. He contended that violence was a part of the social fabric of northern Mississippi and that blacks were especially vulnerable to the prevalent lawlessness. He stressed what he believed to be the sheriff's complicity in the crime, citing the officer's failure to protect the prisoners, pursue the mob, or investigate the lynching. He concluded his report with the observation that local authorities were "incompetent" to cope with such outbursts of interracial violence; only the federal government could "safely intervene in such matters on behalf of justice and fair play."[48]

Although Kester professed to have tried to set the Duck Hill incident in the context of the "historical situation and economic condition in an entire area," this type of analysis, which was an important component of *The Lynching of Claude Neal,* was notably absent.[49] There was the suggestion that Townes and McDaniels were in trouble with some local residents because they had intruded into the illicit liquor traffic popularly regarded as a white man's enterprise. But the author never related the crime to the class struggle or to general economic conditions in the vicinity.

Kester recognized that this report differed from some of his earlier ones. He explained to Walter White that he had written as he did in hopes of reaching a wider popular audience, of providing the kind of material that would assist those seeking passage of federal antilynching legislation, and of concealing the fact that the investigators of the Duck Hill and Marianna incidents were one in the same.[50] Yet, at the heart of the matter lay something more than these rationales suggest. The report reflected subtle but definite changes in Kester's thinking, changes of which he was perhaps not yet fully aware. A few months after the Duck Hill investigation he received a letter from a researcher in the Department of Political Science at the University of Chicago asking his help in determining the "occupational affiliation, nationality, income grouping, church membership and personality types" of participants in lynch mobs and other manifestations of racial intolerance. Although Kester expressed his appreciation for the efforts of scholars trying to understand the dynamics of violence and prejudice, his reply illuminates his doubts about the usefulness of his own work:

> The analysis of individual participation in intolerance movements is an exceedingly difficult and complex problem and one that requires an almost intimate knowledge of the whole social fabric on which the action is cast. I frankly consider my investigations of various lynchings, labor troubles etc. superficial[.] I have been able, particularly in the Claude Neal lynching, the Duck Hill lynchings and the Tuscaloosa lynchings to obtain a fair understanding of the occurences but I do not [c]onsider myself competent to give the microscopic analysis which I believe your study warrants.
>
> While nearly all lynchings or intolerance movements may fall into certain categories or behavior patterns they are often placed there by the wish of the investigator rather than by the nature of the actual facts. disclosed. I am therefore pretty skeptical of the usual "investigation". I do not pretend any knowledge of why humans act the way they do.[51]

Kester's skepticism was the product of years of experience. He had been investigating interracial violence since 1931 and in the process had become thoroughly acquainted with people's capacity for a species of cruelty which defied simple explanation. Although he had interpreted the lynching of Claude Neal as a manifestation of economic problems, he was haunted by the brutality of the lynchers. In Duck Hill he again encountered disturbing evidence of the same propensity for sadism that had so profoundly troubled him earlier. The actions of the mob in these and other incidents seemed to reflect not merely anger or a longing for justice but a thirst for inflicting pain which raised troubling questions about human nature and challenged the validity of purely socioeconomic analyses of racial violence. They appeared to substantiate the neoorthodox reaffirmation of the transcendent reality of evil. Kester began to suspect that if depravity rather than ignorance or poverty lay at the heart of racism, then something more fundamental than education or economic reform would be required to eradicate it, and he wondered about the value of much of his work. These doubts surfaced at a time when he was also beginning to have reservations about the efficacy of his activities on behalf of the Southern Tenant Farmers Union.

CHAPTER 5

■ ## Sharecroppers and ■
Socialism

No facet of his work during the mid and late 1930s captured Howard Kester's imagination more than his efforts on behalf of the Southern Tenant Farmers Union. Although he eventually became disillusioned with the STFU, the union's labors among the rural poor of the Deep South enabled him, at least for a time, to fuse his radical passion for economic justice with his commitment to interracial cooperation and his fundamental faith in the virtue of country life.

One of the most infamous features of southern agriculture in the years between the close of the Civil War and the outbreak of World War II was the development of the ubiquitous system of farm tenancy. Evolving originally out of the economic and social void created by the Confederacy's collapse, sharecropping and similar arrangements ultimately had a devastating effect upon the region. Cotton tenancy led to the exploitation of land and people and to the perpetuation of ignorance, racism, poverty, and provincialism.

As agricultural conditions deteriorated in the late nineteenth century, an ever-increasing number of rural southerners of both races joined the ranks of the landless farmers. Many of these unfortunate tillers of the soil became virtual peasants, tied to the land by their indebtedness to the landlord. While the first two decades of the twentieth century witnessed some improvement in the fortunes of many of those who owned their own land, the lot of most tenants changed little.

In the aftermath of World War I, the realm of King Cotton came under siege from several quarters. Reduced demand, the advent of synthetic fibers, and lower production costs in other parts of the world began to have a detrimental effect upon cotton producers. The Great Depression compounded these problems and placed cotton-producing landowners and tenants alike in an increasingly difficult position. Although many rural southerners failed to recognize the fact, by the thirties the plantation system, once viable because of cheap labor and a worldwide demand for cotton, was virtually obsolete. It survived only because of its integral place in the region's culture and because the planter class had sufficient political influence with the Roosevelt administration to protect itself through government action.[1]

The Agricultural Adjustment Administration (AAA) operated on the premise that the ills of the American farmer could be ameliorated, if not totally cured, by reducing production, thereby substantially raising the income level of most rural residents. In the South, for example, federal officials hoped to reduce cotton acreage by approximately one-third. Although the creation of artificial agricultural scarcity in an era of want was a controversial idea, it proved a boon for Dixie's cotton planters. Not only did the program drive the price of cotton up several cents per pound, but subsidies paid producers for reducing their acreage helped to buffer them against the vagaries of an unstable market. However, they had no such salutary effect upon the hundreds of thousands of tenants across the region.[2]

Initially, subsidies were to be divided equitably between landowner and tenant in proportion to their respective percentages of the year's crop, but from the outset the planters received the lion's share of federal assistance. In 1934 they secured changes in AAA policies that officially reduced the tenant's share of the subsidy to one-ninth of the total. By manipulation and subterfuge the landlord often denied even this modest portion to his powerless minions. Furthermore, New Deal policies that provided landowners with capital and required no sharing of government payments with day laborers tempted planters to place less reliance upon sharecroppers and more upon wage labor. Although forbidden by law from converting tenants to hired hands, plantation owners easily evaded the prohibition. Thus, during the thirties countless tenants fell to the even more precarious status of landless seasonal workers.[3]

By the mid-thirties even those who cultivated cotton in the fertile heartland of Dixie were experiencing the ravages of economic change and depression. Developments in the rich delta country of eastern Arkansas brought into clear focus both the declining fortunes of King Cotton and the evils of tenancy upon which his kingdom rested. In 1935 tenants, the majority of whom were black, constituted approximately 80 percent of the farmers in the area. Their total annual income generally ranged from $240 to $300.[4] The result was a standard of living that Americans usually associated with the impoverished masses of the world's most backward nations. When critics charged that land-owners exploited tenants, the planters responded that their costs were high and profit margins low. While the landed elite habitually exaggerated their own economic difficulties, their traditional defense was now more accurate than in the past. Had it not been for the agricultural policies of the Roosevelt administration, their plight might have become untenable.

It was, however, the tenants, not the landlords, of eastern Arkansas who found themselves most hard-pressed by the depression and the federal government's efforts to cope with it. There, as elsewhere, the Agricultural Adjustment Administration's cotton program undermined the last vestiges of their security by disrupting traditional economic relationships and guaranteeing them little save meager relief payments in compensation. Voiceless and powerless, there seemed little that the landless poor of the delta could do to protect themselves from insensitivity and exploitation. Then, in July 1934 they got a voice, if not much power, when two local Socialists, Harry Leland ("H. L.") Mitchell and Henry Clay East of Tyronza, guided a small band of black and white farmers in organizing the Southern Tenant Farmers Union. Mitchell and East envisioned the union's mission as twofold. To secure more equitable treatment for tenants, it would attempt to unite the disinherited of the delta in order to bring economic pressure to bear upon the planters. At the same time, it would strive through publicity and political pressure to force constructive changes in AAA policy.[5]

From the outset the STFU, though not officially an agency of the Socialist party, was closely associated with it. Norman Thomas visited Arkansas in early 1934 and was deeply moved by the condition of the state's landless unemployed masses. Apparently it was he who first suggested the idea of a union to Mitchell and East. The Socialist leader also funded the research for *The Plight of the Share-Cropper,* which attempted to demonstrate the deleterious effect of New Deal policies on the rural poor. Furthermore, once the union was launched, Thomas nurtured the fledgling organization by periodically channeling funds and personnel to it.[6]

It required little effort to interest young Socialists and other left-wing zealots in the union. Many of them believed this grass-roots movement afforded an opportunity both to minister to the immediate needs of the disinherited and to modify or undermine the economic and political system that was the ultimate source of the tenants' misery. Thus, for a half-dozen years in the mid and late thirties the rural poor of Arkansas and later of Missouri and Oklahoma became a cause célèbre for a host of liberal and radical activists.

Among those attracted to the work of the STFU was Buck Kester. His first contact with the union came in August 1934 when he received a letter from H. L. Mitchell, the organization's secretary, asking for the names of Socialists who might be willing to serve as organizers. Mitchell, who had met Kester a year earlier as a result of their mutual membership in the Socialist party, shrewdly tried to pique Kester's interest in the Arkansas crusade by appealing to his racial, religious, and revolutionary sympathies. He invited him to come over from Nashville and observe the work and "attend one of our meetings with white and black sharecroppers and hear their fundamentalist preachers preach revolution to them."[7]

Any movement that fused religion and radicalism was certain to capture Kester's imagination, but a variety of CERJ responsibilities prevented him from immediately casting his lot with the STFU. Throughout the next few months he stayed abreast of the organization's progress through correspondence with Mitchell and former Vanderbilt classmate Ward Rodgers, who was now active in its work. The more he heard of the union's efforts, the more impressed he became. By late fall he was convinced that it was "a thoroughgoing proletarian movement" which had "great promise of becoming a powerful instrument for the deliverance of the terribly oppressed farmers throughout this area."[8]

Reports of a rising tide of planter terrorism in Arkansas only intensified Kester's desire to throw himself into the fray. He planned to go to the assistance of the comrades in the delta in November, but his investigation of the Claude Neal case prevented him from doing so. Shortly after his return from Marianna, he wrote to Mitchell apologizing for his failure to visit the troubled area and promising to do his best to arrive early in the new year. Meanwhile, he did what he could to help in absentia by collecting used clothing for the membership and assisting in an American Civil Liberties Union attempt to organize a defense committee for the union.[9]

In late January 1935 Norman Thomas requested that Kester investigate the situation in eastern Arkansas for the Socialist party. Thomas especially wanted reliable information about the effectiveness of efforts to defend union organizers and members arrested by local authorities on a variety of charges. The Socialist leader wished not only to protect the union and to be certain that justice was served but also to see that the cases were handled with sufficient expertise to preclude intervention by the Communist International Labor Defense.[10] Thomas provided Kester with the impetus he needed to set aside other CERJ responsibilities and make the anticipated but long-delayed trip to the delta.

As he drove westward from Nashville toward Memphis, Kester may have remembered Mitchell's earlier admonition to "bring your artillery." If so, he judged the suggestion imprudent, for he paused at the Mississippi River long enough to discard a handful of shells left in his car from a recent hunting trip. He knew that hostile authorities might misinterpret the presence of such items and jail him as a violent revolutionary.[11] After taking this precaution, he drove across the river into a world which would absorb most of his time and energy during the next few years.

Within less than a week Thomas's emissary had completed a preliminary investigation of conditions in the area. Kester reported a number of incidents in which union organizers or sympathizers had been the victims of harassment or violence. As evidence he cited the arrest, trial, and conviction of Ward Rodgers following an allegedly incendiary speech in the town of Marked Tree and the beating and arrest of Lucien Koch and Bob Reed, representatives of Commonwealth College, a labor school in Mena, Arkansas, who had been attempting to address a union meeting in Crittenden County. He also pointed out the difficult position of rank-and-file members, several hundred of whom had been the victims of punitive evictions by indignant landlords.[12]

In spite of these difficulties, Kester's assessment of the situation was essentially positive. The wave of repression sweeping the delta neither surprised nor discouraged him. Several months before arriving on the scene he had written to Mitchell:

Those of us who are trying to do something in behalf of the disinherited must be prepared to face the black terror of the reactionaries. It is probably a necessary phase through which our people must pass before they will become class conscious enough to throw this yoke off. It is terrible to contemplate what is in store for many. It is probably inevitable and we may as well take it on the chin and smile. Our day will come and it probably isn't so far distant either.[13]

Thus, like a sectarian eschatologist anticipating the apocalypse, this romantic young radical interpreted current hardship as indicative of future triumph. Planter harassment and terrorism were to be regarded with concern but not despair.

One reason for Kester's cautious optimism about the future of the Southern Tenant Farmers Union was his initially favorable impression of its constituency and leadership. In early February he attended the organization's annual convention, at which members revised the constitution, established a legal defense committee, drew up a model contract, and made plans for the relief of evicted sharecroppers. He reported to Thomas that the proceedings were characterized by a "magnificent spirit" and complimented the leadership, much of which seemed to be drawn from the rank and file, for its "intelligence and earnestness." The veteran champion of interracial cooperation found the apparent solidarity of the black and white workers "positively exhilarating, a great spiritual experience," and he was convinced that "the white croppers would fight for a Negro as quickly as they would a white one." [14]

After only a few days in eastern Arkansas, Kester felt that his earlier notion that the STFU was a genuinely interracial proletarian movement with great promise for the revitalization of the rural South had been confirmed. Consequently, he threw himself into its work with characteristic abandon. In addition to gathering and relaying information to Thomas and other interested parties in the Northeast, the CERJ secretary soon occupied an important if ex officio position in the union's councils. In mid-February he wrote to Alice that he had been "called upon to do a thousand things" and was "going from morning to night without any letup whatever." [15]

Both the union's leadership and Kester's sponsors were delighted with his contributions to the STFU. H. L. Mitchell lacked his Socialist coworker's religious convictions and was somewhat amused by what he considered his prudery. He enjoyed relating the story of an occasion on which Kester came to New York City on business and spent the night with him and a woman with whom he was having an affair. During the night the couple awakened and heard sounds coming from Kester's bedroom. They crept to the partially open door and discovered their guest on his knees praying for his sinful friends. In spite of their differences, Mitchell liked and admired Kester for his courage, intelligence, and ability to articulate the sharecropper's cause. Norman Thomas and Reinhold Niebuhr were especially enthusiastic about the CERJ secretary's work among the rural poor, and Thomas proposed that the Committee on Economic and Racial Justice allow him to re-

main with the union indefinitely under Socialist party auspices.[16] Two
circumstances precluded such an arrangement: the party's inability to
raise the funds necessary for his support and Kester's ambivalence about
committing himself exclusively to the union. Nevertheless, from the
mid to the late thirties he devoted much of his time to the STFU.

The conditions in which the landless farmers of eastern Arkansas
lived appalled Kester. He reported that they were often clothed in rags
as soon as they came into the world and remained in them until they
left it. They lived in dilapidated shacks without even such basic amen-
ities as an outhouse. Their church buildings and schoolhouses were no
better and sometimes worse than their dwellings. Malaria, typhoid,
pellagra, and other diseases were rife. The croppers sometimes had to
comb the countryside for miles around in search of firewood. In the
best of times they ate some variant of the traditional fare of the poor—
meat, meal, and molasses—and in hard times were often reduced to
consuming snakes or the tender roots of wild plants. Kester recalled
visiting the home of one sharecropper who invited him to have dinner
with his family. When the food was served, he recognized the meat
placed before him as dog food. Realizing that his host was offering the
best he had and not wishing to embarrass or offend him, he ate it.
After the meal he left as soon as courtesy would allow and, giving way
to the revulsion he felt, became violently ill.[17]

The situation in the Arkansas delta roused in Kester both compassion and indignation. He believed the Southern Tenant Farmers Union
was the sharecropper's best hope and thought it imperative that the
nascent movement not falter in the face of planter hostility. To win the
confidence of members and the respect of friend and foe alike, it must
demonstrate its commitment to the tenants' cause by stepping up its
organizational campaign. Although impressed by men such as Mitchell, East, and Rodgers and by the ability of some of the leaders who
had emerged from the ranks, he recognized that the effort needed more
organizers. With the exception of his work with the miners of Wilder,
he had little firsthand experience either with the labor movement or
with the impoverished masses of the rural South, but he believed that
he could provide the kind of assistance that the STFU required. His
confidence proved well-founded.

As Donald Grubbs has pointed out, "the STFU founders were . . .
aware that uneducated people could be best approached for revolutionary action through their existing values and institutions." In the thirties religion was still perhaps the single most pervasive force in the
lives of the folk of the delta. One white sharecropper, Myrtle Moskop,

recalled, "I was just like the other people over in Wynne. When they first started talking about union, I thought it was a new church."[18] This was an understandable misapprehension since there were few other institutions to which the poor people of the area could belong.

Some of the most effective organizers, such as the black preacher E. B. McKinney and the white seminarian Ward Rodgers, treated the fledgling union almost as if it were a church. They tapped, as black preachers had done for generations, the imagery of bondage and deliverance to convey the message that as the hand of the Lord had freed the children of Israel, the hand of the union would deliver the sharecroppers of Arkansas. In countless meetings, organizers exhorted and listeners shouted as fervor mounted to an ecstatic crescendo resembling in form, if not in substance, a religious experience. Rural and small-town churches, schools, and lodge halls rocked to the rolling cadences of hymns and spirituals adapted to the cause of economic justice.

No one was more skilled at working in such a milieu than Howard Kester. He was thoroughly familiar with the beliefs and practices of southern Protestants of both races. Furthermore, he understood his own social mission in essentially Christian terms. He easily, almost instinctively, couched his radical message in religious rhetoric with which both he and his audiences were comfortable.

Yet religion was not the only avenue by which Kester reached the sharecroppers. His years of interracial work meant that he was relaxed among, and could communicate effectively with, both black and white members. In spite of economic and social differences between himself and the tenants, he could identify with and accept them. Unlike some of the activists who ventured into the delta country to assist the STFU, he was a southerner who understood the region's mores. Consequently, he knew how to winnow the cultural wheat from the chaff. He tended to accept personal and class idiosyncrasies, challenging only those values and attitudes that he deemed unjust. Regarding the tenants as impoverished men and women rather than cultural curiosities or mere pawns in an ideological struggle made it easier for him to empathize with the landless farmers and for them to accept him. Finally, his courage, as well as his compassion for the downtrodden and fervor for their cause, was obvious and won for him the respect of those whom he was trying to help.

Courage proved an indispensable asset not only for winning the support of the sharecroppers but also for coping with the landlords' determination to suppress the union. Perhaps Kester was guilty of a bit of self-aggrandizing hyperbole when, in mid-February, he wrote to

Alice concerning planter hostility toward him, "I have not been mo-
lested though they would like nothing better than to get their hands
on me."[19] However, before many weeks had passed, his highly visible
role in the union's organizing campaign had indeed made him anathema to many of the members and minions of the Arkansas establishment.

The new advocate of tenants' rights first made it clear to local
authorities that he was a force with which to be reckoned in the latter
part of February 1935. The STFU announced that three British
women, the most notable of whom was Jennie Lee, a member of the
House of Commons, were to address a union gathering in Marked Tree.
Town officials then forbade STFU meetings and declared that those who
violated the prohibition would be arrested. Kester, in charge of the
event, simply moved it to a spot five miles out of town. After he and
Lee had addressed the gathering, the two speakers defied local authorities and led the crowd of approximately fifteen hundred people back
to Marked Tree. There Kester, standing on the steps of the mayor's
office, asked union supporters to boycott local merchants until the ban
on STFU meetings was lifted. Although carloads of men allegedly
armed with machine guns lined the street along which the procession
marched into town, no violence occurred and no one was arrested.[20]

In many cases, however, neither Kester nor his associates could
escape the wrath of antiunion forces. In March 1935 Norman Thomas
went to Arkansas to see what was being done on behalf of the tenant
farmers. During the course of his visit he tried to speak at Birdsong, a
small community in Mississippi County. When Kester, who accompanied Thomas, rose to introduce his friend, he got only as far as "Ladies
and Gentlemen . . ." before an antagonist in the crowd yelled: "They
ain't no ladies in the crowd, and there ain't no gentlemen on the platform. That God damned white-headed Yankee son-of-a-bitch can go
back up North where he came from." When Thomas protested that he
had a constitutional right to speak, several men pulled him from the
platform, declaring that they "didn't give a damn about such things as
the Constitution" and that theirs was the "best God damned county,
and the best God damned state in the whole United States." The as-
sailants informed the Socialist leader in no uncertain terms that they
could take care of their laborers and that they "weren't gonna have no
outside interference from any white haired Yankee son-of-a-bitch."[21]
The indignant crowd, having completed its lesson in Arkansas hospi-
tality, forced Kester and Thomas back into their car and escorted them
to the bridge leading across the Mississippi River to Tennessee.

A week or so after this incident, STFU attorney C. T. Carpenter of Marked Tree wrote to Kester, who was temporarily back in Nashville. He reported that since the Birdsong affair, opponents of the union, some of whom reportedly were reviving the Klan, had repeatedly threatened the lives of Kester and other STFU leaders. The attorney did not believe these to be idle threats and considered the danger very real. Carpenter urged the Tennessee Socialist to exercise caution when he returned to Arkansas, suggesting that he come to Marked Tree only during the day and leave before nightfall. To drive home his point, the attorney concluded his somber message on a grim note: "Please remember me very kindly to Mrs. Kester and say to her that I do not want her to be a widow." [22]

Kester took Carpenter's admonitions seriously. He refused to cower before planter threats, but at the same time he had no desire to become a martyr to the cause. Consequently, he and other leaders took measures to minimize the danger to themselves and those with whom they worked. In hopes of being less conspicuous, he and Mitchell bought secondhand clothes on Beale Street in Memphis and often wore them when working in Arkansas. They frequently traveled the back roads of the delta after dark to avoid detection, and except when publicity seemed advantageous or secrecy impossible to maintain, they tried to conceal local union meetings from the landlords. [23]

In spite of such precautions, the risks remained high. This unpleasant reality became all too clear to Kester in early 1936. On January 17 he, STFU office secretary Evelyn Smith, and Memphis attorney Herman Goldberger drove to a black church near Earle to speak to a gathering of recently evicted sharecroppers. Goldberger spoke first without incident. Kester had scarcely begun when a small band of men brandishing ax handles and guns burst into the church. Some of the tenants panicked and leaped through windows, taking glass and sash with them as they fled. Others remained in their places while Kester continued to talk. The intruders, led by a local cotton broker and two deputy sheriffs, moved toward the speaker, demanding to know whether he would come peaceably or whether they would have to take him. He replied that he was breaking no law and if they wanted him they would have to take him. The men then seized Kester and his two companions and forced them into his car. After stationing the two deputies on the running boards, they ordered their captives to follow them to a wooded area outside of Earle. As Kester drove through town, he slammed on the brakes to avoid hitting a dog which trotted across the street in the path of his car. As he did so, one of the deputies holding a gun inches from his head said: "You G. D. S. O. B., you think more of a dog than you do of us white people. I'm minded to blow your brains out right now."

When the little caravan of cars arrived at its destination, a frightened but alert Kester decided that the time had come for him to try to reason with his captors. He explained to the cotton broker that he had harmed no one and had no intention of doing so. Noticing a noose slung over the shoulder of one of the men, Kester reminded the broker that he was a Tennessean and that if he was lynched, the case would be tried in federal court where a number of witnesses could be marshaled to testify against the guilty parties. The abductors may have planned to do nothing more than scare their victim. However, they may well have intended to rid themselves once and for all of a troublemaker. If so, Kester's presence of mind in the face of danger saved his life. After discussing their captive's fate for several minutes, the men tried to extract from him a promise that he would not return to the area. When this failed, they threatened to shoot him on sight if he crossed their path again and then unceremoniously ushered him and his associates out of Arkansas.

News of Kester's abduction and near-lynching soon reached H. L. Mitchell, who immediately wired the story to Norman Thomas. Thomas, delivering an address in New York that evening, read the telegram to his audience. As the story spread, some confusion developed as to Kester's fate. Alice, who was in Nashville and knew nothing of the Earle incident, suddenly began receiving inquiries from friends and associates concerned about Howard's condition and condolences from those saddened by his supposed death. Only after a frantic phone call to STFU headquarters near Memphis did she learn the details of her husband's traumatic experience.[24]

While Kester proved a courageous and talented organizer, whom many of the rank and file came to respect, his most significant contributions to the growth of the Southern Tenant Farmers Union were as fund-raiser, advocate, and publicist.[25] During his decade of work with the Young Men's Christian Association, Fellowship of Reconciliation, and Committee on Economic and Racial Justice, he had become thoroughly integrated into a network of socially concerned individuals and groups concentrated largely in the Northeast. His ties to secular organizations such as the Socialist party, National Association for the Advancement of Colored People, and American Civil Liberties Union facilitated but were not responsible for their cooperation with the union. However, his arrival in the delta gave the STFU a new, important, and largely untapped source of support, the liberal wing of American Protestantism. His friendships with theologians and teachers, denominational and interdenominational leaders, and local clergy and laity provided a conduit through which he could reach a wide audience with the story of the sharecroppers' struggle and simultaneously could solicit support for their cause. This liaison with liberal Christianity proved extremely advantageous for the union. At least in part because of Kester's influence, the Federal Council of Churches, National Religion and Labor Foundation, Fellowship of Southern Churchmen, and a number of denominational social service agencies furnished publicity, money, and supplies for the Arkansas work.[26]

It was not simply his connections with interested and influential people and groups that made Buck Kester an effective fund-raiser. He was the most articulate and persuasive speaker and impassioned writer at the union's disposal. In numerous speeches and articles and in *Revolt among the Sharecroppers,* he depicted the condition of the rural poor, leveled a Socialist critique at capitalism, and attacked the Roosevelt administration for its failure to develop an equitable agricultural program. During the latter thirties he spent much time each year traveling thousands of miles across the South, Northeast, and Midwest. Under the auspices of the League for Industrial Democracy, National Sharecroppers Fund, and Committee on Economic and Racial Justice, he spoke before hundreds of church, labor, and educational assemblies. At the height of his notoriety as an advocate of the tenants' cause, he sometimes reached audiences with national constituencies. For example, the NAACP invited both him and Ward Rodgers to appear before its convention in St. Louis in 1935. Rodgers reported that Kester was "the sensation of the convention." In the spring of 1937 the CERJ secretary delivered an address before the National Press Club in Washington, and later in the year he appeared on the NBC radio forum "America's Town Meeting of the Air." In 1938 and again in 1940 he testified before congressional hearings investigating the condition of rural labor.[27]

One of Kester's addresses apparently contributed to the establishment of a congressional investigating committee. In early 1936 he helped Gardner Jackson, organizer of the National Committee on Rural and Social Planning, and Benjamin C. Marsh, leader of the liberal advocacy group People's Lobby, plan a dinner in Washington, D.C. to make influential people more aware of civil liberties abuses. On the evening of February 21 representatives of agricultural, labor, and religious organizations as well as several members of Congress, including senators Edward P. Costigan of Colorado, Robert M. La Follette, Jr., of Wisconsin, Lewis B. Schwellenbach of Washington, and Burton K. Wheeler of Montana, and representatives Caroline O'Day of New York, Maury Maverick of Texas, and George J. Schneider of Wisconsin, gathered at the Cosmos Club. They heard Kester, the featured speaker, deliver a moving account of the sharecropper's struggle to secure fair wages and decent treatment from the landlords. Kester's description of the reign of terror that the planters had unleashed against the organizers and members of the Southern Tenant Farmers Union and the presence of a sharecropper still heavily bandaged as a result of a beating by union opponents made clear to most of those present the extent to which the economic and social establishment of eastern Arkansas was riding roughshod over the rights of the poor. The Cosmos Club dinner helped to galvanize the sentiment that led a few weeks later to the establishment of the La Follette Civil Liberties Committee.[28]

Kester's pen was as indispensable to the STFU as was his ability as a speaker. When, in the summer of 1936, Arkansas governor J. Marion Futrell excluded STFU representatives from his commission on farm tenancy, union leaders turned to Kester to prepare a report which they could submit to the investigatory body in lieu of representation. After writing furiously for three days with little sleep and only sandwiches and coffee for sustenance, he completed a concise, forceful document reflecting the union's perception of conditions in the delta and embodying its program for reform.

Kester begged the commission to "face facts . . . in the name of truth and justice." He contended that many of the ill effects ascribed to tenancy were actually a result of the South's willingness "to withhold economic, civil, and political privileges from white men" because the region "wished to deny them to colored men." Among other things, the report called for the abolition or regulation of plantation commissaries, the enforcement of legal rates of interest, compensation of tenants for improvements made upon the land they farmed, guarantees of civil liberties, and enforcement of relevant child labor and eviction statutes. Though the report had little impact on the commission's findings, liberals sympathetic to the sharecroppers' cause praised it.[29]

Kester's most eloquent and impassioned plea on behalf of the disinherited came in 1936 with the publication of *Revolt among the Share-croppers*. In this slender volume he sensitively and graphically portrayed the condition of a rural proletariat reduced almost to peonage by King Cotton. Describing tenancy as "a cancerous growth" susceptible to no treatment "short of a major operation," he charged that New Deal agricultural programs at best offered only a palliative. At their worst, as in the case of the Agricultural Adjustment Act, that "bastard child of a decadent capitalism," they actually degraded the tenant by depriving him of his already meager subsistence. The approach embodied in the Bankhead-Jones bill, proposing federal assistance to tenants and sharecroppers seeking to buy their own land, promised little relief. Some of the projects of the Resettlement Administration were perhaps steps in the right direction but were too limited in scope and funding. What was needed was an innovative and comprehensive program subject to the constraints of neither capitalism nor political expediency.[30]

The plan for the deliverance of the tenants advocated by Kester was a derivative blend of socialism and Country Life Progressivism infused with a prophetic passion for social justice. He argued that the viability of the region's agricultural economy depended upon diversification and the adjustment of supply to demand. However, these objectives should be accomplished through an equitable process which enabled all farmers, not just the landed elite, to benefit from stable living. Thoroughgoing residential cooperatives of the type he envisioned not only would foster economic security but also would contribute to the personal and cultural development of the rural poor.[31]

In the closing pages of *Revolt among the Sharecroppers*, Kester suggested that farmers could own their own homes in compact rural villages and collectively farm communally owned land. Residents of such cooperative farms would enjoy all the advantages and few of the disadvantages of contemporary civilization, for agricultural engineers would bring to the people the best possible methods of getting the most from the soil and social engineers would direct them in the achieving of "a high type of social relationship." This revolution would come not through coercion but persuasion. The founding of a few demonstration farms should prove sufficient to inaugurate the cooperative movement that would soon sweep the South.[32]

As Kester's book was going to press, he and several associates, including H. L. Mitchell and Dr. William R. Amberson of Memphis, who were familiar with the critical situation faced by landless farmers in the Cotton Belt decided to establish a cooperative farm. These Socialist visionaries intended their project to serve both as a haven for evicted STFU members and as a model for subsequent collective ventures elsewhere across the South. They hoped to locate the farm in Arkansas under the auspices of the Resettlement Administration but soon abandoned these plans as impractical. They were unable to secure a suitable tract of land in the delta. Furthermore, Resettlement officials in Arkansas and Washington generally had little confidence in any plan emanating from the STFU. The collectivism advocated by Kester, Mitchell, Amberson, and other proponents of the farm was antithetical to the administration's preference for individual homesteads and traditional cooperatives. Consequently, the project that eventually took shape was a private rather than a governmental endeavor.[33]

By the mid-thirties the plight of the black and white sharecroppers of the South had aroused both sympathy and indignation among liberals and radicals throughout the nation. Therefore, raising money for a cooperative farm which might serve simultaneously as an instrument of relief and a model for rural rehabilitation was relatively easy. James Myers, Norman Thomas, Reinhold Niebuhr, and Sherwood Eddy were among the prominent activists who immediately rallied behind the venture and began soliciting money for it. In March 1936 Eddy, a national officer of the YMCA who had enthusiastically embraced the cooperative idea, made a whirlwind trip to the mid-South and purchased a twenty-one-hundred-acre site in northwestern Mississippi about seventy miles south of Memphis.[34]

Although somewhat taken aback by the speed with which Eddy acted, the architects of the project were delighted with the prospect of at last having an opportunity to translate their ideas into action. Founders of what became the Delta Cooperative Farm envisioned it as much more than an economic venture. It was a social laboratory, an educational effort, and, for some at least, an experiment in applied Christianity. To be sure, the economic dimension of the project was important. Planners hoped to train relocated sharecroppers in diversified scientific agriculture so that they could achieve self-sufficiency and a decent standard of living. However, they also wanted to school residents and observers alike in the virtues of democratic socialism and interracial cooperation. The men, women, and children of both races who lived on the farm were to work, worship, study, and play together. Although each family was eventually to own a house and small plot of land, production, marketing, and purchasing were to remain cooperative efforts and profits were to be shared. After a period of adjustment during which the farm's trustees and resident manager would exercise considerable authority, the people themselves were to assume full responsibility for the cooperative's program.[35]

When Buck Kester learned that Eddy had acquired property for the farm, he was elated. He confided to James Myers that he "felt as though the Kingdom was really being born and that something of historic importance was about to make its appearance on the earth."

The endowment of economic and social reform with theological significance was a common thread running through the thought of a number
of the sharecroppers' champions. Many of the Protestant social activists
who supported the STFU regarded themselves as neoorthodox Christian realists. These men and women dismissed the liberal faith in education and moral suasion as naive. They believed that the class struggle
was the only practical means by which to establish a more equitable
socioeconomic order. The new society rising out of the ashes of the old
would not be perfect, but it would represent as close an approximation
of the Kingdom of God on earth as flawed humanity could hope to
achieve. For Kester and its neoorthodox supporters, the Delta Cooperative Farm represented a potential step forward for both the disinherited and society as a whole.[36]

In spite of the great expectations for the venture, the farm proved
a disappointment. Problems began to arise almost immediately. The
settlement of families on the site did not begin until April 1936,
which meant that the first year's cotton and vegetable crops were
planted too late for maximum yields. Then a drought further reduced
the harvest. In 1937 the farm's production of cotton increased, but the
price of the staple plunged, depriving the project of expected and badly
needed operating capital. Meanwhile, expenses continued to mount.
The salaried staff of the medical clinic and school had to be paid.
Equipment seemed in constant need of costly repair or replacement.
The land turned out to be less of a bargain than its purchasers had
thought; almost two-thirds of the property had never been cleared, and
the process of cutting trees, draining swamps, and breaking new
ground consumed both time and money. By late 1937 the farm was on
the verge of bankruptcy.[37]

Not all the difficulties involved finances. In spite of efforts to nurture interracial cooperation, blacks sometimes felt that whites received
preferential treatment, and whites often found it difficult to lay aside
their assumptions of racial superiority. Ill will also stemmed from the
fact that residents of both races came to regard farm director Sam
Franklin as an autocratic, unresponsive leader. This dissatisfaction contributed to an atmosphere of mistrust. When the farm failed to turn a
profit and dividends to cooperative members were meager or nonexistent, some of them charged that Franklin and his associates were no
better than the landlords who regularly cheated them of their earnings.[38]

Problems on the farm contributed to dissension among its trustees.
The potential for discord existed from the outset because not all mem-

bers of the board shared the neoorthodox conception of the project. Dr. Amberson, a professor of physiology at the medical college of the University of Tennessee and later at the University of Maryland, had little sympathy for the religious motivations of fellow trustees Eddy, Niebuhr, and Franklin. He regarded them as impractical Christian ideologues whose determination to impose their values upon the experiment threatened to destroy it. Amberson believed that if the farm was to be of lasting value, it must become a self-sustaining enterprise, not some kind of socioreligious utopia dependent upon northern philanthropy for survival. The apparent financial ineptitude of the farm's management and the trustees' willingness to tolerate its deficiencies appalled him. The professor was astonished when in early 1938, as the Delta project teetered on the brink of bankruptcy, Franklin purchased a second tract of land to launch Providence Cooperative Farm and the trustees prepared to solicit additional contributions to underwrite both projects.[39]

Although board members Arthur Raper and Guy B. Johnson appear to have shared some of Amberson's concerns, he generated the greatest controversy through his vehement and public charges. His colleagues dismissed his impassioned criticisms as idiosyncratic or pathological. When they proceeded with policies he considered disastrous, Amberson in 1939 resigned from the board. While the trustees generally welcomed the resignation, his public letter to the *Christian Century* disclosing the reasons for his disenchantment with the farm embarrassed them.[40]

Kester observed the trials and tribulations of the Delta and later the Providence Cooperative Farm with concern and disappointment. Although he had been instrumental in launching this experiment in cooperative living, he played no direct role in the project's operations once it was established. However, the various parties embroiled in the controversies besetting the endeavor kept him abreast of the situation in Mississippi.

The disputes that swirled about the farms placed Kester in an awkward position. Though ideologically and personally close to the neoorthodox faction on the board of trustees, he concurred with some of Amberson's misgivings. He dismissed as unwarranted the professor's accusations that Franklin and Eddy were guilty of dishonest bookkeeping and fund-raising practices but recognized that the cooperatives's finances were in disarray. He respected Franklin as a dedicated Christian reformer but developed serious reservations about his ability to work effectively with the people he was trying to help. He understood that the Delta experiment was intended to be merely the first of many such ventures but questioned the wisdom of acquiring a second farm before the first was on a sound economic footing.[41]

In spite of these misgivings, Kester refused to concede that the project was doomed and did what he could to salvage it. He believed that much of the dissension plaguing the farms stemmed from misunderstandings and a lack of communication among residents, management, and trustees. Therefore, in 1939 he advocated an independent audit to establish once and for all the state of the farms' finances and a conference at which disputants could air and resolve their differences. The trustees initially failed to heed these suggestions, but developments in 1940 finally forced them to take action.[42]

In January disgruntled members of the cooperatives brought their grievances before the annual convention of the Southern Tenant Farmers Union. They charged that the management was authoritarian, racist, and dishonest. The accusations widened a chasm between the STFU and the cooperatives which had been developing for several years. As a result of the allegations, the union and the farms' sponsors agreed to establish a joint committee to look into the charges.[43] Kester recognized that the Mississippi operations faced many problems but doubted the validity of these particular accusations. Nevertheless, he believed that an inquiry could bring the real difficulties into clear focus and agreed to serve as one of the union's representatives.

The investigators conducted public hearings at both the Delta and Providence sites in mid-May and concluded, in a report written by Kester, that the charges of racism and malfeasance were unfounded. They attributed most of the trouble on the farms to the residents' lack of experience with cooperatives and to management's failure to educate them adequately. Committee members deemphasized financial difficulties and stressed the project's reform objectives when they contended that "we believe that the significance of this undertaking is far too great to be jeopardized by measuring its success or lack of success by the people's ability to become economically self-sufficient. While we do not minimize the importance of the economic angle we believe that the social and spiritual factors are of profound significance and worth and must not be lost sight of by those concerned with the success of the undertaking." The investigators concluded their report with a commendation for Sam Franklin and expressed confidence that the farms' personnel could overcome the numerous economic and social problems confronting them.[44]

The committee's findings reflected the reform impulse that underlay much of the work with the sharecroppers since 1934. Not all the champions of the disinherited shared the same vision of the new order, but they were united in their conviction that the rural proletariat could be marshaled to the cause of a better world. This faith often persisted in the face of evidence to the contrary. Even as the ad hoc panel investigating the Delta and Providence farms expressed its hope for the future, families drifted away from the project, and its chronically shaky finances crumbled. Finally, in the early forties the trustees sold the acreage and equipment of the Delta Cooperative Farm and concentrated on Providence, which evolved from a cooperative into what was essentially a community health and education center.[45]

Meanwhile, problems racked the Southern Tenant Farmers Union itself. When Kester went to Arkansas in early 1935, he had been quite impressed with the caliber of its leadership and the spirit of interracial solidarity among its members. Before many months had passed, however, he began to be concerned first about the clash of personalities among officers and aspiring leaders and later about the specter of racism, both of which threatened to undermine the union.

In April 1935 two members, Walter Moskop and W. H. Stultz, the latter of whom had succeeded Clay East as president of the STFU, brought a range of charges against H. L. Mitchell. The dissidents' allegations ranged from accusations of mismanagement of union funds to complaints that the secretary had declared that he was "tired of the 'God-damn Sons of bitches' bothering and asking him about the union and he thought he would turn it over to the 'God-damn sons of bitches' and let them run it." The STFU's executive committee held a hearing to consider the accusations. During the proceedings Moskop tried to shoot Mitchell, but Kester and another committee member foiled the attempt. Mitchell was exonerated, but the rivalry and bitterness reflected in this incident lingered. Not long thereafter Stultz tried to seize control of the union during Mitchell's absence. Several months later, while the secretary was visiting Commonwealth College, Moskop emptied a revolver at him at close range but failed to do his intended victim any harm.[46]

Racism posed another threat to the Southern Tenant Farmers Union, but leaders and members generally managed to keep it under control. Occasionally the latent tensions between blacks and whites surfaced. In mid-January 1935 one of the organization's pioneer white workers, J. O. Green, suggested a restructuring of the STFU, including the establishment of segregated locals. The union rejected the proposal and expelled Green. E. B. McKinney, one of the STFU's ablest black leaders, occasionally let racism affect his approach to work among the sharecroppers.[47]

The most serious threat to interracial solidarity was related to a larger controversy which engulfed the union in the late thirties. In 1937 leaders of the STFU, feeling that it might be strengthened by affiliation with the national labor movement, tried to join the Congress of Industrial Organizations (CIO). The only way they could accomplish this objective was to become a part of the newly formed United Cannery, Agricultural, Packing, and Allied Workers of America (UCA-PAWA). Kester thought such a step was unwise. He was an idealist who envisioned the Southern Tenant Farmers Union as an "emancipation movement" which should address the spiritual as well as the material problems of the rural poor.[48] He favored membership in the CIO but feared that becoming part of another agricultural organization might dissipate the STFU's energy and divert it from its broader mission to the tenants and sharecroppers. Furthermore, he worried about the role of Communists in the UCAPAWA.

The Communists had paid little attention to American farmers and sharecroppers during the twenties, but in the early thirties they had begun working among the rural poor. In one of their first efforts in the South, they organized the Sharecroppers Union in Alabama but with meager results. Thus, it is not surprising that they became interested in the STFU as soon as it appeared to be having some success. In January 1935 Donald Henderson, leader of the Communist-sponsored Organization of Agricultural Workers, held a meeting in Washington to unite various agricultural groups. The STFU was invited to participate and sent several emissaries, including Mitchell. The International Labor Defense took up the cause of Ward Rodgers after his arrest at Marked Tree, thus making his defense a Popular Front battle. In October 1934 the Sharecroppers Union called for class unity between the Arkansas and Alabama movements to battle the forces of capitalism more effectively and in August of the following year proposed a merger of the two organizations. The STFU rejected the proposal but remained cautiously friendly toward the Alabama union until 1936.[49]

While the leaders and supporters of the Southern Tenant Farmers Union were willing to cooperate in genuine United or Popular Front ventures, they were wary of forming too close an alliance with Communists and fellow travelers. Their caution resulted in part from the traditional enmity between Socialists and Communists. Mitchell, Kes-

and the other Socialists in the STFU had always insisted that it
not an instrument of their party. It was, however, heavily dependent upon Socialist support. The patron saint of the union was Norman
Thomas, and the organization's stance on questions of land tenure and
economic policy reflected the party's position. In addition to this sectarian rivalry, STFU leaders also disliked the Communist contention
that there should be separate organizations for rural wage laborers,
including sharecroppers, on the one hand and small farmers, including
tenants, on the other. They believed that because the line between
tenant and laborer was ill-defined and was frequently crossed, these
groups should be united in a single union.[50]

Presented in 1937 with an opportunity to affiliate with the CIO,
the officers of the STFU had to decide just how closely they were willing to work with Communists. Donald Henderson was president of
UCAPAWA, and Kester feared that if the STFU became a part of this
organization, it would be vulnerable to infiltration and ultimately
domination by the Communists. A majority of the union's members
did not share his concern, and even some who did convinced themselves that joining the ranks of the CIO was worth whatever risks
might be involved.

At a special convention in September 1937, the Southern Tenant
Farmers Union voted to unite with the United Cannery, Agricultural,
Packing, and Allied Workers of America. Affiliation with UCAPAWA
proved disastrous. The STFU leaders believed that their union had
been granted a semiautonomous status. However, Henderson and his
associates exerted more and more control over its personnel, funds, and
operations. Relations between officials of the two bodies steadily deteriorated. On one occasion Kester, the sharecroppers' most articulate
spokesman, was expelled from a UCAPAWA meeting which was considering STFU grievances.[51] In the midst of the growing spirit of acri-
mony, J. R. Butler, president of the STFU, found a document
belonging to Claude Williams, director of Commonwealth College and
a supporter of UCAPAWA, which outlined plans for a Communist
takeover of the STFU. This discovery simply confirmed the suspicions
of Kester and other Socialists that the STFU was threatened by subversion. Butler demanded that Williams resign from the union's executive
council, but he refused, denying that the apparently incriminating
document was anything more than idle theorizing. The council then
tried and expelled him. He countered by organizing a coalition of mal-
contents which he hoped could gain control of the annual convention
of the union and reinstate him, but the effort failed.[52]

By early 1939 Donald Henderson had lost patience with the troublesome Southern Tenant Farmers Union and decided to deal directly and decisively with it. In March he suspended its executive officers and announced that he was reorganizing the STFU district along more democratic lines. Mitchell and Butler then called a special convention of the STFU which voted unanimously for withdrawal from the CIO. Delighted, Kester conducted a mock funeral service for UCAPAWA. As the mourners passed by a cigar box coffin, they sang:

> She's Ashes to Ashes and Dust to Dust
> Here lies A Union We Never Could Trust;
> Ashes to Ashes and Dust to Dust
> This Man Henderson Has Hushed His Fuss.[53]

The struggle with UCAPAWA embittered Kester. He believed it had undermined not only the economic and political power of the STFU but also its interracial solidarity. He was convinced that the Communists had attempted to play upon prejudice in order to divide and conquer. Advocates of affiliation with UCAPAWA had leveled charges of racism at their opponents. Claude Williams had attempted to build a base of support among the black members of the union in his effort to reverse his ouster by the executive committee. In the fight over disaffiliation, supporters of UCAPAWA had tried to divide their opponents along racial lines.[54]

The personal, ideological, and racial conflicts within the STFU depressed Kester not only because by the early forties they had rendered it virtually impotent but also because they damaged or destroyed longtime relationships with many of his radical friends and associates. He played a major role in the expulsion of Williams, and the action cost him the friendship of a man he had liked and respected since their days together at Vanderbilt. A few of the black supporters of UCAPAWA accused him of racism, an accusation that hurt this veteran of interracial work. The Communists charged that he was a reactionary foe of change. When he devoted time to other causes, some Socialists complained that he had deserted the sharecroppers' cause. Weary of political sectarianism and the machinations of individuals and groups vying for control of the union, he longed for personal and social peace and harmony as well as justice. Furthermore, the failure of this "emancipation movement" to resolve the problems of the rural poor raised questions in his mind about the efficacy of revolutionary politics and the class struggle. By the end of the thirties his accumulated experiences during the decade had convinced him that a more fundamental and comprehensive approach to social change was needed if the world was to be made a better place.

CHAPTER 6

■ From Prophetic Radical ■
to Radical Prophet

Buck Kester's disenchantment with the STFU was not an isolated phenomenon. It was merely one facet of a gradual reorientation of his thought and work which began in the latter half of the 1930s. As the decade passed, his commitment to the struggle for economic and social progress in the South remained intense. However, his understanding of the nature of that progress and of the most effective means of achieving it changed.

Kester's career as a free-lance social activist brought him numerous opportunities for service, many challenges, and considerable notoriety, all of which he relished. Yet a gnawing sense of dissatisfaction plagued him. The scope and volume of his activities pulled him in many directions at once and allowed him little time for reflection and self-definition. As early as December 1933, at the height of his radicalism, he confided to Alice: "I'm getting to be a regular chamel[e]on. First I am a preacher, then an educator, again a peace worker, then a social worker, then a radical—'all things to all men' that I 'may win some.' . . . I'm beginning to believe that I hardly know my own mind." [1]

Such episodes of self-doubt were an integral part of Kester's psyche, but they were intensified by the tenuous and often dangerous nature of his endeavors. As he drove alone over the hundreds of miles of desolate country roads that he traversed each year or tossed restlessly in hotel rooms, too tired to sleep, misgivings about his work sometimes overwhelmed him. As the thirties passed, he grew increasingly anxious and dissatisfied. The emotional troughs of doubt and depression became deeper and more protracted, and the compensatory peaks of enthusiasm and exhilaration less frequent. In January 1937 Kester wrote to Alice:

I wish that I could write joyous letters to you but it just doesn't seem to be in me any more. I feel anything but joyful these days and at times I become quite pessimistic about everything and seriously wonder what is the use of carrying on. I suppose it is just me. I don't seem to have the inspiration and courage I had once and everything seems to be in a whirling mess. There are things to live for yes, but they could possibly get along just as well without me. I feel as though I am beginning to make a mess of things, my life, and I don't want that to happen. Somewhere along the line I have made some mistakes, pretty serious ones, and I wonder if the rebound won't be too much. Something is happening to me. What it is, I don't know but that it is happening, I am certain. I have never been quite so restless, quite so uncertain, quite so honest with myself as I am now for some weeks. I am very discouraged. There seems to be something lacking in my life that wasn't some years ago.[2]

The CERJ secretary's ill-defined but unsettling sense of restlessness and discontent stemmed from several sources. One problem that he recognized but did not know how to resolve was the strain his work placed upon his marriage. His activities, especially those on behalf of the STFU, required long periods of separation from his family and proved trying for all. Alice found it quite difficult to cope with his absences. She was well aware of the dangers involved in the union work and sometimes was overwhelmed with anxiety when Howard left Nashville for the Arkansas delta. Moreover, as time passed, the risks he took on behalf of the STFU seemed to her less and less worthwhile. She resented what she regarded as the union leadership's unreasonable demands on her husband's physical and emotional resources. She was troubled by the fact that H. L. Mitchell and other STFU leaders seemed to lack Howard's integrity and sense of religious commitment.[3] Consequently, she believed that his association with the union forced him to make sacrifices of time, energy, and principle that made him not only unhappy but also less effective in his other endeavors.

Alice also became disaffected with the STFU work for another, more personal reason. Since their marriage in 1927, she had shared Howard's dedication to socioeconomic reform in the South. She had attended interracial conferences, served as a volunteer with YWCA projects among the industrial working women of Nashville, distributed food and clothing to striking miners at Wilder, acted as her husband's secretary, and sacrificed her own aspirations for a career in early childhood education to assist him in realizing his goals. The nature of the undertaking in Arkansas and the birth of the couple's daughter, Nancy, in 1934 meant that she could now be only marginally involved in the STFU work. She began to feel extraneous and isolated. Furthermore, when Kester was home from the delta or one of his frequent trips to the Northeast on behalf of the union, he was often so physically exhausted and emotionally drained by the strain of his efforts that he seemed a stranger. This only intensified Alice's sense of estrangement and insecurity. She tried to fill the void by caring for Nancy, developing her secretarial skills, and attending to the voluminous correspondence that Howard's work generated. Yet, she could not prevent the waves of depression from breaking over her, nor could she hide her emotions from her husband.[4]

Kester was torn between his sense of mission and his love for his wife. He believed that he was making sacrifices for the sake of a better world and expected Alice to endure the periodic loneliness and anxiety as her share of the work. When she seemed incapable of coping with the stress, he sometimes responded with self-righteous indignation at her failure and at other times with remorse and guilt at the pain that he caused her. In one such moment of contrition he wrote:

> At times I suppose I have been a tyrant—ill tempered and ill natured. For all my sins I beg your forgiveness and for your continued love and understanding I beg even more. I am a frail creature pulled here and lured there by ill winds and good but even in my blindness I love and have never—I know now—loved anyone else. I have not always understood—do not now always understand and in moments of weakness my weaker self dominates—and then I suffer hell for all my unkindly ways.[5]

Yet, in spite of such regrets, he did not know how to reconcile the conflicting passions of his life.

Another source of the CERJ secretary's malaise was more subtle and complex. The familial, social, and cultural environment into which he had been born was permeated with the values of the Victorian South. Although not free of economic, social, or racial cleavages, Martinsville and Henry County, Virginia, retained a sense of community cohesiveness characteristic of the late nineteenth century. As many southerners of that era understood it, community stability rested more on the character of its citizenry than on coercion or institutional restraints.[6] Therefore, if order and harmony were to be preserved, the family, church, and school must use education and moral suasion to inculcate qualities such as self-discipline, rationality, and ethical purity. Perhaps this notion of an organic society which rested largely on personal and public virtue was more illusion than reality, but it was a vital component of the social fabric of the day.

This Victorian frame of reference shaped Howard Kester's earliest conceptions of himself and of his world. His education and experience had liberated him from some of the cultural influences of his youth, but he was by no means free of his past. To some extent, his heritage now nurtured the seeds of his discontent.

Kester's work with the intercollegiate YMCA and the Youth Section of the Fellowship of Reconciliation during the 1920s brought him into conflict with the racism and militarism of the South. Yet the methods he employed—education and moral suasion—and the goal toward which he strove—a peaceful harmonious society—were not fundamentally inconsistent with the values instilled in him as a child. However, during the thirties the nature of his work changed. Driven by his compassion for the disinherited and influenced by Socialist and neoorthodox thought, he came to accept institutional restraints and coercion in the form of legislation, strikes, and, if necessary, limited violence as integral parts of the struggle for a better world. Furthermore, he conceded that the result of even these tactics might not be a genuinely harmonious society—the Kingdom of God on earth—but one characterized by only a rough approximation of justice. Complex situations such as those he encountered in Wilder, Marianna, and eastern Arkansas confirmed his new understanding. He believed that the problems of these and other troubled areas might be resolved by pressure but not by persuasion, and even if solutions were found, they were likely to be less than ideal.

Although during the early and mid thirties Kester was intellectually committed to a program of social action which was radical by southern standards, he remained emotionally wedded to many of the values of his youth. The psychic tension produced by this situation was manageable as long as he was convinced that he was contributing to the economic and social progress of his region. However, by the late thirties and early forties he had doubts about the significance of his work. It seemed that lynching had not been abolished but merely driven underground. The Ku Klux Klan appeared to be alive and well, at least in some localities. The Socialist party, Southern Tenant Farmers Union, Delta Cooperative Farm, and other organizations whose causes he championed were riddled with personal, ideological, or racial factionalism and were at best having only modest success in coping with the South's problems. Consequently, his enthusiasm for them waned. As this occurred, he began to experience a debilitating sense of anxiety, restlessness, and guilt.

By the spring and summer of 1937 the strain under which he worked had brought Kester to the brink of mental and physical collapse. On doctor's orders he finally took an extended vacation.[7] This protracted period of rest gave him an opportunity to reflect upon his activities over the past decade and to contemplate his role in the future regeneration of the South. Although he failed to grasp its significance, the summer of 1937 was something of a catalytic period, accelerating a process of reorientation which had begun as early as the previous autumn. By late 1936 the apparent futility of his methods and the concomitant burden of guilt had already led him to begin a reappraisal of his work. One manifestation of this reassessment was his ordination as a Congregational clergyman in October of that year. His statement to the Congregational board of examiners seeking to determine his fitness for the ministry illuminates the direction in which his thought was moving. He affirmed his faith in Jesus as "the most complete expression of God's will known among men" and in religion as "the most sufficient, powerful and creative force known among men whereby the individual and society may be brought into the Kingdom of God." He declared that the church, like the God it represented, must be concerned with all of life and that a "realistic, prophetic, creative and socially-dynamic" Christianity must replace the sham religion so prevalent in the contemporary world. He made it clear that he wished to contribute to the reinvigoration of both religion and society and indicated his belief that among the Protestant denominations in the South, the Congregational church most closely approximated the realistic expression of Christianity in which he believed.[8] While his ordination gave Kester the sense of institutional affiliation that he needed, it did not signal an immediate turn toward the church as his primary avenue of service. However, the reorientation that began in 1936 continued in the summer and fall of 1937 and resulted in the gradual reemergence of a sense of religious commitment as the primary component of his activism.

Even in the mid-thirties when Kester considered himself a "revolutionary socialist," his radicalism was more that of the compassionate prophet than the political sectarian.[9] He had always regarded the religious and secular dimensions of reform as inextricably related. However, as he had grown more radical, he had found it increasingly difficult to fuse Christian ethics and socioeconomic goals into a coherent, persuasive plan of action. While southern Protestantism was not devoid of a sense of social responsibility, it lacked a genuinely prophetic tradition which could be tapped to give religious legitimacy to a call for changes in the region. Furthermore, many of the left-wing zealots with whom Kester associated regarded Christianity as either irrelevant or hostile. Therefore, he often deemed it expedient to subordinate the religious element in his activism to a secular appeal for an equitable social order, but he was never entirely comfortable with this subordination.

His quest for a more effective means by which to serve both God and the cause of social justice led Kester to turn his attention to the Fellowship of Southern Churchmen (FSC). The Fellowship was the most radical expression of Christianity in the South during the 1930s. This interracial, interdenominational group originated with the Conference of Younger Churchmen of the South (CYC) that convened at Monteagle, Tennessee, on 27–29 May 1934. James Dombrowski, who conceived the idea for the Monteagle assembly, wished to bring together socially conscious southern Christians such as Kester, Myles Horton, Benjamin Mays, H. Shelton Smith, and Alva Taylor to consider the numerous ills afflicting their region in the depths of the depression.[10]

Though divergent in origin and occupation, the approximately eighty Monteagle conferees shared the conviction that the hour was at hand when Christians would take the lead in the struggle for social and economic justice. Reinhold Niebuhr, who attended the conference, was the spiritual father of the Churchmen. Many members either had been students of Niebuhr or were sympathetic toward his theology and social ethic. Consequently, the group's early critique of southern society reflected the influence of Niebuhrian neoorthodoxy and Christian socialism.[11]

The neoorthodox character of the Southern Churchmen's thought was apparent in the absence of the optimism typical of the early proponents of the Social Gospel. These Christians regarded man as a child of God but also as a sinner and believed that "a more perfect social order, however organized, cannot eliminate the evil in his heart." In their theology, Christ was no mere example of the moral and ethical heights to which individuals could rise, "the reflection in the sky of our inward best"; rather, Christ was "the invasion by God of our hopeless worst." The entire world seemed to them to be "dying from the demonic forces of injustice, poverty, war, racial hatred, class greed, unemployment, and the debauching worship of false Gods."[12] The task of prophetic Christianity, as they understood it, was to take the measure of society against the plumb line of divine justice and, when finding the social order wanting, to decry its shortcomings and to strive for repentance expressed not only in word but in deed.

As the Churchmen measured the society of the thirties against what they regarded as a divine standard, they employed something of a Marxian analysis. They readily accepted the premise that "the collective behavior of men must be understood on the whole in the light of their economic interests." [13] Such an analysis, they believed, was wholly compatible with the sinfulness and greed of humanity. At their second conference, held in Chattanooga, Tennessee, in the late fall of 1934, the prophets couched their social critique in language likely to warm the heart of the most thoroughgoing Marxist. They expressed their conviction that the existing economic order was "increasingly self-destructive"; that it depended for its existence upon "the exploitation of one group by another"; and that it created industrial strife and international war, precipitated unemployment and insecurity, and curtailed "the cultural and educational opportunities of poor people, thus destroying human values, moral and spiritual." They therefore resolved to work for "the abolition of the system responsible for these destructive elements in our common life, by eliminating the system's incentives and habits, the legal forms which sustain it and the moral ideals which justify it." In its place they hoped to establish "a genuinely social economy, democratically planned to adjust production to consumption requirements and to eliminate private ownership of the means of production and distribution wherever such ownership interfered with the social good." [14]

The Conference of Younger Churchmen of the South seemed to Kester to offer the kind of fusion of religious conviction and radical economic and political thought to which he was committed in the mid-thirties. He was elected to the group's first executive committee and played an active role in both of its meetings in 1934. The CYC was dormant throughout 1935 and most of the next year but revived with a conference at Norris, Tennessee, in November 1936. At this meeting the conferees adopted the name Fellowship of Southern Churchmen and established a loose-knit organizational structure to facilitate their work. They elected as officers the clergymen Thomas B. Cowan, president; Abram Nightingale, treasurer; and Howard Kester, general secretary. [15]

Kester was enthusiastic about what he believed to be the Fellowship's potential for stimulating constructive change in the South. In

July 1937, while convalescing from the mental and physical exhaustion that had brought him to the verge of collapse earlier in the year, he wrote to an FSC member at Fisk University:

> During these weeks of relaxation my mind has been drawn increasingly toward the necessity of instilling a deep and powerful religious motivation of a revolutionary nature amongst those individuals and organizations which offer some hope for the future. I am extremely anxious to see the Fellowship of Southern Churchmen act as such an instrument and to express its faith in creative terms in whatever areas of life are open to them. [16]

Organizational and fund-raising work for the STFU and a number of investigations conducted for the National Association for the Advancement of Colored People, American Civil Liberties Union, and Workers Defense League prevented the FSC's newly elected secretary from immediately throwing himself fully into its work, but from 1937 to 1942 he devoted an increasingly large portion of his time and energy to the Fellowship and related endeavors. [17]

The FSC was not an organization with a well-developed program of action. Rather, it was a network which provided information, inspiration, and a badly needed sense of community for a small band of prophetic Christians scattered across the South. Members tried to bring Christian principles to bear on economic and racial conflicts in their vicinity and sometimes called upon one another for assistance. They kept each other abreast of developments in their respective localities and assembled periodically at conferences where they took a collective stand on the problems plaguing their region. As secretary, Kester conducted an extensive correspondence with members, planned the semiannual conferences, edited the FSC's journal *Prophetic Religion,* and wrote and spoke in the name of the Fellowship. In addition to his FSC work, he also edited the *Student Economic Inquiry,* a publication circulated by the Economics Commission of the Student Christian Movement in the South, and spoke about social issues before numerous intercollegiate conferences and on college and seminary campuses across the region.

In November 1940 Kester wrote to the Committee on Economic and Racial Justice that "our emphasis upon a vital religious approach to the problems of southern society is, I believe, more appreciated and understood than ever before." He noted with satisfaction that he had cordial relations with Southern Baptists, Methodists, and Presbyterians and offered as proof the fact that he had invitations to teach at two denominational institutes for rural ministers and teachers and at a Baptist summer camp for young women. He reported requests to assist local churches in developing programs relevant to parishioners' needs and indicated that he was currently making preparations for conferences of theological students in several southern urban centers and for a summer school for ministerial aspirants planning to work in rural areas.[18]

Kester did not regard the gradual reorientation of his endeavors as a retreat from social activism. In his annual report to the Committee on Economic and Racial Justice in October 1937 he had written, "I have always held that religious convictions should be implemented through economic and political action and that economic and political movements need the dynamic, prophetic and cleansing force of religion."[19] However, whether he recognized it or not, he was beginning to move toward an evolutionary conception of social change which rested more on the redemptive and healing power of Christianity than on the class struggle. He was becoming increasingly dissatisfied with the idea of striving merely for an equitable society characterized by a precarious equilibrium of countervailing powers. Such a goal was shallow, limited, and one-dimensional. Something more fundamental, something that addressed the needs of both the spirit and the body, was necessary if humanity was to realize its potential. What was required was a program of social action which aimed at the cultivation of an organic society based on a spirit of mutual concern and cooperation. In the late thirties he wrote of the new order he envisioned:

I want decent homes, decent schools, for old and young alike, health clinics, and kindly country doctors, freedom from the tyranny of oppressors on the land or in the courts of justice; freedom from drudgery and monotonous toil, from loneliness, emptiness, and despair. I want to see men possessed of the knowledge that they are loved and wanted; that they have talents which are needed in building the world of tomorrow. . . . I want to see men liberated from the tyranny of ignorance and poverty, to see them bless the earth with intelligent labor, and love, and honest sweat and to enjoy the rewards of their toil in peace and security. . . . I want to see every man call his brother "friend" and mean it.[20]

The organization of labor and political action in the interest of economic and social reform each had its place in the crusade for a new order, and Kester did not intend to abandon either. However, he thought that meaningful change must rest not merely on a scheme for the redistribution of wealth and power but on a comprehensive program of community building which would touch every aspect of life. He believed that the society of which he dreamed could become a reality if individuals like those with whom he worked in the Fellowship of Southern Churchmen built "without hate, without malice, and without violence and with understanding and a love that evokes love and trust." "Through an aroused fire-cleansed Christianity burdened with the message and spirit of the prophets," he could see a new life for his oppressed brothers and sisters.[21] Humanity could, of course, never achieve either personal or social perfection, but dedicated Christian men and women could build a better world.

As Kester's thought evolved, he became more and more disenchanted with the radical politics of his day. During the late thirties southern and some national Socialist leaders continued to regard him as a key party figure in the South. They sought his advice, requested his presence at meetings, and called upon him to perform a variety of tasks. He lectured for the League for Industrial Democracy, conducted investigations for the Workers Defense League, and, as a member of the Socialist National Executive Committee in 1937, helped Norman Thomas purge the Trotskyite faction from the party's ranks.[22] Yet as the decade drew to a close, his Socialist work became increasingly perfunctory. He was confused and frustrated by the ideological schisms enervating the party. He sometimes had difficulty relating to Socialists outside the South, especially those in the urban Northeast. As religious convictions reemerged as the dominant motif in his activism, he found the secularism of many Socialists disturbing. In October 1938 he wrote to Alice concerning the party: "How I do wish there was some vigor and fire and realism in it. I find it hard to get excited any more. I feel that it must reorient its entire program and procedure if it is to be at all significant on the American scene." Given this lack of enthusiasm, it was not surprising that when, in 1939, Norman Thomas broached the subject of Kester becoming party secretary for the South, he was not interested. He believed that to do so even on the part-time basis suggested by Thomas would commit him to a program which he now believed too narrowly political to be effective.[23]

Kester's reaction against communism was much more pronounced than his drift away from socialism. For a time in the early and mid thirties he had believed that the sectarian strife between Socialists and Communists had dissipated the strength of both movements to the detriment of the disinherited. Therefore, first as secretary of the FOR and then of the CERJ, he had sometimes encouraged cooperation among representatives of the two groups. Between 1933 and 1936 he had participated in several United and Popular Front endeavors, including the United States Congress against War in New York City in 1933 and the Conference on the Social and Economic Aspects of the Race Problem at Shaw University in 1934.[24]

His participation in such radical convocations and the vehemence of his antiestablishment rhetoric led some of Kester's associates to conclude that he was on the verge of joining the Communist party. Like many idealists of the depression era, the young southern activist had flirted with the idea of becoming a Communist and, at the height of his radicalism, had visited Earl Browder, party secretary in the United States, in hopes of getting a better understanding of this political movement.[25]

Kester sympathized with many of the Communists' objectives but could never see his way clear to join the party. Although he tried to avoid sectarian squabbling, he was never entirely free of the traditional Socialist prejudice against communism. In addition, he was repelled first by what he believed to be the party's exploitation of southern racism for political purposes and later by the Communists' apparent attempt to gain control of the STFU. By the late thirties one of the most important reasons for his rejection of the extreme Left was the fact that communism's materialistic philosophy and opportunistic tactics were incompatible with his understanding of Christianity. He made this quite clear in early 1939 when he wrote to Francis Pickens Miller, secretary of the Southern Policy Committee, an organization founded in the mid–1930s to study the economic and social problems of the South:

> While the goal of Communism is one to which I subscribe I cannot accept nor sanction the methods which they espouse and employ in achieving their goal. The doctrine that the end justifies the means is, in my judgment, one of the most damnable and one of the most insane ideas that ever possessed the human brain or ever entered the human heart. . . .
>
> Finally, as a Christian or as one who tries in his feeble way to be a Christian I find in the theory as well as the practices of Communism a complete negation of my basic Christian faith.[26]

Ultimately Kester rejected not only party membership but also United and Popular Front activities. By the late thirties he opposed all collaboration with the Communists or their fellow travelers and was extremely suspicious of any group in which he thought they might be involved. This attitude contributed to his break with Highlander Folk School and the Southern Summer School for Women Workers, both of which he believed followed the Communist party line, and it was largely responsible for his misgivings about the Southern Conference for Human Welfare (SCHW). In November 1938 he attended the first meeting of this concerned group of liberals and radicals that convened in Birmingham to consider a variety of regional problems. He quickly became "convinced beyond a shadow of a doubt" that it "was conceived and in the main executed by persons who were either members of the Communist Party and known as such, and well known and not so well known fellow-travelers." He thought that the proceedings of the gathering were "in perfect accord with the present line of the Communist Party" and regarded denials that it was a moving force in the gathering as "utter non-sense." He believed the party was trying to manipulate the majority of well-meaning but unsuspecting conferees for its own ends. Rumors that Joseph Gelders, whom he believed to be a Communist and a prime mover behind the conference, had used Kester's name without authorization to raise funds for the event did nothing to allay his suspicions.[27]

The bitter struggle for control of the Southern Tenant Farmers Union undoubtedly caused Kester to exaggerate the dangers posed by Communists and fellow travelers, but his apprehensions did not represent an isolated case of paranoia. A number of other southern liberals and Socialists associated with the conference shared some of his apprehension. Francis Pickens Miller wrote to Kester shortly after the Birmingham meeting: "The question which haunted me most was, 'who is in control of the conference?' The more I saw and heard, the more I became convinced that the persons who appeared to be in control were not actually in control."[28]

Frank Porter Graham, chairman of the SCHW, believed it only fair to allow Communists to participate in the organization's activities, but he was unwilling to allow them to manipulate it covertly. He took charges of subversion seriously enough to spend considerable time trying to determine their accuracy, and Kester was one of the people to whom he turned for relevant information. In 1939 he wrote to the CERJ secretary requesting that he designate those leaders whom he believed to be Communists or fellow travelers. Kester supplied the names of only seven individuals. He conceded that they constituted only a small proportion of the leadership but warned that commitment, discipline, and secrecy rather than numbers were the keys to Communist success. He declared that he had no objections to the party openly striving to achieve its goals but opposed its covert, subversive methods. He contended that those who recognized the radical threat must expose it in order that the masses not be confused or mislead.[29]

Kester's concern over the possible damage a small number of Communists might do to otherwise promising movements extended even to the Fellowship of Southern Churchmen. The prophets who had assembled at Monteagle and Chattanooga in 1934 for the early meetings of the Conference of Younger Churchmen of the South had been consumed with a passion for social change and had worried little about the political orientation of the conferees. A Communist party leader from Alabama attended the proceedings in Chattanooga and emerged from the sessions declaring, "I felt like a conservative in that crowd." However, the men who assumed the leadership of the FSC in the late thirties were increasingly suspicious of and hostile toward Communists and fellow travelers. These Churchmen rejected the pure materialism of classical Marxism. The prophets understood both their means and ends to be different from those of mere secular reformers. Most of them now regarded communism as a naive political religion based upon a superficial understanding of human nature and the universe and directed toward goals that, if achieved, would resolve none of the fundamental problems of society. They shared the conviction that human beings, though creatures of God, are also sinners. Any blueprint for social change that failed to take into account the Lordship of God and human sinfulness was doomed to perpetuate evil and injustice. Therefore, the guiding principle behind a reorganization of society should not be a secular economic or political philosophy but an ideology based on Christian principles.[30]

In April 1938, after an FSC conference at Raleigh, North Carolina, at which suspect persons had applied for membership, Kester warned the executive committee that individuals and groups wishing to use the FSC as a vehicle for the dissemination of their political ideologies were trying to infiltrate the organization. He cautioned that if the Fellowship was to remain a "straightforward prophetic religious group every effort must be made to prevent this from happening." Committee members concurred. Fellowship chairman Thomas B. Cowan wrote to Kester with characteristic flourish and hyperbole: "I get woefully tired of communists and their wooden horses being drawn into the Troy of Christian Conferences. Let us tear down the walls and engage them in the open. Better to die fighting in the open than die like a rat in a trap baited with communistic utopianism, materialism, and disregard for the individual. . . . On with the fight let compromise be unrefined!"

Herbert King, a black FSC leader, wrote in a similar vein: "If there be some who in respect to their devotion to the Lord have not witnessed thereunto I believe there is Scriptural admonition to the effect that the Lord himself will spue them out of his mouth. We could do it and save the Lord the trouble."[31]

By late 1938 Fellowship members had decided to bar purely secular activists from their ranks. In December, at a meeting in Berea, Kentucky, they adopted a statement of principles written by Kester, Cowan, and Berea College professor Walter Sikes that clearly set forth the religious basis for Fellowship members' approach to social problems. The conferees required all persons wishing to join the group to sign the statement and authorized the FSC's executive committee to screen applicants before issuing them membership cards.[32]

Buck Kester's growing preoccupation with the role of religion in the revitalization of the South and his mounting skepticism about the efficacy of exclusively economic or political forms of social action troubled many of his associates. They failed to grasp how a culturally fettered Christianity might be released and transformed into a force for positive change and regarded any attempts to rally Christianity to the cause of social justice as a waste of time and energy. Kester's drift away from the STFU frustrated H. L. Mitchell who tried to persuade the CERJ to pressure him into devoting more time to the union. Norman Thomas reportedly believed that his friend might have been an important figure in the future of the South had he not departed from his initial course. Frank McCallister and Dave Clendenin of the Workers Defense League complained of Kester's loss of interest in the organization's work. Genuine hostility developed between him and some of his former comrades in radicalism who believed that he had gone off on a "Jesus jag."[33]

Even some members of the CERJ thought that their secretary was beginning to neglect other more conventional and reliable means of promoting social change in the South. Several of them were especially uneasy about what appeared to be his disenchantment with the STFU in particular and the class struggle in general. Their concern grew in 1938 when Howard and Alice informed their sponsors that they were considering the possibility of moving from Nashville to Black Mountain, North Carolina.[34]

Several longtime members questioned both the wisdom and implications of the move. Increasing the physical distance between himself and the work in the Arkansas delta symbolized for many of his backers the way in which Kester had already begun to distance himself psychologically from the STFU. Bradford Young, vice-chairman of the CERJ, believed not only that the secretary was important to the union but also that his labor work lay at the heart of his appeal to church and student groups. Young felt that if Kester deemphasized this dimension of his activism, he would diminish his effectiveness in other areas as well.[35]

The Kesters believed the committee's concern was unfounded. They had convinced themselves that relocating to western North Carolina would be beneficial for both professional and personal reasons. A base of operations there would facilitate the CERJ's work in all of the South east of the Mississippi. They argued that it was in this part of the region that racism, economic injustice, rural decay, and reactionary religion posed the greatest problems. Furthermore, the cleaner, dryer air of the mountains should have a salutary effect upon Howard's chronic and increasingly debilitating asthma, thus making him a more effective spokesman for the causes he championed. Finally, the couple desperately longed for something approximating the normal home life they had never had. They hoped that restricting Howard's activities largely to the Southeast and owning their own home and a few acres of land nearer to the heart of the work might provide them with a greater measure of security and stability than they had known at any time since their marriage. With all these presumed benefits in mind, they purchased a small acreage and built a house in High Top Colony, a community originally established by YMCA workers on the periphery of the Blue Ridge Assembly grounds near Black Mountain.[36]

Kester resented the reservations expressed by some members of the CERJ. He believed that his northeastern supporters did not understand the South and his relationship to it, and he felt that the questions they raised reflected a lack of confidence in him. He was particularly disturbed by the committee's apparent skepticism about the potentially creative power of southern Protestantism and by its failure to share his conviction that genuine change in the South required action on a broad front. It seemed to him as though members were obsessed with the STFU to the detriment of every other facet of reform. In January 1939 he wrote to Elisabeth Gilman, treasurer of the CERJ: "It is but natural for those who have no interests but that of the Union to feel that every minute I spend away from Memphis is time wasted. They see nothing of value or use out side of the Union. My experience is wider, and I believe deeper; my horison is larger and my interests greater." To the committee at large he wrote: "There may be some who feel that our work is slowing down or that we are not 'packing the same whallop' we did a couple of years ago. . . . Our complete absorption in the work of the Southern Tenant Farmers' Union lent a certain glamour and romance to our work. The glamour period is over but we are still in the front line trenches as is everyone who seeks to build fundamentally in this area. If you have any misgivings I can but say that I have none for I have never felt more confident of the real value of our work than now." [37]

Some committee members did have misgivings, but they liked and respected their secretary. For the moment, they acquiesced in his judgment that he should give more of his time to student and religious groups. However, dissatisfaction continued to mount. In 1941 Elisabeth Gilman wrote to Reinhold Niebuhr, chairman of the CERJ, expressing reservations about raising money for a program to promote economic and racial justice when a major part of Kester's time was now devoted to "religious undertakings." She conceded that such work had its place but pointed out that this was not what the CERJ had been established to do. She also complained that she was unable to get information from the Kesters, whom she charged, with some justice, either ignored her inquiries or took exception to them. [38]

By the early 1940s a number of key committee members, including Young and Niebuhr, shared Gilman's conviction that Kester had strayed too far from the CERJ's original goals and that they now had too little information about and control over his activities to warrant their continued support. Therefore, the CERJ concluded that responsibility for Kester's projects should lie with the group to which he now devoted most of his time. In the spring of 1941 the committee invited the Fellowship of Southern Churchmen to become Kester's sponsor. He found the idea attractive, and the small, loose-knit association of radical Christians was delighted with the prospect of having his services on a full-time basis. The FSC's only reservation stemmed from uncertainty about its ability to fund the work. After considerable deliberation the Fellowship decided to accept the proposal. In November 1941, at a meeting at Union Theological Seminary, representatives of both groups completed the transfer of responsibility and the CERJ disbanded. [39]

The dissolution of the Committee on Economic and Racial Justice signaled the culmination of the most dramatic and controversial period of Howard Kester's career. Throughout much of the 1930s he had been a leader among the social activists of the South, involved in almost every phase of radical reform in the region. The work had taken a heavy toll on his health, strained his marriage, and engendered within him enormous tension. Since the forces he challenged constituted his own social and psychological matrix, he had to contend not only with much popular opposition but also with an anxiety born of uncertainty about his own social and religious role. By the late thirties and early forties he was searching desperately for some way to alleviate these difficulties without sacrificing his commitment to family, church, or the cause of social justice in the South. He hoped that through the Fellowship of Southern Churchmen he might achieve the sense of fulfillment for which he longed.

CHAPTER 7

■ From Prophet to Professor ■

Buck Kester found his labors on behalf of the Fellowship of Southern Churchmen rewarding but not as satisfying as he had hoped
or expected. He was proud of the prophetic stance that the FSC
took against many of the injustices of the day. He enjoyed speaking
about economic and social problems before groups of college and university students and felt comfortable working among church folk in an
attempt to awaken them to their social responsibility. On the other
hand, the constant travel, habitual fund-raising for the support of his
work, and frequent absences from home grew increasingly burdensome. Consequently, after little more than a year, he and Alice began
searching for some other position that would provide both economic
security and an opportunity for continued meaningful service. During
the 1940s and early 1950s their quest led them to three promising
jobs, all of which ultimately proved disappointing.

As secretary of the Fellowship, Kester was instrumental in the
attempt of several members to develop a religious basis for the rehabilitation of the rural South. His interest in, and understanding of, this
effort illuminates the intellectual distance that he had traveled since
the height of his radicalism a few years earlier and helps to explain the
direction in which his career moved after he left the FSC. In the late
thirties and early forties he and some of the Christian activists with
whom he worked began rethinking their approach to the problems of
the millions of people living on the land. They did not reject the significance of the class struggle but believed that the philosophical foundations on which its champions based their efforts were too simplistic.
They contended that materialism, urbanization, ignorance, and the
failure of secular and religious leadership lay at the heart of the rural
South's problems. For them the Christian activist's role was no longer
simply that of revolutionary prophet but also that of community plan-
ner and pastor. For these Christians the prophetic demand for social

justice was coupled with and sometimes overshadowed by a pastoral plea for stewardship. They returned to an emphasis on comprehensive community development similar to that of the Country Life movement of the Progressive era. They believed as had some earlier Country Life apostles that the church had a vital role to play in community rehabilitation.[1] However, they placed a greater emphasis than had their Progressive predecessors on developing a religious basis for their practical program of rural revitalization. In 1941 several leaders of the Fellowship of Southern Churchmen gathered in the community of Big Lick on the Cumberland Plateau of eastern Tennessee. Those present, clergymen Thomas Cowan, Eugene Smathers, and A. L. DeJarnette, Professor Walter Sikes of Berea College, and Fellowship secretary Howard Kester, founded Friends of the Soil (FOS), a satellite of the FSC with a national constituency but a predominantly southern leadership. Six years later, this organization had only 218 members, of whom probably a third were from the South, but it is noteworthy because of its membership's distinctively religious interpretation of the problems of the countryside.[2] Writing in the FSC journal *Prophetic Religion* in 1945, Francis Drake, administrative secretary of Friends of the Soil, summarized its goals as

> to lead men to regard the earth as holy and man as the steward of the Eternal; to assist the rural church to minister to the total life of the rural community; to work for the reclamation and conservation of the soil and other natural resources and to seek by word and deed to restore man to his divine earthright to the end that justice may be established on the land and a richer, fuller and a more abundant life may be the lot of all.[3]

In short, what FOS members sought to develop was a gospel of Christian stewardship.

The apostles of this gospel of stewardship believed that one of the greatest problems facing the South and the nation was a materialistic attitude toward the land. It seemed to them that an abundance of land had encouraged Americans to think of it as a limitless resource to be exploited rather than as a finite one to be wisely managed. Developments in agricultural technology, while potentially beneficial, had in most cases only facilitated this process of exploitation. Furthermore, American agriculture was increasingly a business rather than a way of life and as such stressed efficiency and economy rather than the human factors in farming. A materialistic approach to agriculture contributed to the growth of large-scale land ownership, a trend that was driving millions of small farmers and tenants off the land and thus denying to them their birthright.[4]

These agrarian Christians believed that a second, related problem plaguing the countryside was the deterioration of rural community life. This was a result not only of agricultural changes that uprooted people but also of urbanization that lured them away. The accelerating process of community decay was detrimental not only to rural America but to the nation as a whole, for the countryside was the seedbed of American values and institutions. Modernization threatened to destroy such fundamentals as the home, church, and community; self-reliance and individual responsibility; and even democracy itself. Rural life was being mined of its resources and people, and American life was being undermined by the process.[5]

Nowhere were these developments more apparent than in the South, but the leaders of Friends of the Soil and the Fellowship of Southern Churchmen were convinced that there was still hope for the countryside. They believed that not only a wise use of technology but also a unifying vision of country life were needed if it was to be restored. The Protestant church could not provide technological expertise, but it might, despite its past failures, contribute important elements to a holistic vision of rural culture.

A fundamental component of this Christian agrarian ideology was a proper understanding of what its advocates regarded as "the common trinity of life: God, the Earth, Man." God was for them "the Sovereign Lord of Life," the creator of "the universe, the earth and all its creatures." The earth as his creation was therefore "sacred and holy." The survival of humanity depended upon a recognition of "the power of God manifest in soil and air, sun and water, plant and animal." The abuse of natural resources was a "denial of the Fatherhood of God and the brotherhood of man." The consequences of such a denial were "revealed in the hunger and insecurity, the fear and violence" that plagued millions of people.[6]

Men and women living upon the land should have respect not only for it but for one another. They should cooperate in their daily endeavors and deny to no one who wished it access to the "sacred soil." Man's relationship to the earth was a moral one, and "to deprive any child of God access to the soil or to rob him of the fruits of his labors" was to "take from him his rightful share of his Father's world." "Bread, brotherhood, and beauty" could be achieved only by man's "intelligent and creative cooperation with the forces of God resident in the land and its resources, and with one another."[7] The Christian was therefore to think of himself as the steward of the land and of the people who lived upon it.

Kester and his associates who espoused such an essentially religious view of life believed it to be both more practical and more relevant to rural problems than the theories and tactics of secular reformers. They were convinced that one of the major difficulties with "radical movements" was their "unrealistic approach to the problems of the soil and of the folk who live on the soil." At the same time, they readily conceded that the Protestant church, having denied its social responsibility, had been equally unrealistic in its mission to country parishioners. Yet the church was traditionally an integral part of southern society, and as such it might, if properly directed, play a unique role in the reconstruction of the region's rural culture. The church was not, however, to become simply a means to an end, that of enhancing the quality of rural life. Its fundamental task remained "to lead men to God through Jesus Christ and bring the totality of their life under the sway of His sovereign will." Such a mission had implications beyond the promotion of piety and church attendance. Believing as they did that "one's attitude toward the soil, toward work, toward his brother man, his scale of values, all are determined by his attitude toward God, his faith and conviction regarding the meaning of life, in other words, by his religion," the apostles of stewardship considered it the task of the church to infuse religion with a sense of social responsibility. Rural security and prosperity lay in the capacity of the church to "motivate its people so that their common tasks in everyday rural life" became "ministries for the glory of God and for the advancement of His purposes." The duty of the rural church was to build Christian communities upon "fertile and holy earth."[8]

Such an understanding of Christian responsibility was rare in the South during the 1940s. Therefore, those who believed their faith had important implications for the revitalization of the countryside first had to find some means of propagating their ideas among rural churchmen. Some institutions, such as Scarritt College and the School of Religion at Vanderbilt University, provided at least a modicum of training for country clergy and lay workers. Generally, however, the religious community in the region paid little heed to the plight of the rural parishioner. Kester was correct when he charged that "the Protestant Church has regarded the country as a place from which everyone, including the minister of God, should escape." The country church, he contended, was usually more readily identifiable with its adjoining graveyard than with the living people to whom it was to minister.

What was needed was a pastorate "equally at home in the field as in the pulpit as able to deal with the problems of eroded land as those of wasted people."[9]

To develop this kind of leadership, Kester dreamed of the establishment of a rural training center for ministers to be known as the "Seminary in the Cornfield." This school, which was to supplement and to expand upon the instruction received in conventional seminaries, not only would inculcate the religious philosophy of its planners but also would train students in such areas as community organization, rural sanitation and health, soil reclamation and conservation, the fundamentals of construction, agricultural economics, and the care and management of the family farm.[10] Pastors trained in such a school could minister to both the physical and the spiritual needs of their parishioners.

As Kester began thinking of leaving his position with the Fellowship of Southern Churchmen, he hoped to find a job which in some way would enable him both to test and to propagate his ideas about the way in which an enlightened Christianity might contribute to the reinvigoration of rural community life. He believed he had found such an opportunity when in 1943, through the auspices of their friend Ethel Paine Moors, a member of the board of trustees of Penn Normal Agricultural and Industrial School, the Kesters received appointments to this venerable but struggling institution.[11] The school for blacks on St. Helena Island, just off the coast of South Carolina, had been founded in 1862 and was one of the humanitarian endeavors undertaken by the emissaries of Yankee civilization who swept onto the Carolina Sea Islands in the wake of the Union army. These religious and cultural missionaries not only sought to minister to the material and spiritual needs of the South's former bondsmen but also hoped to prove to a skeptical public that the freedmen could become self-reliant, responsible citizens.

Shortly after the turn of the century, the school's facilities were expanded and its curriculum was reorganized to conform to industrial education theories then current among those interested in black education. The concept of industrial education was a product of the fusion of late nineteenth- and early twentieth-century philanthropy, piety, prejudice, and progressivism. Northerners and southerners alike perceived black people as inferior beings whose degradation posed a threat to both cultural values and social stability. Most liberal whites believed that industrial education was the key to the elevation of the black and thus to the preservation of American civilization. Although manual training and racial accommodation were integral parts of this approach to education, its paternalistic advocates did not envision it as the mere vocational training of an inferior people. Many of them sincerely believed that by teaching the value of hard work and disciplined orderly living, they were building character. Furthermore, since for them the idea of social responsibility was an important component of the integrity that they sought to nurture, they were confident that they were laying the foundation for the development of stable communities among the South's black masses.

An educational program which aimed not at equality but at the development of character and community among a subordinate people appealed to the prejudices not only of white southerners but of many northern philanthropists as well. As Elizabeth Jacoway, chronicler of the Penn experiment, has pointed out, northern supporters of industrial education wanted not only to uplift blacks but also to keep them in the South until the civilizing process was completed.[12] Thus, the Penn School project was an exercise in both moral regeneration and social control.

For four decades Rossa Belle Cooley and Grace Bigelow House, who directed operations at Penn, labored to make their school a model educational institution and the nucleus of an exemplary rural black community. They expanded the curriculum to include more agricultural, industrial, and home economics instruction. Over the years they reached out to the community in a variety of ways. The school hosted farmers' conferences, encouraged the development of demonstration farms, sponsored teacher training institutes, brought a nurse and a doctor to the island, provided nutritional information, organized producer and consumer cooperatives, established a credit union, and provided low-cost used clothing for island residents. Although the Penn student body never included more than a fraction of the students on St. Helena, by the twenties the school touched the lives of most of the islanders and to some degree had become the educational and community development showcase of which trustees and administrators had dreamed. It attracted the attention of rural reconstructionists and individuals who fancied themselves racial liberals and of those who envisioned the Penn program as a model for similar efforts among the people of Africa. Thus, the school assumed responsibility for the enlightenment of not only its students and the island community that it served but also a steady stream of domestic and foreign observers.

Even as Penn's reputation grew, the relevance and effectiveness of its work diminished. The boll weevil destroyed St. Helena's traditional cotton economy. This problem was compounded by the fact that the agricultural depression of the twenties and thirties, along with inclement weather, hampered economic diversification, thus undermining the dream of establishing an independent black yeomanry upon the land. By the early 1940s two world wars, a bridge that ended St. Helena's isolation, and a new mood of confidence and self-reliance among black residents had begun to bring the island into the twentieth century, thereby rendering the school's educational and community-oriented paternalism obsolete.[13]

Most of the Penn trustees failed to recognize that the school had become an "anachronism." They attributed its increasingly obvious educational and financial problems to other causes. A majority of them reluctantly concluded that Misses Cooley and House were now too old to administer the school effectively. Therefore, they began the search for fresh leadership that could bring to the job a combination of youthful energy, sense of Christian commitment, and experience in the fields of education and race relations.

When Ethel Paine Moors brought Howard and Alice Kester to the attention of her colleagues on the board of trustees, they were not as certain as she that the couple was right for the positions they were seeking to fill. These essentially conservative men and women had reservations about the Kesters' radical past and worried about their lack of educational and administrative training. The Kesters' charm allayed these doubts, as did glowing letters of recommendation from such widely respected educators and social activists as Benjamin Mays of Morehouse College, Liston Pope of the Yale Divinity School, Walter White of the NAACP, James Myers of the Federal Council of Churches, and Fred Brownlee of the Congregational Christian church. White wrote to Francis R. Cope, chairman of the trustees, "There are no two people in the United States who could be better as principals of Penn School." Brownlee characterized Kester as "one of God's saints," "a 'little' (stature) Abraham Lincoln—of the people, for the people, with the people." Only John Nevin Sayre of the Fellowship of Reconciliation interjected a word of caution. He described the Kesters as "sincere Christians" and commended Howard as "a man of outstanding courage and devotion to the cause of interracial justice." He expressed reservations about his ability as an administrator, however, when he suggested that "he belongs . . . more among the prophets than the organizers."[14]

Although the trustees recognized that there was perhaps some truth in Sayre's appraisal, they felt compelled to secure new leadership for Penn as soon as possible and concluded that the Kesters' assets more than compensated for their deficiencies. In July 1943, by a unanimous vote, they appointed Howard principal and Alice supervisor of the academic department. [15]

When the Kesters assumed their responsibilities in January 1944, they actually knew very little about Penn School. Their only direct contact with the institution had come during a brief visit to St. Helena in May 1943. Like many visitors they were initially very impressed with what they found. Howard wrote in the Fellowship of Southern Churchmen newsletter:

Few schools in America can lay so valid a claim to being schools. Here education is life, not just preparation for it. This immensely significant program of education that encompasses all of life was buttressed and undergirded by a deep consciousness of the power of democracy, a profound faith in the ability of common folk to solve their own problems in a spirit of cooperation and fair play, and an unyielding confidence in the power of Christianity to lift men, women and children from self love to community well being. Here indeed is a laboratory and a workshop which has already yielded immensely rich rewards and which more than ever stands as a light house for those who want enlightenment and understanding in the academies of darkness. [16]

Although not oblivious of the problems at Penn, the couple generally saw what they wanted to see. They persuaded themselves that here was a school in a rural environment which provided a holistic education, combining academic instruction with practical training in a milieu permeated by Christian and democratic values. They believed they had found a place to invest their God-given talents with "the utmost joy," and they were convinced that it was his will that they do so. Thus, they approached their task with enthusiasm and optimism. Shortly after his selection as principal, Howard wrote, "The opportunities are almost endless and we hope that at St. Helena we may be able to make some further contribution to the manifold problems besetting our world today, and which will continue into tomorrow's tomorrow." [17]

The Kesters' first challenge was not the sad state of the world but the poor condition of Penn. In his initial report to the trustees in January 1944 Howard catalogued the school's difficulties as he understood them. The instructional departments were poorly integrated, inefficient, and not cost-effective. The physical plant needed repair. The library contained too few books and scarcely any current periodicals. The farm was not productive. The academic department did not adequately train students either to seek additional education elsewhere or to remain on St. Helena. Religious instruction was inferior, and student morale was low.[18] In short, he felt that Penn no longer made a contribution worthy of its reputation and to do so would require radical changes. The new principal pointed out that St. Helena was an island in transition and that Penn must find a way to bridge the gap between the old and the new.

Kester believed that the school's leadership had two choices. It could continue to operate Penn as a distinctly rural school serving the St. Helena community. A local orientation would necessarily mean closer cooperation with South Carolina's educational authorities and perhaps even eventually turning the school over to the state. He believed this would be a mistake because it would destroy the unique practical and spiritual quality of Penn's educational program. The other possibility, favored by Kester, was to transform Penn into a private academy which would provide a quality education for black children from throughout the Sea Islands and across the South. He also hoped that its farm and agricultural training facilities could be used to equip rural clergymen to minister more effectively to the economic and social needs of their parishioners.[19]

The Kesters had scarcely begun to try to resolve Penn's most pressing problems when they began to encounter resistance from islanders and trustees alike. Some of the school's staff opposed the couple's efforts to make its operation more efficient. Many islanders felt that the new administrators cared little for Penn's community service program. The trustees differed in their assessment of the Kesters' performance.

In March 1945 three trustees, John Silver, William Cadbury, and Paul W. Brown, Jr., visited Penn and were pleased with conditions there. They reported that although the Kesters were deeply committed to Penn's tradition of community development, they believed that their first responsibility was to rehabilitate the school itself. The observers commented favorably on efforts to strengthen the academic department through curricular and administrative changes and reported that Howard's agricultural innovations had made the school's farm prosperous at last. They acknowledged that some islanders and staff members were disgruntled but contended that both school personnel and island residents generally approved of the Kesters' administration.[20]

A few of the trustees, such as chairman Francis Cope, believed that the Kesters were making too many changes too quickly. Cope was convinced that there was much disaffection among Penn personnel and islanders in general. On a visit to St. Helena in March 1946 Cope was far less impressed than his colleagues had been a year earlier. He was pleased by what Howard had accomplished with the school's farm but was concerned about the condition of the industrial training work and had misgivings about Alice Kester's administration of the academic department. He regarded her as a bright and attractive woman but felt that she was dictatorial and tactless in handling the staff and lacked an appreciation for Penn's traditional mission to St. Helena.[21]

Although the fault did not lie entirely with the school's administrators as Cope believed, he was correct that there was widespread and growing dissatisfaction among Penn staff members and islanders. They regarded the Kesters as outsiders bent on changing things in ways that they judged detrimental to the school and the St. Helena community. In June 1947 members of the Penn Graduates Club wrote a letter to the trustees in which they declared:

> Recently our concern over the condition of Penn School has been keen. The loss of some of our trades and agricultural training; the decrease in the health and character building program; the absence of a school spirit among students; the absence of that splendid cooperative spirit for which Penn School is famous; have resulted in a wider breach between school and community and a loss of more than one hundred students to other schools. Naturally a change in our program was expected and when that change was presented to us for endorsement, after a brief study we not only endorsed it, but pledged ourselves to stand back of it and give our fullest cooperation; for we believed that if the best in the old and the best in the new could be combined, it would make for a better Penn School. We seem to have lost so much of that old community—Penn's program which has meant the life to both, and so far, we have seen no definite move toward the new program, and things do not seem to be improving.

Club members concluded their letter with a request that conditions at the school be studied.[22]

The Kesters did not believe Penn's problems to be their fault. They made no apologies for their policies, feeling that they had arrived on the scene too late to do anything more than "to fight fire and to patch up the foundations."[23] However, they agreed that the school was in trouble and concurred in the opinion that a careful evaluation of its program was needed. At Howard's suggestion, the trustees asked Professor Ira De Augustine Reid, editor of *Phylon* and chairman of the

Department of Sociology at Atlanta University, to direct the study and make suggestions for the school's future. Reid and his associates submitted a report in which they contended that Penn School as it currently existed had outlived its usefulness. They recommended that Penn's formal educational functions be turned over to the state of South Carolina, which could now do the job more efficiently and economically. They concluded that the school's future value lay in such community development functions as guidance, library services, recreation, social welfare, and adult education. Although the report came as a surprise and a disappointment to many associated with Penn, the trustees accepted the appraisal of the survey team and prepared to adjust the program to changing times. Under other circumstances the Kesters might have found the projected mission of the institution attractive, but they were weary of the problems they had encountered there. Believing this moment of transition to be an opportune time to leave, the couple resigned at the March 1948 meeting of the board of trustees. On 6 May 1948, Penn Normal Agricultural and Industrial School was reorganized as Penn Community Services Incorporated.[24]

The St. Helena experience was one that the Kesters put behind them with considerable relief. Although they had hoped to find at Penn a situation which would afford them both security and an opportunity for service, they quickly became disillusioned. Their lack of experience as educators and administrators contributed to their difficulties. They were also somewhat insecure and sensitive to criticism even when it was intended to be constructive. But the problems at Penn were not of the Kesters' making. Although the school had enhanced the quality of life on St. Helena during its eighty-six-year history, neither its trustees nor its administrators had kept abreast of the changing times. They failed to realize that the missionary paternalism and theories of industrial education that had characterized the endeavor since the turn of the century had lost whatever relevance they had once had. Elizabeth Jacoway accurately assessed conditions at Penn:

When Miss Cooley and Miss House stepped down from their forty year reign as St. Helena's undisputed rulers, the Penn School trustees turned over to their successors an impossible situation. The school's productive funds had been seriously eroded and its income generating power had become ineffective. The staff was feeling disillusioned and abused and most of the younger recruits had abandoned their posts on St. Helena for more lucrative positions elsewhere. The program was not only out of touch with the needs of the modern world, it no longer satisfied the needs of the not so modern island of St. Helena. And, probably most important, the community wide feeling of pride in Penn School—and the heady feeling of participating in a significant educational experiment—had been lost. Penn School would never be the same again and the future would hold only pain for those who sought to sustain what might have died with dignity.[25]

Unfortunately, the Penn School episode was not the last unpleasant experience the Kesters were to have as educators, but for the moment they turned their attention to what was for them a new and very different kind of work. During the latter 1940s governmental and private agencies in several countries began attempting to relocate persons displaced by World War II and its aftermath. Among the private organizations that accepted this challenge was the Congregational Christian Service Committee. In early 1949 denominational officials invited Kester to become the director of its part of this project. Howard welcomed the offer in part because he had been unemployed since leaving Penn School several months earlier and in part because he believed the position provided an opportunity to make a significant contribution in a chaotic world. In the spring he and Alice moved to New York City to begin this new work. Kester's responsibilities included distributing materials, explaining the program, soliciting sponsors for displaced persons, helping to orient newly arrived refugees, and coping with the bureaucratic details of their placement. Alice became the hostess of the Congregational Christian church's International Service Centre, a temporary hostel for, among others, displaced persons arriving in the United States and European and American students involved in exchange projects designed to foster international understanding and cooperation. In this position she not only managed the day-to-day operations of the Centre but ministered as best she could to the needs of an often lonely and sometimes confused or frightened clientele.[26]

For the most part, the Kesters liked their work in New York. Not only did they encounter interesting people from many nations, but they had a larger income and a greater measure of financial security than at any time since their marriage in the late 1920s. The couple could occasionally enjoy a meal in a nice restaurant or visit one of the shops along Fifth Avenue. Eventually, however, Howard began to feel that the frustrations exceeded the rewards. It was often difficult to secure reliable sponsors for displaced persons. Only about a fifth of the Congregational Christian churches participated in the program. Furthermore, the success of the Congregational Christian Service Committee's project was dependent upon the efficiency with which a number of other national and international public and private agencies operated. The program as a whole was cumbersome, inefficient, and disappointing. Although his superiors recognized the difficult situation with which he had to contend and were satisfied with his work, Kester, who was never very patient, soon grew discouraged with the complexity of the task and slow pace of progress. After slightly more than a year, he resigned his position to undertake another educational endeavor in the South.[27]

In July 1950 Howard assumed the directorship of the John C. Campbell Folk School in Brasstown in the mountains of southwestern North Carolina. The school, founded in 1925 by Olive D. Campbell and Marguerite Butler Bidstrup, was modeled after Danish projects in adult education. Its objective was to "awaken, enliven and enlighten" the southern Appalachian people whom it served, thereby giving them the ability to improve the physical and spiritual quality of their lives. When the school formally opened in December 1927, its curriculum included instruction in surveying, scientific agriculture, forestry, bookkeeping, home economics, health, recreation, and the three Rs, as well as lectures in history, literature, economic geography, natural history, and government. The school had no formal requirements for admission, nor did it give examinations or grades. The education it offered was not intended as vocational training nor was it meant to prepare students for college. Rather, it was designed to equip them to live richer, more rewarding lives in their own rural communities. Campbell, like Penn, also tried to reach out beyond its student body and serve as a stimulus to community development.

The school provided nursing and library services to area residents until state and local governments assumed these functions. It tried to stimulate economic progress by promoting producer, consumer, and financial cooperatives among the farmers of the area and also by encouraging the mountain folk to use and to enlarge upon their tradition of craftsmanship as a source of income. Over the years the school encouraged the development of a variety of handicrafts, including hand weaving, vegetable dying, wood and iron working, pottery making, enameling on copper, stitchery, jewelry making, and most importantly wood carving. The Brasstown carvers eventually achieved national renown for the quality of their work. School founder Olive Campbell was instrumental in the organization of the Southern Highland Handicraft Guild.

The Campbell Folk School eventually served not only the people of Brasstown and nearby communities but also local leaders from throughout the nation who were interested in rural revitalization. Over the years teachers, ministers, and agricultural extension workers attended short courses that emphasized the cultural enrichment of rural life. Those enrolled learned folk games, dances, and music; studied crafts; and discussed rural problems.[28]

By the time Howard Kester became director of Campbell, it was plagued by a variety of problems, some of which were similar to those that he had encountered at Penn. The chief difficulty seems to have been that the institution had not adapted to changing times and many of its leaders and staff failed to recognize that fact. The expansion of state and federal services in the areas of education, public health, and agricultural extension work meant that some of the original functions of the school were no longer relevant. Furthermore, while Campbell had done a good job of preserving and developing an appreciation of southern Appalachian culture and had translated some of the region's traditions into satisfying and lucrative pursuits, it had been only marginally successful in revitalizing the larger economy of the area it served. As a result, it had failed to stem the flow of youth from the mountains and had not adequately trained the people in the techniques of group action and community building needed to develop the kind of life that the school held up as its goal.[29]

The Kesters did not go blindly into the situation at Brasstown. Dagnall Folger, a longtime friend and his predecessor as director of the folk school, wrote Howard in 1949 explaining the reasons for his resignation. He complained that Campbell's leaders and their allies on the board of directors refused to allow him to do the job that needed to be done. He believed that they had an unrealistic commitment to a traditional folk school program which had little appeal to residents of the area. Folger concluded that he could not recommend the Campbell job to anyone, especially a friend, unless the school's directors were willing to allow his successor the freedom necessary to make adjustments to the changing times. He cautioned Kester that he should make a thorough investigation of the situation before taking the position and reminded him that Campbell's woes were compounded by the increasingly difficult problem of raising funds for such schools.[30]

Kester recognized that the circumstances at Brasstown were less than ideal, but he and Alice were looking for a measure of economic security, along with an opportunity to serve the people of the rural South. Howard believed that the position offered not only a chance to minister to the needs of a mountain community but perhaps also to establish in a rather isolated setting a base of operation for the rural, interracial, and religious work to which he was so deeply committed. The couple also found attractive the school's location in the southern Appalachians a relatively short distance from their home in Black Mountain. These circumstances, combined with the fact that Howard believed that the directors had granted him the latitude necessary to administer the school effectively, persuaded him to accept the position.

When he arrived in Brasstown in the summer of 1950, the new director immediately began meeting with the staff and examining the facilities, organizational structure, and books of the school. He soon discovered that Folger had not exaggerated the problems and quickly concluded that Campbell's organization was inefficient and costly, its finances were in disarray, and many of its programs were ineffective or irrelevant. He began making organizational and administrative changes designed to facilitate communication, clarify responsibilities, and consolidate financial operations.[31] He also began trying to develop meaningful and economically viable programs for the school. It seemed to him that expanding state agricultural and educational services had undermined much of Campbell's appeal. The school already had difficulty attracting a sufficiently large and stable student body to fund its operations. Philanthropy was an unsound foundation upon which to build because contributions to private secondary or nontraditional educational endeavors were increasingly difficult to secure. The school survived only because of a temporary infusion of students and funds from postwar Veterans Administration training programs. Kester was convinced that once this source of revenue was depleted the future looked bleak unless fundamental changes were made.

In a report to the board of directors in October 1951, Kester made a series of recommendations for Campbell's future. He pointed out that relations between the school and community were strained and suggested that to play a significant role in the lives of area residents, it must overcome these tensions and become the nucleus for a thoroughly democratic program of community development which integrated local residents into every phase of decision making. He contended that Campbell could provide a much-needed service by establishing a medical cooperative and health center. He argued that both its farm and craft shop should be managed so that they would make a significant contribution to the economic security of the school and the community. The farm could provide needed food for the student body and function as an agricultural laboratory. By expanding their markets and level of production, the shops could provide training in various crafts and generate income for the school. As for the problem of developing a stable student body, Kester believed that Campbell had a natural constituency in veterans; young people desiring specialized training in agriculture, craftsmanship, or community development; handicapped persons; and local residents. He also believed that the school's facilities might be used as a training center for rural teachers and preachers.[32]

Kester thought that he had gotten the Campbell board of directors to grant him considerable leeway in administering its programs. He soon found that he had no more freedom of action than had his predecessor. Tension soon developed between the Kesters and Olive Campbell and her supporters among the staff and directors. These individuals believed that Kester was attempting to make too many changes too quickly and that he did not understand the folk school's mission. Although he had support among some of the school's directors, Olive Campbell held the real power, and without her approval he could do little. Campbell and her longtime associates Georg and Marguerite Bidstrup became disenchanted with their new administrator. Tensions ran high between the Kesters and this trio. The latter believed Howard was not "a folk school man." He in turn considered the Bidstrups obstructionists who wanted to control the school and was convinced that the aging Olive Campbell would support them in every dispute.[33]

The situation at Campbell was not unlike that at Penn. The school had not kept abreast of changing times. Although its leadership recognized that the school was in trouble, it could reach no consensus about how best to address its problems. Some of the institution's directors were willing to accept innovation and adjustment; others, led by the Bidstrups and Campbell, were reluctant to do so. This situation meant that anyone coming in from the outside intending to advocate reforms faced a difficult, if not impossible, task. Folger had left because his educational philosophy differed from that of the old guard and it was unwilling to make any concessions. Howard Kester eventually resigned for similar reasons. It is true that his lack of well-developed educational theories, impatience, penchant for doing things his own way, and lack of tact in dealing with opposition complicated his problems. However, it is unlikely that anyone committed to genuine change could have had much more success as long as the old leadership remained entrenched.

By the fall of 1951 the situation had become untenable for the Kesters. In October, Fred Brownlee, a longtime friend and one of the school's directors, wrote to Howard that "it seems to me that I would be a truer friend if I told you that I think you are bound to find the situation impossible, making you less able rather than more able to give your best under the circumstances." He suggested that Howard might find both the economic and the psychological security that he needed in a college pastorate at a place like Berea. Although disappointed by his failure to effect changes at Campbell, by late 1951 Kester recognized that Brownlee was correct. As a result, he tendered his resignation but suggested that he would like to remain at the school until March 1952 in order to wrap up some loose ends. However, at its December meeting the board of directors accepted Kester's resignation effective at the end of the month and elected his nemesis Georg Bidstrup his successor.[34]

After two disappointing episodes as an educator, punctuated by a brief and only marginally satisfying interlude as Congregational Christian Service director of displaced persons, Buck Kester made a desperate attempt to go home again. Although he wanted a stable and secure life-style for himself and his family, he missed the role of prophetic activist that he had once played. In the early fifties he decided that there was no place for him except the "Christian movement," by which he meant the fragile but tenacious struggle for social change on the periphery of southern Protestantism. He hoped to find again some way in which to try to awaken the social consciousness of the churches and thereby contribute to the progress of his region. Therefore, he was delighted when in 1952 the Fellowship of Southern Churchmen offered him what he believed would be a chance to resume his former mission. Unfortunately, his return to the Fellowship, like so many facets of his career, proved a transitory and bittersweet experience rather than a gratifying climax to a life of Christian social service.[35]

Nelle Morton, who succeeded Kester as secretary, had resigned in 1949 because of illness and financial insecurity, leaving the FSC with no full-time executive.[36] When Kester made it known that he was looking for another job, the group offered him his former post. The position was especially attractive because, of all the organizations he had served over the previous quarter century, the work of the Fellowship came closest to satisfying Kester's need to live a life dedicated to Christian service while at the same time trying to effect changes in the South. Furthermore, he had a rather proprietary attitude toward this cadre of religious activists. In October 1951 he wrote to Alice: "The FSC is in a sense our own child. We built it with nothing but hope and plans and ideas."[37] While he may have underestimated the contributions of others, his appraisal of his and Alice's importance to the fledgling Fellowship was accurate in many respects. In the late thirties he had been the figure around which the Fellowship coalesced. He was its chief apostle and recruiter while Alice attended to much of the administrative detail, and without the couple's efforts it might well have languished. As it grew and matured during the 1940s, however, the character of the group changed.

Nelle Morton lacked Kester's prophetic temperament and had no desire to be the kind of free-lance activist that he had been. Rather, she was a skilled organizer and administrator who thought that to be really effective the members of the Fellowship of Southern Churchmen must act as catalysts within their local communities, quietly but persistently promoting the kind of economic and social changes they believed consistent with the Gospel.[38] Under Morton's leadership the FSC became better organized and its constituency and program expanded dramatically. Although its membership never numbered more than a few hundred middle-class men and women, this interracial, interdenominational company of believers courageously challenged regional attitudes and traditions in innumerable, if undramatic, ways in an era before such activities became chic.

The FSC office, which was in Chapel Hill, North Carolina, during Morton's tenure as secretary, kept in close touch with liberal groups throughout the nation and became a clearinghouse for information and a channel of communication among individual members and Fellowship cells scattered across the South. Through its labor, race relations, and rural reconstruction commissions, the Fellowship conducted investigations and produced reports, pamphlets, and articles calling attention to deficiencies in southern life. At their periodic conferences and in the pages of their journal, *Prophetic Religion,* FSCers took liberal stands on the controversial economic and social issues of their day and attempted to get the churches to rethink their theological positions with regard to them. To acquaint young people of both races with one another and with regional problems, they sponsored industrial and agricultural work camps and organized interracial, intercollegiate student councils in urban centers across the South from Jackson, Mississippi, to Richmond, Virginia. Perhaps more important than their collective and public stance was the vast amount of behind-the-scenes activity in which they engaged.

Some members offered their services as mediators in labor crises in hopes of securing peaceful but equitable resolutions of such disputes. Others living in rural areas attempted to enhance the quality of country life by organizing cooperatives, securing better medical service, and encouraging local churches to become centers of community development. In the years before the civil rights movement, many of these Christians sought to undermine their region's racial mores in a number of ways. Members of both races traveled and ate together in violation of law and custom. Whites opened their homes to black travelers denied public accommodations. They encouraged the integration of local governments, schools, churches, public meetings, and restaurants. Whenever racial tensions flared, they worked quietly but persistently to defuse explosive situations before they erupted into violence.[39]

When Howard Kester once again became secretary of the Fellowship in 1952 he found it a considerably different group from that which he had served in the late thirties and early forties. The FSC no longer had the character of a prophetic remnant railing against injustice with Kester as the foremost prophet. It had become a small but far-flung organization of Christian liberals seeking to act individually and collectively as a kind of leavening agent for economic and social change in the region.

While such developments were in some respects heartening, they were not without costs. An increase in membership meant greater diversity of opinion and a more varied agenda, which sometimes undermined the spirit of fellowship. Disagreement over the importance of a conference center is a case in point. During the late forties and early fifties many members felt the need for a place where they could hold interracial gatherings unencumbered by regional prejudice. In 1948, thanks to a gift from an interested benefactor, the FSC was able to purchase a 385-acre tract of land in western North Carolina near Black Mountain for this purpose. Over the next several years much time, energy, and money went into the development of this site, to the delight of some members who believed such a retreat essential and the chagrin of others who felt that the Fellowship was becoming a place rather than a dynamic Christian movement. Another difficulty stemmed from subtle differences in temperament and style between some of the preachers, teachers, and assorted activists scattered across the South who constituted the early membership and FSC members from the liberal academic community of the Chapel Hill–Durham area who dominated the group in the late forties and early fifties. Still another source of tension was the impatience of younger zealots with what they regarded as the timidity of some of the pioneer prophets.[40]

Kester's personality, propensity for independent action, and proprietary attitude toward the Fellowship did not equip him to deal effectively with the kind of organization that it had become. He was a preacher and teacher, not an organizer and administrator. He was not skilled at mediating among contending points of view. He was irritated by associates who did not share his vision of the Fellowship and often interpreted differences of opinion as personal criticism. Consequently, although many Fellowship members regarded him as something of a folk hero, they sometimes found his style of leadership difficult to accept.

While the altered character of the FSC posed a problem for Kester, this was not the most significant challenge that he faced. Economic and social conditions in the South were different from those of the late thirties and early forties. The FSC secretary had devoted most of his career to promoting better relations between blacks and whites. Although his vision was no less grand or fundamentally sound than it had always been, by the 1950s the rising tide of change had swept him aside. Like many of the Christian liberals with whom he had long been associated, Kester was heartened and perhaps a little surprised by the Supreme Court's desegregation decision in *Brown* v. *Board of Education of Topeka*. In October 1954 he wrote to the members of the Fellowship:

It is, I believe, a rare social phenomenon that an organization whose basic concepts were a mere two decades ago regarded as radical, if not revolutionary, sees them established in the fundamental law of the land, and furthermore, sees a broad section of the people accept it as good, sound and wholesome democratic and Christian doctrine. Let us rejoice that the law, which generally sanctifies custom and morality, has set aside fiction and established the fact of every man's right to freedom, equality and justice squarely in the basic law of the land, and called this nation, including the church of the living God, to give heed to its long-neglected ideals of righteousness, mercy and love.[41]

Kester cautioned that those who had for so long committed themselves to the struggle for equality and fraternity should not now become complacent on the assumption that their ideas had carried the day. Their goal would never be achieved unless committed Christians continued to labor. Although he knew that a long and potentially painful period of adjustment lay ahead, the FSC secretary was rather optimistic in the months after the *Brown* decision. He felt that a substantial number of southerners were prepared to accept the court's ruling and to begin implementing it. However, as the segregationist White Citizens' Councils proliferated in the Deep South and the tide of massive resistance to integration began to rise throughout much of the region, his mood grew more somber.

In the fall of 1955, after returning from a 3,600-mile trip across the South, Kester issued to the members of the FSC a "Report on Mississippi" describing something of the backlash in the Magnolia State and other parts of Dixie. He reported violence against blacks, ostracism and intimidation of people working at the interracial Providence Cooperative Farm, and the purge of liberal ministers by lily-white congregations bent on maintaining the status quo. He felt that the white reaction was not simply a matter of recalcitrance. Rather, the Supreme Court's ruling that integration should be implemented with "all deliberate speed" had frightened and antagonized a region which needed time to cope with a radical departure from its traditions. Furthermore, he believed that the *Brown* decision had been rendered in a cultural vacuum. No indigenous secular or religious institutions existed to help southerners accept and adjust to the changes mandated by the justices. Though Kester considered integration both legal and right, he felt that the emphasis on immediacy and the lack of preparation were delaying the realization of the desired goal.[42]

Although the Lower South appeared unyielding in its opposition to social change, Kester thought it unwise to relinquish the area to polarized forces, symbolized on the one hand by the courts and on the other by the White Citizens' Councils. He believed it imperative to build an indigenous base of support for integration. He was confident that the nucleus of such a movement already existed among the "'gradualists' or 'moderates'" who were repelled by the extremists on both sides. If these people were carefully educated in their democratic and Christian responsibilities and organized to support peaceful change, "a bit of patience, faith and common sense" could "work a miracle of human integration, respect and good will where neither edict nor bayonet can move men against their will."[43]

Kester believed that FSC members throughout the South should make a concerted effort to organize those men and women in their vicinities who were prepared to accept integration and to marshal them to facilitate a smooth transition into a new era of race relations. He also hoped it would be possible for a few FSC members to be freed to travel across the region to help develop a network which would encourage communication and build a sense of community and strength among beleaguered moderates and liberals. All this must be done quietly, however, in order not to endanger either individuals or the goal toward which they strove.[44]

The means by which Kester proposed to deal with the interracial crisis of the mid and late 1950s were not radically different from those he had employed as a YMCA and FOR activist in the 1920s. Now, as then, he planned to use education and moral suasion to achieve social change. In a manner reminiscent of the nineteenth-century romantic reformers, he hoped to convert rather than to coerce the South into doing what was right. A change of heart, not a change in the law, was the only effective way to establish a just, peaceful, and harmonious society. Like the Victorian that in some ways he was, he believed that social cohesion depended upon the virtue of the people, not on intimidation or force.

In one important respect Kester's thinking had changed. In the twenties he had questioned the social relevance of the institutional church and for a time in the early thirties had dismissed it as inconsequential in a revolutionary world. However, with the reorientation of his work along religious lines in the late thirties and early forties, he began to hope that the church might yet be invigorated and raise a prophetic voice against injustice. As the momentous events of the fifties began to unfold, he thought that perhaps white southern Protestantism might be purified in the fires of turmoil and play a role in the salvation of the South. If the church was for southern blacks one means to the end of freedom and equality, the civil rights movement was for Kester a means by which white southern Protestantism might save its own soul. He viewed the struggle gathering momentum in the region as one of almost epic proportions in which both democracy and Christianity were on trial. Southerners' actions had implications not only for the future of the region but for that of mankind. The betrayal of democratic and Christian values might well hasten the spread of communism and the demise of freedom around the world.

Now that the battle against social, political, and religious inequity and hypocrisy was joined, the time had come for Christians at last to confront the ethical implications of their faith. Kester concurred in the judgment of one Mississippi parson that a great many southern church folk had "checked their brains and their guts at the door." However, he was not without hope, for there were others, a minority to be sure, like another Mississippi pastor who told his bishop and his parishioners that he would excommunicate anyone who joined the White Citizens' Councils. Although he was well aware of the scarcity of such courage, Kester did not think this was the time to "tear one's hair over the perversity of Christians in the South." Liberals instead should carefully examine the situation and begin to develop a comprehensive program of organization and education within the religious community to facilitate change. He declared, "We will keep hammering away in the church, at the church, with the church in the knowledge that we stand on solid ground and with the ages and not on the sand which already slips away as the rains descend and the winds of a new day blow with might."[45]

In an era of economic boycotts, public demonstrations, and other forms of nonviolent direct action, such tactics had little appeal outside the Fellowship, and even within its ranks some of the younger, more zealous members questioned their efficacy. Indeed, the group found it increasingly difficult to define its role in the South. As race relations and the civil rights struggle became a cause célèbre for liberals regionally and nationally, the FSC was unable to develop a compelling plan of action. Working behind the scenes may have made it more effective in an earlier era, but now its lack of visibility and failure to develop programs for which it could claim credit meant that it had little appeal for many contemporary black and white activists and that foundations tended not to take it very seriously. Furthermore, its goal of developing a genuine spirit of Christian fraternity which transcended racial or class consciousness seemed to many reformers of the day a remote and ephemeral dream in a land where a color line based on both statute and sentiment bisected not only secular but also religious institutions.

Thus, by 1957, with both its membership and resources dwindling, the Fellowship had reached a crisis. A year earlier, Kester, tired of the financial insecurity that went with the position of executive secretary, troubled by the FSC's inability to generate support, and upset by the dissatisfaction of some members with his leadership, had informed the executive committee that he wished to resign. He agreed to remain until after a proposed Conference on Christian Faith and Human Relations, the last major project of the Fellowship as it then existed.[46]

This three-day conference, cosponsored by the Tennessee Council of Churches, convened in Nashville on 23 April 1957. Its purpose was to bring together Christian leaders from across the South to consider racial integration in the context of their faith. Organizers invited roughly 4,500 clergy and laymen, but only about 300 people from twelve states, approximately a quarter of whom were black, gathered to discuss how they as Christians might facilitate the integration of their region.[47]

At their first session, conferees received a telegram from President Eisenhower which read in part: "It is important that new plans and effective programs be considered if we are to make the service of God and neighbor meaningful in our generation." Over the next two days a number of prominent southern religious educators and clergymen addressed the assembly. Merrimon Cuninggim, dean of Perkins School of Theology at Southern Methodist University in Dallas, argued that the South was "the best laboratory in the world" in which to test both Christianity and democracy. Contending that southerners had overemphasized the problems posed by integration and underestimated the opportunities it presented, he told the conferees that they "must move ahead with courageous prudence," acting as "Christians first and southerners second." Professor Kelley Barnett of the Episcopal Theological Seminary of the Southwest in Austin, Texas, observed that the South was "the last stronghold of Protestant Evangelical piety." The fact that southerners still took their religion seriously meant that they could be "led, but not driven" to understand that their "ultimate loyalty" was "not to Jim Crow but to Jesus Christ." Benjamin Mays, president of Morehouse College in Atlanta, called upon local churches to adopt an open admissions policy based not on race or class but solely on a profession of faith. Martin Luther King appeared briefly before the gathering and paid tribute to those clergymen in the South who in the face of threats and violence had pioneered in "Christian race relations." He pointed out that segregation "scars the soul of the segregator and the segregated" and called not merely for justice but for understanding and reconciliation.[48] In a series of seminars the men and women who assembled in Nashville discussed the Christian's role in defusing racial tensions and in the peaceful integration of churches, schools, and other institutions of community life. They agreed on the need for interracial ministerial associations, church-sponsored institutes on race problems, and the opening of channels of communications between the races.

The moderate and liberal Christians who gathered in Nashville recognized the need to avoid carelessly antagonizing their adversaries, but the stance they took inevitably precipitated hostile reactions. The opinions expressed by a contributor to an Alabama newspaper were undoubtedly typical of those of many white southerners. The writer condemned the proceedings as "degrading to both races." The indignant author contended correctly that the conferees did not reflect the opinions of the vast majority of southern churchmen and charged that the meeting was

as bad in its way as is meeting of the Ku Klux Klanners in their way, perhaps worse, because rabblerousing in the name of religion is even more to be condemned than rabblerousing in the name of patriotism. And this was a rabble-rousing meeting. It was completely integrated. . . . It contemplated with scorn, derision, sarcasm and satire all those who are not for complete and immediate integration. No moderate approach for them. You are not a Christian if you do not believe in integration. You do not believe in democracy if you do not believe in integration. You are just not fit to associate with high-minded, decent people if you do not believe in integration.[49]

On the other hand, most of those who attended the conference seem to have found it a rewarding experience. One participant declared that it was "more Christ centered" than any such gathering he had ever attended. Martin Luther King wrote to Kester: "It seems to me the we must do more of this type of thing if we are to solve the tremendous problem that faces us in the South. I still have faith in the church and the Christian ministry, and if the problem is solved the church must stand at the forefront of the struggle. Let us continue to hope and pray that the bright daybreak of freedom and brotherhood will emerge in the not-too-distant future."[50]

Buck Kester spent much of late 1956 and early 1957 raising funds, soliciting sponsors, and planning the program for the Nashville conference. Although the response was modest, the subject and tone of the gathering made it a fitting benediction to his career as social critic and reformer. He was ending where he had begun, championing the cause of racial equality and fraternity in the name of the Gospel of Christ. During the previous thirty years he had been both witness and contributor to enormous changes in his region, but now he felt that the time had come to turn his attention to other things.

The line between preacher and teacher is ill-defined, and Kester's work had always had an educational dimension. He liked and had faith in young people and believed that he could use his experiences to help them better understand and cope effectively with an increasingly complex and challenging world. Although his years at Penn and Campbell had been disappointing, he decided to turn once again to academics as an avenue of service.

Thanks to the efforts of longtime friend and Fellowship member Walter Sikes, administrators at Eureka College, a small Disciples of Christ school in Illinois, learned of Kester's interest in an educational position. They believed him to be the kind of man for whom they had been searching and offered him an appointment as director of student life and an opportunity to do some teaching.[51]

Kester looked forward to his new job but found it difficult to leave the South. In August, just before departing for the Midwest, he wrote to Will Campbell of the National Council of Churches: "This business of pulling up stakes and severing ties is rough on this old hardened southerner. I never knew until recently how really deep my attachment to all the things—good and bad, the noble and the damnable—that make the South what it is until I started packing a week or so ago."[52]

Kester left the Fellowship of Southern Churchmen with mixed emotions. He considered the last five years that he had spent in its service among "the richest and happiest" in his life, but at the same time they had been disappointing. He recognized that the FSC had not realized either his own expectations or those of many other members, but he believed that some things of significance had been accomplished. He was pleased by the progress made toward the completion of the Fellowship's interracial conference center, which seemed so badly needed amid the white backlash developing in the South in the aftermath of the *Brown* decision. Of far greater satisfaction was his conviction that southern liberals had come to regard the Fellowship as a pioneer Christian movement which could be counted on in times of trouble. He knew that difficult years lay ahead both for the FSC and the South but was convinced that beyond them lay a brighter future for men and women of hope and goodwill.[53]

Kester initially enjoyed his work in Illinois. In addition to his duties as director of student life, he taught sociology and history. He found the students a joy and the teaching a challenge. However, he soon grew dissatisfied with certain aspects of the job. Like many small colleges with limited resources, Eureka expected much work for little pay. Kester felt that his salary of approximately five thousand dollars was inadequate given the extent of his responsibilities and the time and energy they required. His relatively limited income made it necessary for Alice to work as secretary of the Eureka Christian Church and for him to serve as a supply pastor as often as his busy schedule would permit. The matter of compensation was not the only or perhaps even the most important source of his discontent. He regarded some of the college's leadership, especially its president Ira Langston, as too conservative and inflexible, and he found the atmosphere at the school increasingly uncongenial. Furthermore, the bitter winters of northern Illinois were even more inhospitable than the climate at Eureka. Finally, both he and Alice never ceased to miss the South and the kind of work they had done there.[54]

As early as January 1958 Kester wrote to Will Campbell: "We keep getting too busy to get really homesick but we long for some good southern talk and some pot licken' food that you could really enjoy rolling your tongue over. We are enjoying the work very much. The students are a challenge as well as a joy but no substitute for the fuss and turmoil to which I am accustomed." He tried to cope with the longing he had for the South and his past work there by recognizing that the Midwest too had many social problems yet to be resolved and by convincing himself that he might play a role in their resolution. In 1960 he wrote to Reinhold Niebuhr: "My inability to participate in the turmoil and strife now engaging the South would be burdensome indeed were it not for the fact that the work to be done here provides troublesome ground: the problem is nation-wide. In many communities here, Negroes may not rent or buy land, stay over night or be served in restaurants. The opportunity to get my oar in is almost constant and at times most heartening."[55]

Even as he penned these words, Kester was already so dissatisfied with Eureka that he was searching for another job. Thanks to the assistance of a friend in the Northeast, he had begun corresponding with officials of InterAmerican University of Puerto Rico about becoming a teacher or administrator there. Although it would not enable him to return to the South, the position was attractive because it would allow him to continue working with young people and perhaps to contribute to the rehabilitation of an area in which economic and social problems were rife. At the same time he was negotiating with representatives of the Disciples of Christ who were seeking an executive director for Christmount Christian Assembly, their conference center near Black Mountain, North Carolina. He preferred the educational position, but the Disciples offered him a job in the spring of 1960.[56]

Although he and Alice were delighted to be back in the southern Appalachians, Kester never really enjoyed the Christmount work. His responsibilities ranged from menial chores about the grounds to fundraising but were largely administrative. Organizing and publicizing conferences and administering the center on a daily basis were the sort of detailed routine tasks that caused him to be "bored almost to tears." He had spent much of his life in the eye of one storm or another, and he now missed the fray and felt a little guilty that he was not contributing to the momentous changes occurring in his region. In the spring of 1961 he confided to a friend that he felt "very much like a slacker in not having a hand in some crucial situation." He consoled himself with the knowledge that he had helped to eliminate racial barriers at Christmount and in the belief that some of the center's projects, such as its school for rural ministers, were significant. But he considered these "minor efforts" that provided "the barest interior satisfactions." As he witnessed what appeared to be the "accumulating divisions and ten-sions throughout the World" he hoped to find a job which might yet allow him a "more vital participation in the molding of thought and action" than his present one.[57]

Kester felt that his age, Alice's frail health, the couple's need for a reliable income, and the changing tenor of reform in the South pre-cluded a return to the free-lance activism of his youth. Nevertheless, he believed that there were avenues of service still open to him, and by the early sixties the field of education seemed the most viable one. In spite of his lack of extensive graduate training, he professed compe-tence in a number of disciplines, including history, ethics, religion, and philosophy. The veteran activist suspected that college administra-tors were hesitant to hire him because of his past work on behalf of race and labor, but it may have been his lack of a graduate education as much as his past radicalism that gave them pause. In any case, he finally got a chance to return to the classroom in 1964 when in addition to his Christmount work he became a part-time instructor in history and geography at Montreat-Anderson College, a small two-year Pres-byterian school near Black Mountain. In 1965 he joined the faculty on a full-time basis as a social science professor and later served for three years as dean of students.[58]

Kester's chief contribution to the college community lay not in the power of his intellect or in his work as an administrator but in his strength of character and the breadth of his experience. He was an unconventional teacher. He would come into the classroom, a cup of strong black coffee in his hand, sit down on the edge of his desk, and begin talking about the subject of the day while he tapped the floor with his boots and smoked one cigarette after another. He assigned newspaper and magazine articles in addition to or sometimes in lieu of chapters from textbooks. He taught as much from his own experience as from the work of scholars and occasionally was moved to tears as he recounted a particularly poignant instance of injustice or inhumanity encountered in the course of his work. Some students disliked the un-structured character of his classes, but many others were fascinated and a few were inspired.[59] The intellectual and social atmosphere at Mon-treat was more conservative than that at many schools in the late six-ties, but even there the restlessness and idealism sweeping American campuses were becoming apparent. There was something about the spirit of this rebel of an earlier generation with which students could identify. While he did not always approve of their life-style and tactics, Kester understood and appreciated the ideals and aspirations of the civil rights and Vietnam-era protestors.[60] He tried to nurture the burgeoning social consciousness of his students by relating subject matter to contemporary issues and by conveying to them the notion that if the world was to be a better place, it was committed Christians who must make it so.

Kester had accepted the position of dean of students at Montreat-Anderson very reluctantly and never particularly enjoyed the responsibilities it entailed. He disliked having to play the role of disciplinarian and found most administrative tasks boring. He was, however, enthusiastic about teaching and was sufficiently good at it to receive from the college's president, C. Grier Davis, a nomination to *Outstanding Educators of America,* an annual awards publication recognizing the nation's foremost teachers and scholars.[61] His satisfaction with this facet of his work was marred only by Alice's declining health. Over the years she had endured loneliness, anxiety, danger, hostility, financial insecurity, and misunderstanding for the sake of a better world. She had frequently suffered from a variety of physical problems that were undoubtedly compounded by the emotional strain inherent in the couple's life-style. By the late sixties she was virtually incapacitated by cerebral arteriosclerosis, and in the spring of 1970 she died.[62]

With Alice's death something died in Howard as well. Nancy Kester Neale, who witnessed her parents' interaction from a unique vantage point, once characterized their interdependence by describing her father as "fire and wind" and her mother as "earth and water."[63] For more than forty years the couple had a relationship which was sometimes romantic, at other times turbulent, but always undergirded by a profound love. Alice's temperament and talents complemented those of her husband and were essential to his work. He was a dreamer who disliked being encumbered with details and was often impatient with those who did not share his vision. She was practical, well-organized, and somewhat more receptive to different points of view. She was a coworker, administrative assistant, editor, and counselor, as well as a friend and lover. Since most of her contributions were behind the scenes and less dramatic than Howard's, they were sometimes unappreciated by contemporaries and are now difficult to document, but they were significant nonetheless.

Had he been able to continue to work, Kester might have coped more effectively with the emptiness he felt. Although he resigned as Montreat-Anderson's dean of students in 1970, the pleasure he took in working with young people and his need for a decent income would probably have kept him in the classroom for another year or two had it not been for his health. In 1971 he suffered a heart attack which forced him to retire from the college's faculty.

During the remaining six years of his life, Kester had much time to reflect upon the causes to which he and Alice had dedicated themselves. As he looked back over the previous half century, he was ambivalent about the significance of his work. In moments of despair he brooded over the fact that in spite of the efforts of liberal and radical crusaders, militarism, racism, and economic injustice were rife. Yet he recognized that the South of the 1970s was not that of the 1920s, and he believed that his generation of reformers had contributed much to the change. Disappointed, at times even bitter, because the labors of earlier activists had been largely overshadowed by the civil rights and antiwar movements of the 1950s and 1960s, he did what he could to set the record straight.

Kester, who had hoped that at least some of the socioeconomic and religious activities in which he was involved might someday prove historically significant, had scrupulously kept most of his correspondence and had urged associates to do likewise. Now he devoted a considerable portion of his time to organizing his files, granting interviews to researchers, giving an occasional talk, and doing some writing. The Committee of Southern Churchmen, spiritual heir to the Fellowship of Southern Churchmen, encouraged him to write a history of the FSC and partially underwrote the project. The task of preparing this manuscript was to some degree therapeutic since it helped to give both structure and purpose to the life of a man who did not deal well with retirement. Yet his health was frail, and he found it difficult to sustain the physical and emotional energy required to write a book. The product of his labor, an unpublished manuscript entitled "Radical Prophets: A History of the Fellowship of Southern Churchmen," is a valuable source of information, but it is poorly organized and sometimes confusing and lacks the literary vitality of some of Kester's earlier prose. He nevertheless managed to convey a sense of the courage and commitment of an almost forgotten cadre of unconventional southern Christians.

Work and reflection could never fill the void in Kester's life. He longed for the kind of companionship he had known with Alice. Years earlier, when the couple had been apart so much, they had attempted to transcend the miles separating them and commune with one another by each gazing at a special star at the same time every evening.[64] Undoubtedly, there were now many nights when an aging and lonely man looked at that same star, remembered what once had been, and pondered the meaning of the experiences that he and his wife had shared. As his life drew to a close, only the love of his scattered family and friends and for a brief time the care of his second wife, Elizabeth Moore Kester, ameliorated the pain caused by deteriorating health, chronic loneliness, and periodic bouts of depression. On 12 July 1977, Kester died of complications related to an abdominal aneurysm.

EPILOGUE

Howard Kester was born at a time when southern civilization was beginning an era of erratic but significant economic, social, and cultural change, and his life and work reflect the inconsistencies, strains, and tensions concomitant with such transitional epochs. The cultural and familial milieu of his youth provided much of the inspiration for his activism and helped to shape his understanding of what life in the South should be. However, it also imposed social limitations and contributed to the development of psychological parameters that made it difficult for him to define his religious and social mission satisfactorily and constricted the scope of his vision as a reformer.

Kester was steeped in the values of a rural and small-town culture generally satisfied with social norms characteristic of the nineteenth century but committed to a notion of progress sometimes incompatible with tradition. During his childhood, Martinsville and Henry County, Virginia, were caught up in the optimistic fervor for economic growth and diversification and regional rehabilitation typical of the New South and Progressive movements. As a result, the values and attitudes of the area were beginning to change, but for the most part they remained those of a community which thought of itself in largely organic terms. There was social stratification based on such factors as race, wealth, or occupation, and there were beginning to be signs of class consciousness. However, ties of friendship and kinship, as well as a sense of homogeneity and mutual responsibility for the welfare of the whole, remained important cohesive forces.

Evangelical Christianity was a pervasive feature of southern civilization at the turn of the century, and no facet of Kester's heritage was more important for his subsequent development than his religious training. At home and in the community he was exposed to the beliefs and practices of white southern Protestantism. His sensitivity to this Christian ethos was heightened by his awareness that his parents had dedicated him to the ministry at his christening. He grew up believing that he should and would someday occupy the respected and influential position that clergymen usually enjoyed in the South of his youth.

The progressive optimism of communities such as Martinsville and Beckley undoubtedly contributed to Kester's confidence that the economic and social life of his region could be improved. The Progressive era's emphasis on service, his family's active concern for the less fortunate, and his conception of the minister as a community leader convinced him that he bore considerable responsibility for building a better world. Yet certain inconsistencies between material goals and cultural norms and between Christian ideals and religious realities in the South made it difficult for him to develop an integrated vision of society and to define his role as an advocate of change.

As a fledgling activist Kester's approach to economic and social problems reflected something of the highly personal and paternalistic character of reform in his region. However, by the mid–1920s his education and student work with the YMCA and Presbyterian church caused him to begin to abandon the benevolent paternalism of his youth and early college years for a more fundamentally critical Christian liberalism characterized by a faith in the socially constructive power of education and moral suasion. While religious idealism lay at the heart of his new approach to his region's problems, he was skeptical of institutional southern Protestantism's relevance to the process of social revitalization. By the late twenties and early thirties his work with the Youth Section of the Fellowship of Reconciliation, contact with a number of activists in Nashville, and the deterioration of economic and social conditions in the South convinced Kester that his liberalism had been naive. Consequently, he turned to the class-oriented ideology of the Marxists, but he never felt wholly comfortable with his new position. Communism's materialism and assertion that the end justifies the means were antithetical to his essentially Christian point of view. Furthermore, the Marxian class analysis of problems, even that of the version of socialism which he embraced, was inconsistent with his basically organic view of society. Thus, as socialism's model of reality and the tactics it dictated seemed increasingly ineffectual, he rejected them for others more compatible with the values of his youth.

If Kester was never wholly comfortable among the ranks of radical political activists, neither was he entirely at ease with the religious role that circumstances imposed upon him. As his education and experience engendered in him an unconventional conception of his own mission and that of the church, he found the ministry an increasingly elusive goal.

Southern Protestantism during the late nineteenth and early twentieth centuries was not void of a sense of social consciousness, but it usually defined reform in pietistic or paternalistic terms. The handful of radical Christians who wanted to serve the church found it difficult to tap into their region's religious tradition. The man of God in the

South was either a pastor or an evangelist, not a social critic. For Kester to become a minister, he would have had to sacrifice his prophetic convictions or reshape his ministerial post to conform to his unorthodox understanding of his responsibilities. He could not do the former, and most parishioners could not accept the latter. As a result, a conventional pastorate was not open to him, and he was forced to redefine his role in the church and the South. He tried functioning within the Christian tradition but outside institutional southern Protestantism by becoming a peripatetic activist and prophet, but this proved unsatisfying. Church folk accustomed to thinking in pietistic or paternalistic terms usually failed to grasp the prophetic dimension of their faith. At the same time, most secular activists were skeptical of the creative potential of southern Protestantism. Kester grew increasingly disillusioned with pursuits that failed to satisfy his religious needs and seemed incompatible with his ideas about meaningful social change.

By the late thirties his profound frustration, along with the physical and psychological strain his activities placed upon both him and his family, produced a shift in the emphasis of his work. He became convinced that reformers should strive for a just and harmonious organic society based on the ethical precepts of Jesus and the prophets. He turned to the Fellowship of Southern Churchmen because he believed its prophetic perspective and the sense of Christian fraternity that existed among its members offered him a unique opportunity to work with kindred spirits and to make a lasting contribution to the quality of life in his region. However, the Fellowship's financial difficulties during World War II, as well as his and Alice's growing desire for a more stable life-style and their wish to try their hand at social and religious work within the context of a local community, prompted him to seek other avenues of service.

Several of the alternatives that Kester chose proved disappointing. In the case of both Penn School and the Campbell Folk School, he assumed the directorship of institutions born out of idealism and compassion for the disadvantaged but which by the middle decades of the twentieth century were out of touch with the times. Whether his temperament and experience equipped him for administrative responsibilities under any conditions is debatable, but in the circumstances in which he found himself his efforts were doomed. In both instances, he and Alice were perceived as outsiders by trustees and staff members who were reluctant to relinquish power and uncertain about the direction in which they wanted their schools to move. When he returned to the Fellowship of Southern Churchmen, Kester encountered a difficult situation similar to that at Penn and Campbell, but his role in it was different.

In the thirties the FSC had been radical by southern standards, but by the fifties its philosophy and tactics seemed passé to many activists. As the civil rights movement gained momentum, other more dramatic and aggressive groups took the lead in the quest for economic and social justice and began siphoning off the funds and tapping the pool of potential members once available to the Fellowship. Kester was deeply committed to the struggle for civil rights, but he believed that more than mere legal equality was necessary if the South was to experience genuine racial peace and justice. A spirit of Christian fraternity which transcended racial or class distinctions was his goal, and he thought that moral suasion was as important as civil disobedience, legislation, or judicial decisions in achieving this objective. Such an approach to social change seemed impractical and inadequate to most of the leaders of the civil rights movement.

Three decades earlier, Kester had been a radical prodding moderates to be more daring in their efforts on behalf of social justice for black southerners. Now, however, he appeared moderate, even conservative, to many of his contemporaries. He never fully understood the degree to which circumstances in the South had changed and therefore was unable to give the FSC the kind of innovative leadership it required in the fifties.

Thus, at a crucial juncture in the history of the South and nation, Kester's career as prophet and reformer came to an end. His life and work attest to the existence of a liberal dimension in southern Protestantism during the first half of the twentieth century and to the complexity of the problems faced by the men and women who constituted this admittedly peripheral element. Even when they seemed to their peers to be quite radical, these individuals sometimes were embroiled not only in a battle against the prejudice and complacency of their region but also in a personal struggle against culturally determined definitions of religion and reform that they had absorbed at an early age.

For Kester the interior conflict was as challenging as the external one. His courage and commitment enabled him to cope with opposition, but his cultural heritage made it difficult for him to develop a coherent vision of a better world and to define his role in realizing it. His organic view of society meant that he was never entirely comfortable with the class consciousness that informed much of the radical activism of his day. His tendency to think of country life largely in social and cultural terms prevented him from developing a program of rural rehabilitation consistent with the economic and demographic changes occurring in the South. The faith in education and the power of persuasion characteristic of much of his work was out of step with the pressure politics and civil disobedience that were the corollaries of activism in modern America. Like the evangelical reformers of the nineteenth century, he wanted to convert, not coerce; like the Victorians, he aspired to a society built upon virtue, not force. Finally, while he often spoke and acted as prophet, Kester was shaped by a southern Protestantism which had no genuinely prophetic tradition. Therefore, he sought, through the various groups with which he was connected, something like a pastorate. The Fellowship of Reconciliation, Socialist party, Committee on Economic and Racial Justice, Southern Tenant Farmers Union, Fellowship of Southern Churchmen, and the various educational institutions with which he was affiliated functioned as surrogate parishes for him. In each he searched for what he believed the church had denied him, the opportunity to serve both God and the cause of social justice, but none of these surrogates ever proved entirely satisfying.

Kester was not an ideologue or fanatic but a compassionate dreamer who longed for some means by which to translate his vision of a new order into reality. He believed that only in conjunction with others could he hope to have a significant impact upon the South. Yet his temperament was such that he was frequently most effective when he acted alone. Restless and impatient, he was not ordinarily a skilled organizer or administrator. Possessing a prophetic conviction that he had grasped the truth, he was sometimes intolerant of other activists who did not share his point of view. Articulate, courageous, and sensitive to the economic and social injustices in his society, he was in fact best suited to play the role of prophet and teacher.

In spite of difficulties and self-doubts, for more than three decades Howard Kester sacrificed health, wealth, and sometimes happiness in order that the disinherited of his region might have a better way of life. His activities may have made a difference in the lives of some of the miners of Wilder, the tenant farmers of eastern Arkansas, the black and white collegians who heard him speak, or the people who read his book and his articles. He did not, however, immediately affect changes in the economic system or social mores of his region. Yet his labors were no less significant for that fact. He and the generation of activists

with whom he worked built bridges across the color line, called attention to the plight of the poor of both races, and in countless ways
prodded the conscience of the South. In doing so they laid foundations
upon which future generations of reformers could build.

Abbreviations

Notes

Selected Bibliography

Index

ABBREVIATIONS

ACLU Archives   American Civil Liberties Union Archives, Seeley G. Mudd Library, Princeton University, Princeton, N.J.

Chancellor's Files, V.U.   Record Group 3, Files: Office of the Chancellor, Vanderbilt University, Vanderbilt University Archives, Heard Library, Nashville

FOR Papers   Fellowship of Reconciliation Papers, Peace Collection, Friends Historical Library, Swarthmore College, Swarthmore, Pa.

FSC Papers   Fellowship of Southern Churchmen Papers, Southern Historical Collection, Library of the University of North Carolina at Chapel Hill

HAK   Howard Anderson Kester

HAK Papers and *HAK Papers–Restricted*   Howard Anderson Kester Papers, Southern Historical Collection, Library of the University of North Carolina at Chapel Hill

NAACP Records   National Association for the Advancement of Colored People Records, Manuscript Division, Library of Congress

SOHPC   Southern Oral History Program Collection, ser. B, Southern Historical Collection, Library of the University of North Carolina at Chapel Hill

STFU Papers   Southern Tenant Farmers' Union Papers, Southern Historical Collection, Library of the University of North Carolina at Chapel Hill

WDW Files   Willis D. Weatherford Files, Southern Historical Collection, Library of the University of North Carolina at Chapel Hill

YWCA Records   Young Women's Christian Association, National Board, Historical Records, YWCA Headquarters, New York

NOTES

Introduction

1. Jacquelyn D. Hall, *Revolt against Chivalry: Jessie Daniel Ames and the Women's Campaign against Lynching* (New York, 1979); Morton Sosna, *In Search of the Silent South: Southern Liberals and the Race Issue* (New York, 1977); Anthony P. Dunbar, *Against the Grain: Southern Radicals and Prophets, 1929–1959* (Charlottesville, Va., 1981); Frank Adams, *Unearthing Seeds of Fire: The Idea of Highlander* (Winston-Salem, N.C., 1975); John P. McDowell, *The Social Gospel in the South: The Woman's Home Mission Movement in the Methodist Episcopal Church, South, 1886–1939* (Baton Rouge, La., 1982); John M. Glen, *Highlander: No Ordinary School, 1932–1962* (Lexington, Ky., 1988).

2. Samuel S. Hill, *Southern Churches in Crisis* (New York, 1967); John Lee Eighmy, *Churches in Cultural Captivity: A History of the Social Attitudes of Southern Baptists* (Knoxville, Tenn., 1972); Kenneth K. Bailey, *Southern White Protestantism in the Twentieth Century* (New York, 1964); John B. Boles, "Religion in the South: A Tradition Recovered," *Maryland Historical Magazine* 77 (Winter 1982): 388–401.

3. Hill, *Southern Churches in Crisis*, 171.

Chapter 1

1. [HAK], "Early Life of Howard Kester," [1940], 1, HAK Papers.

2. U.S. Bureau of the Census, "Henry County, Va.," *Manuscript Census of 1900, Twelfth Census of the United States, Schedule No. 1—Population,* microfilm; U.S. Bureau of the Census, "Montour County, Pa.," *Manuscript Census of 1870, Ninth Census of the United States,* microfilm; Jane Elizabeth Kester, interview with author, Roanoke, Va., 27 June 1981; HAK, interview by Jacquelyn Hall and William Finger, 22 July 1974, transcript, SOHPC (hereafter cited as transcript of interview with HAK, 22 July 1974).

3. "Kester Reunion," *Tablet* (Millville, Pa.), 14 Sept. 1904, Howard Anderson Kester Papers, Black Mountain, N.C., in possession of the family.

4. HAK, "Early Life of Howard Kester," 1; U.S. Bureau of the Census, "Amherst County, Va.," *Manuscript Census of 1870, Ninth Census of the United States,* microfilm; interview with Jane Kester; Nancy Kester Neale, interview with author, Boone, N.C., 24 May 1985; transcript of interview with HAK, 22 July 1974.

5. Interview with Jane Kester; Raymond P. Barnes, *A History of Roanoke* (Radford, Va., 1968), 284.

6. Transcript of interview with HAK, 22 July 1974; interview with Jane Kester; untitled responses of HAK to questions submitted by John Stark Bel-

lamy, author of "If Christ Came to Dixie: The Southern Prophetic Vision of Howard Anderson Kester, 1904–1941" (M.A. thesis, University of Virginia, 1977), Kester Papers (Black Mountain) (hereafter cited as "Responses").

7. "Martinsville, Virginia" (Adv.), *Henry County Bulletin,* 5 May 1910.

8. U.S. Bureau of the Census, "Henry County, Virginia," *Thirteenth Census of the United States, Taken in the Year 1910,* vol. 7, *Agriculture 1909 and 1910* (Washington, D.C., 1913), 814; interview with Jane Kester; HAK, "Early Life of Howard Kester," 1–2; Bellamy, "If Christ Came to Dixie," 13.

9. Daniel Walker Howe, introductory essay in *Victorian America,* ed. Howe (Philadelphia, 1976), 3–28; Daniel J. Singal, *The War Within: From Victorian to Modernist Thought in the South, 1919–1945* (Chapel Hill, N.C., 1982), 3–33.

10. Interview with Jane Kester; transcript of interview with HAK, 22 July 1974.

11. "Responses," Addendum: 1, 5.

12. HAK to Alice Harris, 7 Oct. 1926, HAK Papers–Restricted; "Responses," 3, 2.

13. HAK, "Early Life of Howard Kester," 1; interview with Jane Kester; John Egerton, *A Mind to Stay Here: Profiles from the South* (New York, 1970), 76.

14. In terms of the sociologists' *Gemeinschaft-Gesellschaft* or community-society model, Martinsville, although moving in the direction of *Gesellschaft,* retained many characteristics typical of *Gemeinschaft* (Robert A. Nisbet, *The Sociological Tradition* [New York, 1966], 71–82.)

15. Transcript of interview with HAK, 22 July 1974; "Responses," Addendum: 2.

16. Interview with Jane Kester.

17. "Responses," 1; interview with Jane Kester.

18. Bellamy, "If Christ Came to Dixie," 5–6.

19. Ibid., 18, 14–15.

20. HAK, "Early Life of Howard Kester," 2–3; Bellamy, "If Christ Came to Dixie," 19–20; interview with Jane Kester.

21. Interview with Jane Kester.

22. Bellamy, "If Christ Came to Dixie," 19–20.

23. U.S. Bureau of the Census, "Population—West Virginia," *Thirteenth Census of the United States, Taken in the Year 1910,* vol. 3, *Population* (Washington, D.C., 1913), 1038; U.S. Bureau of the Census, "Population—West Virginia," *Fourteenth Census of the United States, Taken in the Year 1920,* vol. 3, *Population* (Washington, D.C., 1922), 1108; "Big Steps toward Good Roa[d]s," "New Chief Engineer of Road Construction Here," 4 Jan. 1917, "Fourteen Counties Mined over 1,000,000 Tons Each," 18 Jan. 1917, "Six Years Road Building Progress in West Virginia," 24 May 1917, *Raleigh Register.*

24. "Government Alert as Nation Faces Greatest Coal Strike," "How

Government Met Coal Strike," 6 Nov. 1919, "Strike Is Off by Order of Mine
Union Leaders," 13 Nov. 1919, "Miners Slow to Resume Work," 20 Nov.
1919, "Coal Miners' Strike Ended," 11 Dec. 1919, *Raleigh Register;* Egerton,
A Mind to Stay Here, 73.

25. U.S. Bureau of the Census, *Thirteenth Census,* 3, *Population,* 1038;
Fourteenth Census, 3, *Population,* 1108.

26. Transcript of interview with HAK, 22 July 1974; unidentified manuscript fragment, n.d., Kester Papers (Black Mountain).

Chapter 2

1. HAK, "Early Life of Howard Kester," 6.

2. Orville Wentworth Wake, "A History of Lynchburg College, 1903–
1953" (Ph.D. diss., University of Virginia, 1957), 63–67.

3. Ibid., 184, 185.

4. "Who's Who," *Critograph,* 11 Oct. 1924. Kester recalled in a letter to
Alice Harris on 3 Aug. 1926 (HAK Papers–Restricted) that his pacifism,
critique of what he deemed hypocrisy within the church, and fraternization
with black students, some of whom he had brought to the Lynchburg campus, had alienated a number of students and faculty members.

5. HAK, "Early Life of Howard Kester," 1, 3; McPherson to Holt Kester,
21 April 1972, Kester Papers (Black Mountain).

6. Bellamy, "If Christ Came to Dixie," 28.

7. HAK to George Washington Carver, 4, 14 July 1924, George Washington Carver Papers, Hollis Burke Frissell Library, Tuskegee University, Tuskegee, Ala.; Otis K. Rice, *West Virginia: A History* (Lexington, Ky., 1985),
191.

8. Bellamy, "If Christ Came to Dixie," 30, 32, 33.

9. William H. Morgan, *Student Religion during Fifty Years: Programs and
Policies of the Intercollegiate Y.M.C.A.* (New York, 1935), 146–47.

10. Ibid., 147; Bellamy, "If Christ Came to Dixie," 35; "The American
Student Pilgrimage to Europe (YMCA), the Year 1923: Travelogue, Events,
Impressions, Expressions, Friendships; Composite Notes, as Culled from Dia-
ries by Ray Legatte during the Spring of 1949," 25, Kester Papers (Black
Mountain).

11. "The American Student Pilgrimage to Europe," 27; transcript of interview with HAK, 22 July 1974.

12. "The American Student Pilgrimage to Europe," 13, 29–32.

13. Transcript of interview with HAK, 22 July 1974.

14. HAK, "Radical Prophets: A History of the Fellowship of Southern
Churchmen," n.d. (photographic copy in possession of author; original in
possession of Nancy Kester Neale, Boone, N.C.), 87.

15. Wilma Dykeman, *Prophet of Plenty: The First Ninety Years of W. D.
Weatherford* (Knoxville, Tenn., 1966), 74.

16. Morgan, *Student Religion during Fifty Years,* 29–30, 133, 135-37.

17. Forrest D. Brown, "Indianapolis Student Volunteer Convention," *Blue Ridge Voice* 5 (Dec. 1923/Jan. 1924): 17, 16–18, 28; Morgan, *Student Religion during Fifty Years,* 30, 155–56.

18. George Brown Tindall, *The Emergence of the New South, 1913-1945* (Baton Rouge, La., 1967), 183.

19. Transcript of interview with HAK, 22 July 1974.

20. Weatherford to Ben M. Cherrington, 20 July 1925, WDW Files.

21. Juliette Derricote to Ruth Scandrett, 22 Oct. 1926, to Mrs. George E. Haynes, 30 Oct. 1924, YWCA Records.

22. HAK, "Radical Prophets," 23; transcript of interview with HAK, 22 July 1974. In the spring of 1926 Kester described Carver as "the man who has been and is to this day the greatest inspiration in my life." In the summer of that year he spent several weeks with Carver at Tuskegee. During this visit the two men began laying plans, which never reached fruition, for the establishment of a George Washington Carver Fellowship, the purpose of which was "to unite all kindred spirits, whatever race, religion or nationality, who behold in the universe the most sublime expression of Love, Truth and Beauty, through which the Great Creator eternally speaks concerning the things that He has created." Over the years Kester went to Tuskegee on a number of occasions during which Carver taught him the pleasurable hobby of painting with pastels, watercolors, and oils and contributed to his work by suggesting ways in which science and technology could be used to enhance the quality of life in the rural South (Linda O. McMurry, *George Washington Carver: Scientist and Symbol* [New York, 1981], 210–11; HAK, "Early Life of Howard Kester," 4).

23. J. J. King to Willis D. Weatherford, 19 June 1926, WDW Files.

24. Weatherford to Ben M. Cherrington, 29 July 1925, to Ruth Scandrett, 20 May 1926, ibid.

25. Benjamin Mays, *Born to Rebel* (New York, 1971), 127–28; Benjamin Mays, interview with author, Atlanta, 11 Aug. 1982.

26. Lefferts A. Loetscher, *The Broadening Church: A Study of Theological Issues in the Presbyterian Church since 1869* (Philadelphia, 1957), 136–48; HAK, "Early Life of Howard Kester," 5.

27. Allyn Russell, "J. Gresham Machen, Scholarly Fundamentalist," *Journal of Presbyterian History* 51 (1973): 46–48, 50–52.

28. Ibid.; HAK, "Early Life of Howard Kester," 5.

29. "Responses," Addendum: 19–20.

30. Transcript of interview with HAK, 22 July 1974.

31. Bellamy, "If Christ Came to Dixie," 53; HAK, "Early Life of Howard Kester," 6.

32. Vincent G. Burns, "Brother Bill," *Christian Century* 45 (20 Sept. 1928): 1133–35; HAK, "Early Life of Howard Kester," 5–6; Bellamy, "If Christ Came to Dixie," 51; HAK to Alice Harris, 7 Aug. 1926, HAK Papers.

33. HAK, "Early Life of Howard Kester," 6–7; Maud H. Paris, interview with author, Warner-Robbins, Ga., 20 May 1985.

34. HAK, "Radical Prophets," 22–23; Wilson Newman, telephone interview with author, 15 Jan. 1983.

35. Harris to HAK, 18, 23 June 1926, HAK to Harris, June 1926, HAK Papers.

36. Transcript of interview with HAK, 22 July 1974; "This Is to Tell You of the Work of the Nashville Student Forum," n.d., Membership Continuation Committee, Nashville Interracial Student Forum to "Dear Friend," 11 Oct. 1924, YWCA Records.

37. Student Interracial Committee Report, 1926 (misdated 1924), YWCA Records.

38. "Report of Katharine Butler, Feb. to May 1927," ibid.; A. Whitney Griswold, *The Far Eastern Policy of the United States* (New York, 1938), 386–87.

39. Walter L. Fleming to Chancellor Kirkland, 31 March 1927, Chancellor's Files, V.U.; "Report of Katharine Butler, Feb. to May 1927," YWCA Records.

40. "Report of Katharine Butler, Feb. to May 1927," YWCA Records; Fleming to Kirkland, 31 March 1927, Chancellor's Files, V.U.

41. Kirkland to Brown, 20 Jan., 6, 7 April 1927, Brown to Kirkland, 23 April 1927, Chancellor's Files, V.U.; transcript of interview with HAK, 22 July 1974.

42. "[FOR] Statement of Purpose," 6 Dec. 1930, telegram, Don M. Chase to HAK, 1 Jan. 1927, HAK to Alice Harris, 11 Jan. 1927, Francis Henson to Alice and Buck Kester, 12 April 1927, HAK Papers; Brown, "Indianapolis Student Volunteer Convention," 18; "The Fellowship of Reconciliation (Fellowship of Youth for Peace): An Explanation," Feb. 1924, FOR Papers.

43. "The Fellowship of Reconciliation (Fellowship of Youth for Peace): An Explanation," Feb. 1924, FOR Papers.

44. Seattle Stowater to Dear Friend, [1926?], Central Committee to members, 10 May 1926, "Two Peace Societies Unite," Oct. 1926, ibid.

45. Jones to HAK, 27 Nov. 1926, HAK Papers; transcript of interview with HAK, 22 July 1974.

46. HAK to Harris, 30 Nov. 1926, draft note, HAK to Jones, undated, telegram, Chase to HAK, 10 Jan. 1927, HAK to Alice Harris, 11 Jan. 1927, HAK Papers.

47. Alice H. Kester to HAK, 8 Jan. 1927, ibid.; Program, General Conference of FOR including Youth Section (Sept. 8–11, 1927), FOR Papers.

48. Sydney E. Ahlstrom, ed., *Theology in America: The Major Protestant Voices from Puritanism to Neo-Orthodoxy* (Indianapolis and New York, 1967), 66–72.

49. "The Force of Love," [late 1920s], FOR Papers.

50. Interview with Maud H. Paris; transcript of interview with HAK, 22 July 1974.

51. HAK to Alice H. Kester, 14 Nov. 1928, HAK Papers.

52. HAK, "Early Life of Howard Kester," 7; "Meeting of the Executive Committee of the Fellowship of Reconciliation, Thursday, April 5, 1928 . . .," John Nevin Sayre Papers, Peace Collection, Friends Historical Library, Swarthmore College, Swarthmore, Pa.

53. Newman to HAK, 18 May 1929, Kester Papers (Black Mountain).

54. Carver to HAK, 2 April 1929, Carver Papers.

55. HAK to Alice H. Kester, 28 Feb., 5 March 1929, HAK Papers; HAK, "Early Life of Howard Kester," 7. Ethel Moors was the wife of John F. Moors, a wealthy investment broker, philanthropist, member of the Harvard Corporation, trustee of Radcliffe College, and community leader of Boston. In the late twenties she became interested in Howard Kester's efforts on behalf of social justice in the South. On several occasions over the next quarter century, she provided modest financial assistance not only for his work but also directly to the Kesters to help with such personal matters as the purchase of a site for a house in western North Carolina and the education of their daughter.

Chapter 3

1. HAK to Alice H. Kester, 6 June 1929, HAK Papers.

2. Stanley Lincoln Harbison, "Social Gospel Career of Alva W. Taylor" (Ph.D. diss., Vanderbilt University, 1975), 214–16; Paul K. Conkin, *Gone with the Ivy: A Biography of Vanderbilt University* (Knoxville, Tenn., 1985), 370–73.

3. Dunbar, *Against the Grain,* 29; Bellamy, "If Christ Came to Dixie," 77.

4. HAK, "Early Life of Howard Kester," 8; "Notes on the Work of the Fellowship of Reconciliation, May 1, 1931 [fragment]," Sayre Papers; Minutes of the Executive Committee, 14 March 1931, Minutes of FOR Executive Council Meeting, 1 May 1931, FOR Papers.

5. Donald B. Meyer, *The Protestant Search for Political Realism, 1919– 1941* (Berkeley, Calif., 1960), 50.

6. HAK, "Early Life of Howard Kester," 8.

7. Bellamy, "If Christ Came to Dixie," 98–100; transcript of interview with HAK, 22 July 1974.

8. Egerton, *A Mind to Stay Here,* 78.

9. Clarence Senior to HAK, 12 Oct. 1931, Socialist Party Papers, Manuscript Department, William R. Perkins Library, Duke University, Durham, N.C.; Alice Kester to "Folk Back Home," 21 July 1932, copy in possession of author.

10. James R. Green, *Grass-Roots Socialism: Radical Movements in the South-*

west, 1895–1943 (Baton Rouge, La., 1978); Clarence Senior to Myles Horton, 29 Dec. 1932, Socialist Party Papers.

11. HAK to Clarence Senior, 10 Oct. 1931, Socialist Party Papers; HAK to Alice Kester, 13 Oct. 1931, HAK Papers.

12. "Annual Report of Howard Kester, Southern Secretary, Annual Conference of the Fellowship of Reconciliation, October 1933," Sayre Papers (hereafter cited as "Annual Report of Howard Kester . . . October 1933"); "For Congress," *Nashville Tennessean,* 6 Nov. 1932.

13. "Final Davidson Vote," *Evening Tennessean,* 10 Nov. 1932; HAK to Clarence Senior, 4 Feb. 1932, Socialist Party Papers.

14. "Annual Report of Howard Kester . . . October 1933."

15. Ibid.; Dunbar, *Against the Grain,* 2; "Crawford Called to Nashville for Report on Ambush," *Nashville Tennessean,* 28 Oct. 1932.

16. Helen Dahnke, "Their Leader Dead, Wilder's Striking Miners Say Their Cause 'Goes Marching On,'" *Nashville Tennessean,* 7 May 1933.

17. "Annual Report of Howard Kester . . . October 1933."

18. Dahnke, "Their Leader Dead," *Nashville Tennessean,* 7 May 1933.

19. Sayre to HAK, 22 April 1932, 6 Feb. 1933, J. B. Matthews to HAK, 22 Nov. 1932, HAK Papers.

20. Taylor to Sayre, 26 Dec. 1932, Alva Wilmot Taylor Papers, Disciples of Christ Historical Society, Nashville, Tenn.

21. Taylor to Myers and Spofford, 18 May 1933, ibid.

22. Ibid.

23. "Their Leader Dead," 7 May 1933, "President of Union Killed at Wilder," 1 May 1933, "Union Men on Warpath," 1 May 1933, untitled, May 1933, Don West, "A Fallen Labor Chief," n.d., newspaper clippings, ACLU Archives; Myles Horton to Alva Taylor, [1932?], Taylor Papers.

24. "Union Men on Warpath," 1 May 1933, newspaper clipping, ACLU Archives.

25. HAK, "Radical Prophets," 10; Fran Ansley and Sue Thrasher, "The Ballad of Barney Graham [interview of Della Graham Smith and Barney Graham, Jr.]," *Southern Exposure* 4 (Spring 1976): 137; HAK, "'Barney' Graham," *Labor Advocate* (Nashville), 4 May 1933.

26. "President of Union Killed at Wilder," 1 May 1933, "Barney Graham Shot by 'Shorty' Green in Coal Strike Zone," n.d., newspaper clippings, ACLU Archives.

27. Barnett [to the newspapers of Nashville], encl. in Barnett to James Myers, 2 May 1933, ibid.

28. Myers to Baldwin, 9 May 1933, HAK to Baldwin, 13 May 1933, ibid.; Lewis to Taylor, 9 May 1933, Taylor Papers.

29. HAK to Roger Baldwin, n.d., unsigned to HAK, 16 May 1933, ACLU Archives.

30. ACLU to HAK, 31 May, 6 June 1933, Allen Turnblazer to Lucille Milner, 17, 22 July, 1933, ibid.; HAK, "Radical Prophets," 10.

31. HAK, "Radical Prophets," 9–10.

32. Taylor to [?] Irby, 12 Aug. 1933, Taylor Papers.

33. HAK, interview by Mary Fredrickson, 25 Aug. 1974, transcript, SOHPC.

34. "Annual Report of Howard Kester . . . October 1933."

35. Meyer, *The Protestant Search for Political Realism,* 203–16.

36. "Annual Report of Howard Kester . . . October 1933."

37. Sayre to HAK, 30 Oct. 1933, Sayre Papers.

38. "Annual Report of Howard Kester . . . October 1933."

39. HAK to Sayre, 2 Nov. 1933, Sayre Papers.

40. J. N. Sayre to Alice H. Kester, 21 Dec. 1933, ibid.

41. Ibid.

42. HAK to J. N. Sayre, 2 Jan. 1934, ibid.

43. HAK to Claude Williams, 18 Nov. 1934, HAK Papers; HAK to Carver, 13 March 1934, Carver Papers.

44. David A. Shannon, *The Socialist Party of America: A History* (New York, 1958), 211–14.

45. "An Appeal to the Socialist Party from 47 Members," *World Tomorrow* 17, no. 8 (12 April 1934): 1.

46. HAK to Tess Sinovich, 21 July 1934, to Reinhold Niebuhr, 23 Oct. 1934, HAK Papers.

47. HAK to Tess Sinovich, 21 July 1934, ibid.; HAK to J. N. Sayre, 2 Jan. 1934, Sayre Papers.

48. Robert Moats Miller, *American Protestantism and Social Issues, 1919–1939* (Chapel Hill, N.C., 1958), 96–97; Alice Kester to John N. Sayre, 11 Jan. 1934, Sayre Papers.

49. Alice Kester to Wilson Newman, 8 March 1934, HAK Papers.

50. "Suggested Program for the Committee on Racial and Industrial Justice," n.d., ibid.

51. "Annual Report of Howard Kester . . . October 1933."

Chapter 4

1. HAK, "Radical Prophets," 82–86.

2. HAK to "Dear Friend," 3 Feb. 1930, "The Meaning of LeMoyne," 15 Jan. 1930, Sayre Papers.

3. HAK to Wilson Newman, 19 Nov. 1929, HAK Papers; "The Meaning of LeMoyne," 15–16, Sayre Papers.

4. Claud Nelson to HAK, 18 May 1932, HAK Papers.

5. "Minutes of the Council Meeting of the F.O.R. of March 14, 1931," Sayre Papers.

6. HAK, "Early Life of Howard Kester," 7–8.

7. HAK to "Dear Friend," 27 April 1931, "Fellowship of Reconciliation Retreat, LeMoyne College, Memphis, Tennessee, March 25, 26, 27, 1932," HAK Papers.

8. "Toward Peace, Justice, and Understanding: The Story of Fellowship Activities Submitted to the National Council at the Annual Conference on 'Disarmament and the New Defense,' October 15–18 [1931]," Sayre Papers.

9. HAK to Alice H. Kester, 29 July, 30 July 1931, to "Dear Friend," 15 Aug. 1931, HAK Papers.

10. HAK to "Dear Friend," 15 Aug. 1931, ibid. For the battle between the NAACP and the ILD for control of the Scottsboro defense, see Dan T. Carter, *Scottsboro: A Tragedy of the American South*, rev. ed. (Baton Rouge, La., 1979), 52–54, 61–62, 85.

11. HAK to "Dear Friend," 15 Aug. 1931, HAK Papers.

12. "Toward Peace, Justice, and Understanding: The Story of Fellowship Activities Submitted to the National Council at the Annual Conference on 'Disarmament and the New Defense,' October 15–18 [1931]," Sayre Papers.

13. Ibid.

14. "Annual Report of Howard Kester . . . October 1933."

15. HAK to Jackson, 9 Feb. 1933, HAK Papers.

16. HAK to Mr. and Mrs. John Bergthold, 16 Nov. 1934, ibid.

17. Henson to HAK, 10 July, 26 Oct. 1934, to Ira Reid, 11 July 1934, ibid.

18. "Findings of the Negro-White Conference Held at Shaw University, Raleigh, N.C., Nov. 30–Dec. 2, 1934," ibid.

19. White to HAK, 5 Aug., 18 Aug. 1931, HAK to White, 5 Sept. 1931, NAACP Records.

20. HAK to White, 5 Sept. 1931, ibid.

21. James R. McGovern, *Anatomy of a Lynching: The Killing of Claude Neal* (Baton Rouge, La., 1982), 42–45.

22. Dothan *Eagle*, 26 Oct. 1934, cited in ibid., 74.

23. Ibid., 76–92.

24. Ibid., 115.

25. HAK to Alice H. Kester, 5 March 1934, HAK Papers; White to Leon Ransom, 1 Nov. 1934, NAACP Records, cited in McGovern, *Anatomy of a Lynching*, 126; telegram, White to HAK, 30 Oct. 1934, telegram, HAK to White, 30 Oct. 1934, telegram, White to HAK, 31 Oct. 1934, White to HAK, 31 Oct. 1934, NAACP Records.

26. HAK, "Radical Prophets," 102–3; HAK to Walter White, 7 Nov. 1934, NAACP Records.

27. HAK to Alice Kester, 11 Nov. 1933, HAK Papers; McMurry, *George Washington Carver*, 217.

28. HAK, "Radical Prophets," 101–2.

29. HAK, *The Lynching of Claude Neal*, 30 Nov. 1934, 3, NAACP Records.

30. Ibid., 5.

31. Ibid., 7; HAK to Mr. and Mrs. John Bergthold, 16 Nov. 1934, HAK Papers; HAK to White, 7 Nov. 1934, NAACP Records.

32. HAK, *The Lynching of Claude Neal*, 7.

33. Telegram, Roy Wilkins to White, 9 Nov. 1934, telegram, White to HAK, 17 Nov. 1934, White to HAK, 27 Nov. 1934, to Eleanor Roosevelt, 20 Nov. 1934, to Romeo Dougherty (editor, *Amsterdam News*), 12 Dec. 1934, NAACP Records.

34. Carter to Sholtz, 10 Nov. 1934, Lynching File, ser. 278, Florida State Archives, cited in McGovern, *Anatomy of a Lynching*, 112; Brill to Walter White, 24 Nov. 1934, NAACP Records.

35. Henry C. Patterson to White, 24 Nov. 1934, cited in McGovern, *Anatomy of a Lynching*, 130; Mencken to White, 30 Nov. 1934, NAACP Records.

36. McGovern, *Anatomy of a Lynching*, 144; Bellamy, "If Christ Came to Dixie," 146; Virginius Dabney, "Dixie Rejects Lynching," *Nation* 145 (27 Nov. 1937): 581.

37. McGovern, *Anatomy of a Lynching*, 142–44.

38. Walter White to Homer S. Cummings, 29 Oct. 1934, NAACP Records; "Senators Told Cummings Flouts Law They Introduced," 2 Nov. 1934, newspaper clipping, "Prominent Writers Protest Florida Lynching," Nov. 1934, newspaper clipping, Harry F. Ward, Arthur Garfield Hayes, and Roger N. Baldwin to Franklin Roosevelt, 29 Oct. 1934, ACLU Archives; McGovern, *Anatomy of a Lynching*, 119.

39. McGovern, *Anatomy of a Lynching*, 121–23.

40. Ibid., 135–39.

41. Telegram, Walter White to HAK, 30 Jan. 1934, HAK Papers; telegram, Roy Wilkins to Walter White, 15 Feb. 1934, NAACP Records; U.S. Congress, Senate, Committee on the Judiciary, Subcommittee on S. 1978, *Hearings . . . on S. 1978: A Bill to Assure to Persons within the Jurisdiction of Every State the Equal Protection of the Laws, and to Punish the Crime of Lynching*, 73d Cong., 2d sess., 1934, pt 1.

42. HAK to Katherine Gardner, 26 Nov. 1934, HAK Papers.

43. HAK to Henson, 21 July 1935, ibid.

44. Roy Wilkins to HAK, 6 June 1935, HAK, "The Struggle against Peonage," 26 June 1935, ibid.

45. Williams to Alice H. Kester, 31 Dec. 1935, ibid.

46. HAK to White, 20 Sept., 10 Oct. 1939, ibid.

47. HAK, "Lynching by Blow Torch (A Report upon the Double Lynching at Duck Hill, Miss., April 13, 1937)," 1–7, ibid.

48. Ibid., 7–8.

49. HAK to Walter White, 8 May 1937, NAACP Records.

50. Ibid.

51. L. E. Gleeck to HAK, 22 July 1937, HAK to L. E. Gleeck, 27 July 1937, HAK Papers.

Chapter 5

1. Donald H. Grubbs, *Cry from the Cotton: The Southern Tenant Farmers' Union and the New Deal* (Chapel Hill, N.C., 1971), 14–16.

2. Ibid., 17–19, 25.

3. Ibid., 19–25.

4. Ibid., 7–8, 10.

5. HAK, *Revolt among the Sharecroppers* (New York, 1936), 55.

6. Grubbs, *Cry from the Cotton,* 28–29.

7. Mitchell to HAK, 8 Aug. 1934, HAK Papers.

8. HAK to Mr. and Mrs. John Bergthold, 16 Nov. 1934, ibid.

9. HAK to Mitchell, 23 Nov. 1934, to Mr. and Mrs. John Bergthold, 16 Nov. 1934, ibid.; H(arry) L(eland) Mitchell, observations recorded for author, Montgomery, Ala., 23 June 1988. H. L. Mitchell claims that Kester made a brief stop in eastern Arkansas on his way back from investigating the Claude Neal lynching. Documentary evidence suggests that this was probably not the case. He may, however, have paid a quick visit to size up the situation later in the fall.

10. Thomas to HAK, 26 Jan. 1935, HAK Papers.

11. Mitchell to HAK, 24 Nov. 1934, ibid.; Bellamy, "If Christ Came to Dixie," 96.

12. HAK to Thomas, 2 Feb. 1935, Socialist Party Papers.

13. HAK to Mitchell, 23 Nov. 1934, HAK Papers.

14. HAK to Thomas, 2 Feb. 1935, Socialist Party Papers; excerpt of HAK to Alice H. Kester, in Elisabeth Gilman to Reinhold Niebuhr, 15 Feb. 1935, Reinhold Niebuhr Papers, Manuscript Division, Library of Congress.

15. HAK to Mr. and Mrs. John Bergthold, 16 Nov. 1934, HAK Papers; excerpt of HAK to Alice H. Kester, in Elisabeth Gilman to Reinhold Niebuhr, 15 Feb. 1935, Niebuhr Papers.

16. Observations of H. L. Mitchell; H. L. Mitchell, *Mean Things Happening in This Land: The Life and Times of H. L. Mitchell, Co-Founder of the Southern Tenant Farmers Union* (Montclair, N.J., 1979), 142; Niebuhr to Elisabeth Gilman, 1 March 1935, Niebuhr Papers.

17. HAK, *Revolt among the Sharecroppers,* 39–43; HAK, "Radical Prophets," 12–13.

18. Grubbs, *Cry from the Cotton,* 64. Grubbs cites documentary evidence attributing this remark to Myrtle Moskop but acknowledges that H. L. Mitchell thinks that Myrtle Lawrence, a more articulate member of the STFU, is more likely to have made it.

19. Excerpt of HAK to Alice H. Kester, in Elisabeth Gilman to Reinhold Niebuhr, 15 Feb. 1935, Niebuhr Papers.

20. CERJ to "Dear Friend," 7 March 1935, HAK Papers.

21. Mitchell, *Mean Things Happening in This Land,* 69, 70.

22. Carpenter to HAK, 16 March 1935, HAK Papers.

23. HAK, "Radical Prophets," 110.

24. Ibid., 105–7; telegram, H. L. Mitchell to Norman Thomas, 17 Jan. 1936, HAK Papers; Grubbs, *Cry from the Cotton,* 91–92. On at least one occasion Kester suggested that the presence of a woman among their captives may have caused the mob to have second thoughts about lynching him (Jerold S. Auerbach, *Labor and Liberty: The La Follette Committee and the New Deal* [Indianapolis, 1966], 44).

25. Bellamy, "If Christ Came to Dixie," 105–6.

26. Reinhold Niebuhr and Elisabeth Gilman to "Dear Friend," 7 March 1935, HAK Papers; Grubbs, *Cry from the Cotton,* 75–76.

27. Roy Wilkins to HAK, 6 June 1935, Gardner Jackson to HAK, 18 April 1937, Marian S. Carter to HAK, 29 Nov. 1937, HAK to Reinhold Niebuhr, 18 Jan. 1938, telegram, Allen Johnson to HAK, [1938], Alice H. Kester to Bill McKee, 29 Feb. 1940, HAK Papers.

28. Auerbach, *Labor and Liberty,* 45–47.

29. Bellamy, "If Christ Came to Dixie," 188–90; Grubbs, *Cry from the Cotton,* 121.

30. HAK, *Revolt among the Sharecroppers,* 26, 88–91.

31. HAK to Genevieve Schneider, 26 March 1936, HAK Papers.

32. HAK, *Revolt among the Sharecroppers,* 92–93.

33. Sam H. Franklin, Jr., *The Delta Cooperative Farm, Hillhouse, Mississippi* (n.p., n.d.), Delta and Providence Farms Papers, Southern Historical Collection, Library of the University of North Carolina at Chapel Hill; Mitchell to Gardner Jackson, 14 Feb. 1936, William R. Amberson to HAK, 17 Feb. 1936, HAK Papers.

34. Amberson to HAK, 17 Feb. 1936, Thomas and Niebuhr to Clarence Pickett, 2 March 1936, HAK to Myers, 10 March 1936, HAK Papers; Thomas M. Jacklin, "Mission to the Sharecroppers: Neo-Orthodox Radicalism and the Delta Farm Venture, 1936–40," *South Atlantic Quarterly* 78 (Summer 1979): 308–9.

35. HAK to Myers, 10 March 1936, HAK Papers; Franklin, *The Delta Cooperative Farm,* Delta and Providence Farms Papers.

36. HAK to Myers, 10 March 1936, HAK Papers; Jacklin, "Mission to the Sharecroppers," 302–5. Some of the Christian activists such as Eddy were not, strictly speaking, neoorthodox but were evangelical liberal heirs of the Social Gospel tradition. Eddy did not worry much about theological designations. On one occasion he wrote of his own beliefs, "I have no desire to be orthodox or 'neo-orthodox,' but neither do I have any aversion to being either" (Sherwood Eddy, *Eighty Adventurous Years: An Autobiography* [New York, 1955], 227).

37. Jacklin, "Mission to the Sharecroppers," 311.

38. Ibid., 314; untitled report of investigatory committee, encl. in HAK to Reinhold Niebuhr, 9 July 1940, HAK Papers.

39. Norman Thomas to Roy Burt and HAK, 18 Jan. 1938, Amberson

to HAK, 5 March 1939, with encl., Amberson, "A Statement to the Board of Trustees, Cooperative Farms, Inc., Feb. 22, 1939," HAK Papers.

40. Reinhold Niebuhr to HAK, 21 Jan. 1938, HAK Papers; Jacklin, "Mission to the Sharecroppers," 312–13; Amberson, "The Delta Farms," ltr. to the editor, *Christian Century* 56 (14 June 1939): 774.

41. HAK to Reinhold Niebuhr, 18 Jan. 1938, Niebuhr Papers; HAK to Alice H. Kester, 5 Jan. 1937, HAK Papers.

42. HAK to Rev. James Myers, 25 April 1939, Niebuhr to HAK, [July 1939?], HAK to Reinhold Niebuhr, 14 Aug. 1939, HAK Papers.

43. "Condensed Statement of Grievances Set Forth at Blytheville, Arkansas, Jan. 1940," encl. in HAK to Sam Franklin, 25 March 1940, Franklin to Reinhold Niebuhr, 12 Jan. 1940, Niebuhr to Board of Directors, STFU, 17 Jan. 1940, Niebuhr Papers.

44. Untitled report of Delta and Providence Farms investigatory committee, encl. in HAK to Reinhold Niebuhr, 9 July 1940, HAK Papers; HAK to Niebuhr, 9 July 1940, to Sam Franklin, 25 March 1940, Niebuhr Papers.

45. Jacklin, "Mission to the Sharecroppers," 314–15.

46. Mitchell, *Mean Things Happening in This Land,* 70–77; transcript of interview with HAK, 22 July 1974.

47. Mitchell, *Mean Things Happening in This Land,* 75; Grubbs, *Cry from the Cotton,* 67, 114, 176.

48. HAK to Norman Thomas, 18 Aug. 1937, HAK Papers.

49. Lowell K. Dyson, "The Southern Tenant Farmer's Union and Depression Politics," *Political Science Quarterly* 88, no. 2 (June 1973): 231–36. Donald Henderson, a former Socialist, had abandoned the party for the ranks of the Communists in 1931. He had been a leader in the Communist National Student League, and in the mid-thirties the party had assigned him to its expanding agricultural work (Harvey Klehr, *The Heyday of American Communism: The Depression Decade* [New York, 1984], 237, 311–12).

50. Grubbs, *Cry from the Cotton,* 82, 166.

51. HAK to Thomas, 27 Sept. 1937, HAK Papers; STFU News Release, n.d., STFU Papers.

52. Norman Thomas to H. L. Mitchell, 29 Sept. 1937, HAK Papers; Mitchell, *Mean Things Happening in This Land,* 153–63.

53. Dyson, "The Southern Tenant Farmer's Union and Depression Politics," 249.

54. Grubbs, *Cry from the Cotton,* 176, 184.

Chapter 6

1. HAK to Alice Kester, 9 Dec. 1933, HAK Papers.

2. HAK to Alice Kester, 11 Jan. 1937, HAK Papers–Restricted.

3. Alice H. Kester to HAK, [1936], 13 Dec. 1936, [1938], 7 Feb. 1938, ibid.

4. Interview with Nancy Kester Neale.

5. HAK to Alice H. Kester, [1936], HAK Papers–Restricted; HAK to Alice H. Kester, 14 Dec. 1936, HAK Papers; Alice H. Kester to HAK, 10 Jan. 1937, HAK to Alice H. Kester, 15 Feb. 1938, HAK Papers–Restricted.

6. Singal, *The War Within*, 21–33.

7. Elisabeth Gilman to Adelaide Case, 28 April 1937, Niebuhr Papers.

8. "Report of Howard Kester, Secretary of the Committee on Economic and Racial Justice for the Twelve Month Period Ending October 15, 1937" (hereafter cited as "Report of Howard Kester . . . October 15, 1937"), HAK, "A Statement of Faith to the 'Examiners' before my Ordination to the Ministry in October, 1936," HAK Papers.

9. HAK to George Washington Carver, 13 March 1934, Carver Papers.

10. HAK, "The First Decade," *Prophetic Religion* 6 (Summer 1945): 4; James Dombrowski to author, 20 July 1979; list of people invited to Conference of Younger Churchmen of the South, Monteagle, Tenn., 28–29 May 1934, encl. in Conference of Younger Churchmen of the South, Monteagle, Tenn., 27–29 May 1934, *Findings*, HAK Papers.

11. HAK, "The First Decade," 4; Thomas B. Cowan, *History of the Fellowship of Southern Churchmen* (n.p., n.d.), 1, FSC Papers; David Burgess, *The Fellowship of Southern Churchmen: Its History and Promise* (n.p., n.d.), 1, ibid.; HAK, interview with author, Montreat, N.C., 15 Nov. 1969.

12. Cowan, *History of the Fellowship*, 7; Cowan to Nelle Morton, 14 Jan. 1949, FSC Papers; "Resolutions," *Prophetic Religion* 1 (Dec. 1937): 3.

13. Reinhold Niebuhr, "The Fellowship of Socialist Christians," *World Tomorrow* 17 (14 June 1934): 298.

14. Cowan, *History of the Fellowship*, 4.

15. Minutes of Meeting of Southern Churchmen, Norris, Tenn., 11–13 Nov. 1936, copy in possession of author; "Cowan Honored at Norris Meet," newspaper clipping in possession of author.

16. HAK to William Faulkner, 29 July 1937, HAK Papers.

17. The Workers Defense League originated in 1936 in response to what its founders professed to be the need for a "genuinely non-partisan labor defense organization dedicated to uniting workers and other people firmly resolved to fight for the democratic rights of labor." Though in theory nonpartisan, the WDL was initially closely tied to the Socialist party (Preamble, "Constitution of the Workers' Defense League," ACLU Archives).

18. HAK to the members of the Committee on Economic and Racial Justice, 8 Nov. 1940, HAK Papers.

19. "Report of Howard Kester . . . October 15, 1937," 3.

20. HAK, "Early Life of Howard Kester," 12.

21. Ibid., 12.

22. Frank McCallister to Elisabeth Gilman, [1939], encl. in Gilman to HAK, 1 April 1939, HAK to Charles M. Wallace, 5 July 1938, Hattie Ross to HAK, 6 Feb. 1939, Minutes, National Executive Committee, Socialist

Party, U.S.A. Meeting, 1–4 Sept. 1937, HAK Papers; A. S. Gilmartin to Roger N. Baldwin, 5 Nov. 1937, ACLU Archives. For a discussion of the Trotskyites and factionalism within the Socialist party, see Shannon, *The Socialist Party in America*, 245, 251–54.

23. HAK to Alice H. Kester, 14 Oct. 1938, Thomas to HAK, 16 May 1939, HAK to Thomas, 26 May 1939, HAK Papers.

24. Dunbar, *Against the Grain*, 49–50. Although often used interchangeably, the terms *United Front* and *Popular Front*, strictly speaking, had different meanings; *United Front* designated cooperation between Communists and Socialists, while *Popular Front* referred to cooperation among Communists and a broad range of groups with whom they thought alliance beneficial.

25. Transcript of interview with HAK, 22 July 1974.

26. HAK to Miller, 19 March 1939, HAK Papers.

27. Ibid., and HAK to Elisabeth Gilman, 31 Dec. 1939, ibid.

28. Miller to HAK, 25 Nov. 1938, ibid.

29. Thomas A. Krueger, *And Promises to Keep: The Southern Conference for Human Welfare, 1938–1948* (Nashville, 1967), 82–83; HAK to Graham, 11 Dec. 1939, Frank Porter Graham Papers, Southern Historical Collection, Library of the University of North Carolina at Chapel Hill.

30. Quoted in Cedric Belfrage, *A Faith to Free the People* (New York, 1944), 142; Burgess, *Fellowship of Southern Churchmen*, 2; interview with HAK, 15 Nov. 1969; Cowan, *History of the Fellowship*, 7.

31. HAK to the Members of the Executive Committee, the Fellowship of Southern Churchmen, 24 April 1938, copy in possession of author; Scotty and Gladys Cowan to the Kesters, 4 May 1938, King to HAK, 23 May 1938, HAK Papers.

32. "Statement of Principles, Fellowship of Southern Churchmen, Adopted in Berea, Kentucky, 1938; Authored by T. B. Cowan, Howard Kester, Walter Sykes," "The Fellowship of Southern Churchmen, Constitution and By-Laws" [1938], FSC Papers.

33. Transcript of interview with HAK, 22 July 1974; Elisabeth Gilman to Reinhold Niebuhr, 28 March 1941, Niebuhr Papers; Donald L. West to HAK, 27 Nov. 1939, HAK Papers. Kester attributed the "Jesus jag" comment to Louise Leonard McLaren of the Southern Summer School for Women Workers (transcript of interview with HAK, 25 Aug. 1974).

34. HAK to Elisabeth Gilman, Adelaide Case, and Reinhold Niebuhr, 22 Aug. 1938, HAK Papers.

35. Young to Dorothy Detzer, 14 Nov. 1938, ibid.

36. HAK to Elisabeth Gilman, 20 Oct. 1939, Alice H. Kester to "Dear Friend," 22 Oct. 1939, ibid.

37. HAK to Rev. Bradford Young, 5 Jan. 1939, to Gilman, 5 Jan. 1939, to the Members of the Committee on Economic and Racial Justice, 27 Oct. 1939, ibid.

38. Gilman to Niebuhr, 28 March, 22 May 1941, Niebuhr Papers.

39. Reinhold Niebuhr to Thomas B. Cowan, 15 April 1941, HAK Papers; Niebuhr to Elisabeth Gilman, 23 May, 18 Nov. 1941, Niebuhr Papers.

Chapter 7

1. The Country Life movement that emerged around the turn of the century in the Northeast and Midwest as a part of the Progressive ferment had a religious dimension. Some of its leaders, such as Kenyon Butterfield, believed that churches could serve as the nucleus for a rational reorganization and revitalization of disintegrating rural communities. These apostles of a rural Social Gospel shifted their religious emphasis from the individual or church to the community at large and were optimistic about the church's potential for constructive change. Although groups such as the Federal Council of Churches, Moravian Brethren, and Presbyterian Church, USA initially displayed considerable enthusiasm for the Country Life movement, in the post–World War I era the opposition of conservatives, urban biases of denominational leaders, and failure of its proponents to develop a sound theological or doctrinal basis for their views enervated the movement within the church (Merwin Swanson, "The 'Country Life Movement' and the American Churches," *Church History* 46 [September 1977]: 358–73).

2. Burgess, *Fellowship of Southern Churchmen*, 2; 1943 membership list, Friends of the Soil, Miscellaneous Series, Eugene Smathers Papers, Special Collections, Heard Library, Vanderbilt University, Nashville.

3. Francis Drake, "Friends of the Soil," *Prophetic Religion* 6 (Winter 1945): 91.

4. Eugene Smathers, "The Church and Rural Security," *Christian Rural Fellowship Bulletin,* no. 86 (Nov. 1943): 1–3.

5. Although their criticism of materialism, reservations about industrialization, and faith in the spiritual virtues of rural life are reminiscent of the Agrarians, there is no evidence that Howard Kester or any of his associates were directly influenced by the Vanderbilt theorists. Kester, who loved the land and the people who lived upon it, was at Vanderbilt during the heyday of the Agrarians and briefly toyed with the idea of taking classes with one or more of them. The burgeoning radical quickly rejected the idea, believing their understanding of the rural South to be too romantic to provide a realistic basis for constructive change in the region. Since he too tended, in his own way, to romanticize country life, had he encountered them a decade earlier or later at a less radical point in his pilgrimage, his response might have been somewhat different (interview with HAK, 15 Nov. 1969).

6. "Suggested Revision of Statement of Friends of the Soil," n.d., 2, FSC Papers.

7. Ibid.

8. Eugene Smathers, "The Land, Democracy, and Religion," *Prophetic Religion* 5 (Feb.–March 1941): 4; Smathers, "The Church and Rural Security," 8.

9. "Regarding the Founding of a Seminary or Religious Center to Provide

Special Training for Rural Pastors, Social and Religious Workers," n.d., 2, 3, HAK Papers.

10. [HAK] to Scotty Cowan, Nelle Morton, Walter Sikes, and Dave Burgess, 10 Feb. 1948, encl. in HAK to Burgess, 10 Feb. 1948, Incoming Correspondence, Regular ser., Eugene Smathers Papers.

11. Elizabeth Jacoway, *Yankee Missionaries in the South: The Penn School Experiment* (Baton Rouge, La., 1980), 243.

12. Ibid., 1–22.

13. For a detailed discussion of the genesis and evolution of Penn Normal Agricultural and Industrial School, see Jacoway, *Yankee Missionaries.*

14. Ibid., 219, 245; White to Cope, 2 July 1943, Brownlee to L. Hollingsworth Wood, 1 July 1943, Sayre to Harold Evans, 16 June 1943, Penn School Papers, Southern Historical Collection, Library of the University of North Carolina at Chapel Hill.

15. "Summer Meeting, July 8, 1943," Penn School Papers.

16. Newsletter, the Fellowship of Southern Churchmen, May 1943, ibid.

17. HAK to Rossa Cooley, 31 May 1943, ibid.; HAK to Pickens Johnson, 28 July 1943, quoted in Jacoway, *Yankee Missionaries,* 243–44.

18. HAK to members of the Board of Trustees, Penn Normal Industrial and Agricultural School, Jan. 1944, Penn School Papers.

19. HAK, "Preliminary Statement regarding the Future Development of Penn School," [1946?], ibid.

20. "Report of Visit to Penn School—John A. Silver, Paul W. Brown, Jr. and William E. Cadbury—March 24 to March 27, 1945," ibid.

21. Cope to L. Hollingsworth Wood, 12 April 1946, to Ethel Moors, 26 June, 17 July 1946, ibid.

22. Graduates Club of Penn School to Our Beloved Trustees, 9 June 1947, ibid.; interview with Nancy Kester Neale.

23. [HAK] to Uncle Bill, 15 Sept. 1946, Penn School Papers.

24. Jacoway, *Yankee Missionaries,* 250.

25. Ibid., 237.

26. HAK, "Report on Displaced Persons Program, May 1, 1949, to May 10, 1950," Alice Kester to Dr. Stein, 1 May 1950, HAK Papers; interview with Nancy Kester Neale.

27. Interview with Nancy Kester Neale; HAK, "Report on Displaced Persons Program, May 1, 1949, to May 10, 1950," Earle H. Ballou, "To the Members of the Executive Committee of the General Council of Congregational Christian Churches," [Aug. 1950], HAK Papers.

28. Pat McNelley, ed., *The First 40 Years: John C. Campbell Folk School* (Atlanta, 1966), 2–55.

29. "A Critical Appraisal of the John C. Campbell Folk School with Suggested Plans for the Future," encl. in D. F. Folger to the Directors, John C. Campbell Folk School, 14 April 1949, HAK Papers.

30. Folger to HAK, 5 July 1949, ibid.

31. [HAK] to M. M. (Board of Directors), 6 Aug. 1950, ibid.

32. HAK to the Board of Directors, John C. Campbell Folk School, 25 Oct. 1951, ibid.

33. [Alice Harris Kester] to Nelle Morton, 23 Nov. 1951, ibid.

34. Brownlee to HAK, 14 Oct. 1951, HAK to Olive Campbell, 12 Dec. 1951, Brownlee to HAK, 21 Dec. 1951, HAK Papers.

35. HAK to Alice Kester, Oct. 1951, ibid.

36. Nelle Morton, telephone interview with author, 7 Dec. 1978.

37. HAK to Alice Kester, Oct. 1951, HAK Papers.

38. Nelle Morton to Tony Dunbar, 3 Jan. 1978, annotated copy in possession of author; interview with Nelle Morton.

39. Nelle Morton to author, 21 Nov. 1978.

40. David Burgess to HAK, 29 March 1948, Nelle Morton to Dr. Thomas, 29 March 1948, Scotty and Gladys [Cowan] to Howard and Alice Kester, 28 July 1949, 22 July 1952, Neal Hughley to HAK, 17 Aug. 1952, HAK to David Burgess, 23 June 1953, HAK Papers; Warren Ashby, interview with author, Greensboro, N.C., 25 Sept. 1978; interview with Nancy Kester Neale.

41. HAK to "Dear FSCer, Friend and Co-Worker," Oct. 1954, FSC Papers.

42. [HAK], "Report on Mississippi," Fellowship of Southern Churchmen Newsletter, Nov. [1955], HAK to "Dear Fellowshipper," [Nov. 1955?], [HAK?], untitled article on Brown v. Board of Education of Topeka, Kansas, [1957], FSC Papers.

43. [HAK], "A Step toward Building a Democratic-Christian Front in the Deep South," encl. in [?] to Gene [Cox], 22 Feb. 1956, ibid.

44. Ibid.

45. [HAK], "Report on Mississippi," 2, 6, ibid.

46. HAK to Gene Cox, 5 Sept. 1956, HAK Papers; "Dear Fellowship Member," 9 Nov. 1956, FSC Papers.

47. "Christianity v. Jim Crow," Time, 6 May 1957, 86–89.

48. "President Spurs Church Move in South to Ease Race Tensions," New York Times, 24 April 1957; Woodrow A. Geier, "Southwide Church Leaders Relate Theology to Interracial Situation," Christian Century 74 (15 May 1957): 628–30; "Proceedings of the Conference on Christian Faith and Human Relations, Nashville, Tennessee, April 23, 24, 25, 1957," HAK Papers.

49. "Not Representative," Clanton Union-Banner, reprinted in Montgomery Advertiser, 12 May 1957, typewritten copy in the HAK Papers.

50. Charles Demere to HAK, 10 May 1957, King to HAK, 31 May 1957, HAK Papers.

51. Sikes to HAK, 23 Jan. 1957, Ira Langston to HAK, 31 Jan. 1957, ibid.

52. HAK to Campbell, 8 Aug. 1957, ibid.

53. HAK to Eugene Smathers, 1 Aug. 1957, ibid. A remnant of the Fellowship of Southern Churchmen survived into the early 1960s. Its heir was Will D. Campbell's Committee of Southern Churchmen.

54. HAK to Walter Davis, 10 Jan. 1960, to Reinhold Niebuhr, 29 Feb. 1960, to Alice Kester, 29 April, 8 May 1960, ibid.

55. HAK to Campbell, 23 Jan. 1958, to Niebuhr, 29 Feb. 1960, ibid.

56. Lorraine Casby to HAK, 3 May 1960, HAK to Hayes Parish, 7 Feb. 1960, Walter Davis to HAK, 19 Feb. 1960, HAK to Davis, 26 April 1960, ibid.

57. HAK to Grace Smith, 26 June, 7 April 1961, to Dr. Ronald C. Bauer, 11 Oct. 1960, ibid.

58. HAK to "Dear Joe," 4 Nov. 1964, C. Grier Davis to HAK, 15 Feb. 1965, "Howard Anderson Kester," statement by Gaines M. Cook, President of Christmount Christian Assembly, 1 Aug. 1965, HAK to Rev. G. Daniel McCall, 1 Aug. 1967, ibid.

59. O. R. ("Pete") Post, interview with author, Montreat, N.C., 5 Aug. 1985.

60. Kester detested what he considered the destructive rhetoric and tactics of Black Power advocates on the periphery of the civil rights movement. In August 1967 he wrote to Montreat-Anderson president C. Grier Davis concerning Stokley Carmichael and H. Rap Brown, "I think you know me well enough to know that I loathe their preachments and actions more than I loathe a mountain copperhead" (HAK to Davis, 20 Aug. 1967, HAK Papers).

61. Virginia W. Buchanan and Elizabeth Maxwell, interview with author, Montreat, N.C., 6 Aug. 1985; Elizabeth Wilson, interview with author, Asheville, N.C., 5 Aug. 1985; Milton ("Bunk") Spann, interview with author, Montreat, N.C., 6 Aug. 1985; Morris Dees to HAK, 26 March 1970, HAK Papers.

62. Maud H. Paris to "Dear Family and Friends," 10 July 1969, HAK to "Beloved," 15 May 1971, HAK Papers.

63. Interview with Nancy Kester Neale.

64. Elizabeth Jacoway to author, 20 Dec. 1989.

SELECT BIBLIOGRAPHY

I. Manuscript Collections

American Civil Liberties Union. Archives. Seeley G. Mudd Library, Princeton University, Princeton, N.J.

Carver, George Washington. Papers. Hollis Burke Frissell Library, Tuskegee University, Tuskegee, Ala. (microfilm).

Chancellor's Office. Files. Vanderbilt University Archives, Heard Library, Vanderbilt University, Nashville.

Delta and Providence Farms. Papers. Southern Historical Collection, Library of the University of North Carolina at Chapel Hill.

Fellowship of Reconciliation. Papers. Peace Collection, Friends Historical Library, Swarthmore College, Swarthmore, Pa.

Fellowship of Southern Churchmen. Papers. Southern Historical Collection, Library of the University of North Carolina at Chapel Hill.

Graham, Frank Porter. Papers. Southern Historical Collection, Library of the University of North Carolina at Chapel Hill.

Highlander Research and Education Center. Papers, 1917–73. Social Action Collection, Archives Division, the State Historical Society of Wisconsin, Madison.

Kester, Howard Anderson. Papers. Black Mountain, N.C. In possession of family.

——. Papers. Southern Historical Collection, Library of the University of North Carolina at Chapel Hill. (Some of these papers are available on microfilm.)

National Association for the Advancement of Colored People. Records. Manuscript Division, Library of Congress.

Niebuhr, Reinhold. Papers. Manuscript Division, Library of Congress.

Penn School. Papers. Southern Historical Collection, Library of the University of North Carolina at Chapel Hill (microfilm).

Sayre, John Nevin. Papers. Peace Collection, Friends Historical Library, Swarthmore College, Swarthmore, Pa.

Smathers, Eugene. Papers. Special Collections, Heard Library, Vanderbilt University, Nashville.

Socialist Party. Papers. Manuscript Department, William R. Perkins Library, Duke University, Durham, N.C.

Southern Tenant Farmers' Union. Papers. Southern Historical Collection, Library of the University of North Carolina at Chapel Hill.

Taylor, Alva Wilmot. Papers. Disciples of Christ Historical Society, Nashville.

Weatherford, Willis D. Files. Southern Historical Collection, Library of the University of North Carolina at Chapel Hill.

Young Women's Christian Association. National Board. Historical Records. YWCA Headquarters, New York (microfilm).

II. Interviews

Ashby, Warren. Interview with author. Greensboro, N.C., 25 Sept. 1978.

Buchanan, Virginia W. Interview with author. Montreat, N.C., 6 Aug. 1985.

Folger, Genevieve M. Interview with author., Asheville, N.C., 5 Aug. 1985.

Kester, Howard A. Interview with author. Montreat, N.C., 15 Nov. 1969.

———. Interview by Jacquelyn Hall and William Finger, 22 July 1974. Transcript, Southern Oral History Program Collection, ser. B, Southern Historical Collection, Library of the University of North Carolina at Chapel Hill.

———. Interview by Mary Frederickson, 25 Aug. 1974. Transcript, Southern Oral History Program Collection, ser. B, Southern Historical Collection, Library of the University of North Carolina at Chapel Hill.

Kester, Jane Elizabeth. Interview with author. Roanoke, Va., 27 June 1981.

Maxwell, Elizabeth. Interview with author. Montreat, N.C., 6 Aug. 1985.

Mays, Benjamin. Interview with author. Atlanta, 11 Aug. 1982.

Mitchell, H(arry) L(eland). Observations recorded for author. Montgomery, Ala., 23 June 1988.

Morton, Nelle. Telephone interview with author, from Claremont, Calif., 7 Dec. 1978.

Neale, Nancy Kester. Interview with author. Boone, N.C., 24 May 1985.

Newman, Wilson. Telephone interview with author, from Chicago, 15 Jan. 1983.

Paris, Maud H. Interview with author. Warner-Robbins, Ga., 20 May 1985.

Post, O. R., IV. Interview with author. Montreat, N.C., 5 Aug. 1985.

Spann, Milton G. and Nancy G. Interview with author. Montreat, N.C., 6 Aug. 1985.

Wilson, Mary Elizabeth. Interview with author. Asheville, N.C., 5 Aug. 1985.

III. Congressional Hearings

U.S. Congress. Senate. Committee on the Judiciary. Subcommittee on S. 1978. *Hearings . . . on S. 1978: A Bill to Assure to Persons within the Jurisdiction of Every State the Equal Protection of the Laws, and to Punish the Crime of Lynching.* 73d Cong., 2d sess., 1934. Pt. 1.

———. ———. Special Committee to Investigate Unemployment and Relief. *Hearings . . . Pursuant to S. Res. 36: A Resolution Creating a Special Committee to Investigate Unemployment and Relief.* 75th Cong., 3d sess., 1938.

IV. Census Materials

U.S. Bureau of the Census. *Fourteenth Census of the United States, Taken in the Year 1920.* Vol. 3. *Population 1920.* Washington, D.C.: GPO, 1922.

———. *Manuscript Census of 1870. Ninth Census of the United States* (microfilm).

———. *Manuscript Census of 1900. Twelfth Census of the United States.* Schedule No. 1—Population (microfilm).

———. *Thirteenth Census of the United States, Taken in the Year 1910.* Vol. 3. *Population.* Vol. 7. *Agriculture 1909 and 1910.* Washington, D.C.: GPO, 1913.

V. Newspapers

Critograph (Lynchburg College, Lynchburg, Va.), 1921–25.

Evening Tennessean (Nashville), 1932–33.

Henry County Bulletin, 1900–1910.

Labor Advocate (Nashville), 1933.

Nashville Banner, 1932–33.

Nashville Tennessean, 1932–33.

Raleigh Register (Beckley, W. Va.), 1917–19.

VI. Magazines

Blue Ridge Voice, 1923–26.

VII. Books

Adams, Frank. *Unearthing Seeds of Fire: The Idea of Highlander.* Winston-Salem, N.C.: J. F. Blair, 1975.

Ahlstrom, Sydney E., ed. *Theology in America: The Major Protestant Voices from Puritanism to Neo-Orthodoxy.* Indianapolis and New York: Bobbs-Merrill Company, 1967.

Auerbach, Jerold S. *Labor and Liberty: The La Follette Committee and the New Deal.* Indianapolis: Bobbs-Merrill Company, 1966.

Bailey, Kenneth K. *Southern White Protestantism in the Twentieth Century.* New York: Harper & Row, 1964.

Barnes, Raymond P. *A History of Roanoke.* Radford, Va.: Commonwealth Press, 1968.

Belfrage, Cedric. *A Faith to Free the People.* New York: Dryden Press, 1944.

Carter, Dan T. *Scottsboro: A Tragedy of the American South.* Rev. ed. Baton Rouge: Louisiana State University Press, 1979.

Conkin, Paul K. *Gone with the Ivy: A Biography of Vanderbilt University.* Knoxville: University of Tennessee Press, 1985.

Cort, John C. *Christian Socialism: An Informal History.* Maryknoll, N.Y.: Orbis Books, 1988.

Daniel, Pete. *Breaking the Land: The Transformation of Cotton, Tobacco, and Rice Cultures since 1880.* Urbana: University of Illinois Press, 1985.

Davis, David C. *Model for a Humanistic Education: The Danish Folk School.* Columbus, Ohio: Charles E. Merrill Publishing Company, 1971.

Dunbar, Anthony P. *Against the Grain: Southern Radicals and Prophets, 1929– 1959.* Charlottesville: University Press of Virginia, 1981.

Dykeman, Wilma. *Prophet of Plenty: The First Ninety Years of W. D. Weatherford.* Knoxville: University of Tennessee Press, 1966.

Dykeman, Wilma, and James Stokely. *Seeds of Southern Change: The Life of Will Alexander.* Chicago: University of Chicago Press, 1962.

Eddy, Sherwood. *Eighty Adventurous Years: An Autobiography.* New York: Harper & Brothers, 1955.

Egerton, John. *A Mind to Stay Here: Profiles from the South.* New York: Macmillan, 1970.

Eighmy, John Lee. *Churches in Cultural Captivity: A History of the Social Attitudes of Southern Baptists.* Knoxville: University of Tennessee Press, 1972.

Fleischman, Harry. *Norman Thomas: A Biography.* New York: W. W. Norton & Company, 1964.

Glen, John M. *Highlander: No Ordinary School, 1932–1962.* Lexington: University Press of Kentucky, 1988.

Governor Treutlan Chapter, D.A.R. *History of Peach County.* Fort Valley, Ga.: Cherokee Publishing Company, 1972.

Green, James R. *Grass-Roots Socialism: Radical Movements in the Southwest, 1895–1943.* Baton Rouge: Louisiana State University Press, 1977.

Griswold, A. Whitney. *The Far Eastern Policy of the United States.* New York: Harcourt, Brace & Company, 1938.

Grubbs, Donald H. *Cry from the Cotton: The Southern Tenant Farmers' Union and the New Deal.* Chapel Hill: University of North Carolina Press, 1971.

Hall, Jacquelyn D. *Revolt against Chivalry: Jessie Daniel Ames and the Women's Campaign against Lynching.* New York: Columbia University Press, 1979.

Hill, Samuel S. *Southern Churches in Crisis.* New York: Holt, Rinehart and Winston, 1967.

Hopkins, C. Howard. *History of the Y.M.C.A. in North America.* New York: Association Press, 1951.

Howe, Daniel Walker, ed. *Victorian America.* Philadelphia: University of Pennsylvania Press, 1976.

Hyfler, Robert. *Prophets of the Left: American Socialist Thought in the Twentieth Century.* Westport, Conn.: Greenwood Press, 1984.

Jacoway, Elizabeth. *Yankee Missionaries in the South: The Penn School Experiment.* Baton Rouge: Louisiana State University Press, 1980.

Kegley, Charles W., ed. *Reinhold Niebuhr: His Religious and Political Thought.* New York: Pilgrim Press, 1984.

Kester, Howard A. *Revolt among the Sharecroppers.* New York: Covici Friede, 1936.

Klehr, Harvey. *The Heyday of American Communism: The Depression Decade.* New York: Basic Books, 1984.

Krueger, Thomas A. *And Promises to Keep: The Southern Conference for Human Welfare, 1938–1948*. Nashville: Vanderbilt University Press, 1967.

Loetscher, Lefferts A. *The Broadening Church: A Study of Theological Issues in the Presbyterian Church since 1869*. Philadelphia: University of Pennsylvania Press, 1957.

Loveland, Anne C. *Lillian Smith, a Southerner Confronting the South*. Baton Rouge: Louisiana State University Press, 1986.

McDowell, John P. *The Social Gospel in the South: The Woman's Home Mission Movement in the Methodist Episcopal Church, South, 1886–1939*. Baton Rouge: Louisiana State University Press, 1982.

McGovern, James R. *Anatomy of a Lynching: The Killing of Claude Neal*. Baton Rouge: Louisiana State University Press, 1982.

McMurry, Linda O. *George Washington Carver: Scientist and Symbol*. New York: Oxford University Press, 1981.

McNelley, Pat, ed. *The First 40 Years: John C. Campbell Folk School*. Atlanta: McNelley-Rudd Printing Service, 1966.

Mays, Benjamin. *Born to Rebel*. New York: Charles Scribner's Sons, 1971.

Meyer, Donald B. *The Protestant Search for Political Realism, 1919–1941*. Berkeley: University of California Press, 1960.

Miller, Robert Moats. *American Protestantism and Social Issues, 1919–1939*. Chapel Hill: University of North Carolina Press, 1958.

Mitchell, H. L. *Mean Things Happening in This Land: The Life and Times of H. L. Mitchell, Co-Founder of the Southern Tenant Farmers Union*. Montclair, N.J.: Allanheld, Osmun, 1979.

——. *Roll the Union On: A Pictorial History of the Southern Tenant Farmers' Union, as Told by Its Co-founder, H. L. Mitchell*. Chicago: Charles H. Kerr Publishing Company, 1987.

Morgan, William H. *Student Religion during Fifty Years: Programs and Policies of the Intercollegiate Y.M.C.A.* New York: Association Press, 1935.

Nisbet, Robert A. *The Sociological Tradition*. New York: Basic Books, 1966.

Rice, Otis K. *West Virginia: A History*. Lexington: University Press of Kentucky, 1985.

Shannon, David A. *The Socialist Party of America: A History*. New York: Macmillan, 1955.

Singal, Daniel J. *The War Within: From Victorian to Modernist Thought in the South, 1919–1945*. Chapel Hill: University of North Carolina Press, 1982.

Sosna, Morton. *In Search of the Silent South: Southern Liberals and the Race Issue*. New York: Columbia University Press, 1977.

Thurmond, Howard. *With Head and Heart*. San Diego: Harcourt Brace Jovanovich, 1979.

Tindall, George Brown. *The Emergence of the New South, 1913–1945*. Baton Rouge: Louisiana State University Press, 1967.

Zangrando, Robert L. *The NAACP Crusade against Lynching, 1909-1950*. Philadelphia: Temple University Press, 1980.

VIII. Articles

Amberson, William R. "The Delta Farms," *Christian Century* 56 (14 June 1939): 774.

"An Appeal to the Socialist Party from 47 Members," *World Tomorrow* 17, no. 8 (12 April 1934): 183–88.

Ansley, Fran, and Sue Thrasher. "The Ballad of Barney Graham [interview of Della Graham Smith and Barney Graham, Jr.]," *Southern Exposure* 4 (Spring 1976): 136–42.

Boles, John B. "Religion in the South: A Tradition Recovered," *Maryland Historical Magazine* 77 (Winter 1982): 388–401.

Brown, Forrest D. "Indianapolis Student Volunteer Convention," *Blue Ridge Voice* 5, nos. 3 & 4 (Dec. 1923/Jan. 1924): 16–81, 28.

Burns, Vincent G. "Brother Bill," *Christian Century* 45 (20 Sept. 1928): 1133–35.

"Christianity v. Jim Crow," *Time* (6 May 1957): 86–89.

Dabney, Virginius. "Dixie Rejects Lynching," *Nation* 145 (27 Nov. 1937): 579–80.

Drake, Francis. "Friends of the Soil," *Prophetic Religion* 6 (Winter 1945): 91–92.

Dyson, Lowell K. "The Southern Tenant Farmer's Union and Depression Politics," *Political Science Quarterly* 88, no. 2 (June 1973): 230–52.

Geier, Woodrow A., "Southwide Church Leaders Relate Theology to Interracial Situation," *Christian Century* 74 (15 May 1957): 628–30.

Jacklin, Thomas M. "Mission to the Sharecroppers: Neo-Orthodox Radicalism and the Delta Farm Venture, 1936–40," *South Atlantic Quarterly* 78 (Summer 1979): 302–16.

Kester, Howard. "The First Decade," *Prophetic Religion* 6 (Summer 1945): 4–5.

Martin, Robert F. "Critique of Southern Society and Vision of a New Order: The Fellowship of Southern Churchmen, 1934–1957," *Church History* 52, no. 1 (March 1983): 66–80.

———. "A Prophet's Pilgrimage: The Religious Radicalism of Howard Anderson Kester, 1921–1941," *Journal of Southern History* 48, no. 4 (Nov. 1982): 511–30.

Niebuhr, Reinhold. "The Fellowship of Socialist Christians," *World Tomorrow* 17 (14 June 1934): 297–98.

"President Spurs Church Move in South to Ease Race Tensions," *New York Times* (24 April 1957).

"Resolutions," *Prophetic Religion* 1, no. 1 (Dec. 1937): 3–4.

Russell, Allyn. "J. Gresham Mechan, Scholarly Fundamentalist," *Journal of Presbyterian History* 51 (Spring 1973): 41–69.

Smathers, Eugene. "The Church and Rural Security," *Christian Rural Fellowship Bulletin,* no. 86 (Nov. 1943): 1–8.

————. "The Land, Democracy, and Religion," *Prophetic Religion* 5 (Feb.–March 1941): 4–7.

Swanson, Merwin. "The 'Country Life Movement' and the American Churches," *Church History* 46 (Sept. 1977): 358–73.

IX. Theses and Other Unpublished Materials

Bellamy, John Stark. "If Christ Came to Dixie: The Southern Prophetic Vision of Howard Anderson Kester, 1904–1941." M.A. thesis, University of Virginia, 1977.

Harbison, Stanley Lincoln. "Social Gospel Career of Alva W. Taylor." Ph.D. diss., Vanderbilt University, 1975.

Kester, Howard A. "Radical Prophets: A History of the Fellowship of Southern Churchmen," n.d. Photographic copy in possession of author; original in possession of Nancy Kester Neale, Boone, N.C.

Wake, Orville Wentworth. "A History of Lynchburg College, 1903–1953." Ph.D. diss., University of Virginia, 1957.

Index